ALSO BY BENSON BOBRICK

∽◊∾

Master of War: The Life of General George H. Thomas

The Fated Sky: Astrology in History

Testament: A Soldier's Story of the Civil War

Wide as the Waters: The Story of the English Bible and the Revolution It Inspired

Angel in the Whirlwind: The Triumph of the American Revolution

Knotted Tongues: Stuttering in History and the Quest for a Cure

East of the Sun: The Epic Conquest and Tragic History of Siberia

Fearful Majesty: The Life and Reign of Ivan the Terrible

Labyrinths of Iron: Subways in History, Myth, Art, Technology, and War

Parsons Brinckerhoff: The First Hundred Years

the

Caliph's

SPLENDOR

Islam and the West in the Golden Age of Baghdad

BENSON BOBRICK

SIMON & SCHUSTER

New York   London   Toronto   Sydney   New Delhi

Simon & Schuster
1230 Avenue of the Americas
New York, NY 10020

First Simon & Schuster hardcover edition August 2012

SIMON & SCHUSTER and colophon are registered trademarks
of Simon & Schuster, Inc.

For information about special discounts for bulk purchases,
please contact Simon & Schuster Special Sales at
1-866-506-1949 or business@simonandschuster.com.

The Simon & Schuster Speakers Bureau can bring authors
to your live event. For more information or to book an event,
contact the Simon & Schuster Speakers Bureau at
1-866-248-3049 or visit our website at www.simonspeakers.com.

Designed by Joy O'Meara

Maps by Paul Pugliese

Manufactured in the United States of America

10 9 8 7 6 5 4 3 2 1

Library of Congress Cataloging-in-Publication Data
Bobrick, Benson, date.
    The caliph's splendor : Islam and the West in the golden age of Baghdad /
Benson Bobrick.
        p.   cm.
    Includes bibliographical references and index.
1. Islamic Empire—Foreign relations—Byzantine Empire.   2. Byzantine
Empire—Foreign relations—Islamic Empire.   3. Islamic Empire—
History—750–1258.   4. Byzantine Empire—History—527–1081.   5. Islam—
Relations—Christianity.   6. Christianity and other religions—Islam.   7. Harun
al-Rashid, Caliph, ca. 763–809.   8. Charlemagne, Emperor, 742–814.   I. Title.
    DS38.6.B63 2012
    327.53049509'021—dc23   2011044430
ISBN 978-1-4165-6762-2
ISBN 978-1-4165-6806-3 (ebook)

To my agent, Russell Galen

and

My longtime editor, Bob Bender—
Twin pillars of support for my writing over the years.

CONTENTS

CHRONOLOGY

B.C.

ca. 1700— Approximate time of the patriarch Abraham and his son Ishmael, whom Jews and Arabs alike regard as the progenitors of their race

ca. 853— An Assyrian inscription marks the first material record of the Arabs in history

A.D.

70— Roman capture of Jerusalem

330— Foundation of Constantinople

527–628— Intermittent war between the Persians and the Byzantines

ca. 570— Birth of Muhammad

622— The Hegira, the flight of Muhammad from Mecca to Medina, marking the beginning of the Islamic era

630— Muhammad and his followers take Mecca

632— Death of Muhammad. Abu Bakr chosen as first caliph.

633–647— Arabs conquer Syria, Iraq, Persia, North Africa, and Egypt

661— Ali, the fourth caliph, assassinated at Kufa; Umayyad Caliphate begins

680— Massacre at Karbala

691–694— Construction of the Dome of the Rock in Jerusalem

710— Westernmost India becomes the eastern frontier of Islam

711— Muslims cross the Strait of Gibraltar into Spain

732— The Arab invasion of France is checked by Charles Martel at Poitiers

742— Charlemagne born at Aachen

750— Foundation of the Abbasid Caliphate. Accession of Saffah.

754— Accession of Mansur

756— Independent Emirate of Cordova established

762— Foundation of Baghdad

763— Birth of Harun al-Rashid

775— Accession of Mahdi

778— Charlemagne leads expedition into Spain

780— Death of Byzantine Emperor Leo IV. Constantine VI, still
a child, nominally succeeds. His mother Irene takes charge
as regent.

785— Accession of Hadi

786— Accession of Harun al-Rashid

797— Constantine VI deposed. Irene becomes empress.

800— Charlemagne crowned Holy Roman Emperor in Rome

802— Irene deposed. Nicephorus crowned.

803— Fall of the Barmaks

809— Death of Harun al-Rashid. Accession of Amin. Civil war.

813— Death of Amin. Accession of Mamun.

814— Death of Charlemagne

827— Muslim conquest of Sicily begins

833— Death of Mamun

929— Ahd al-Rahman III of Spain adopts title of Caliph

1000— Mahmud of Ghazna invades northern India

1061— Normans take Messina in Sicily

1085— Christians take Toledo, Spain

1099— Crusaders occupy Jerusalem

1187— Saladin defeats the Crusaders and recaptures Jerusalem

1258— Baghdad overwhelmed and destroyed by the Mongols.
End of the Caliphate.

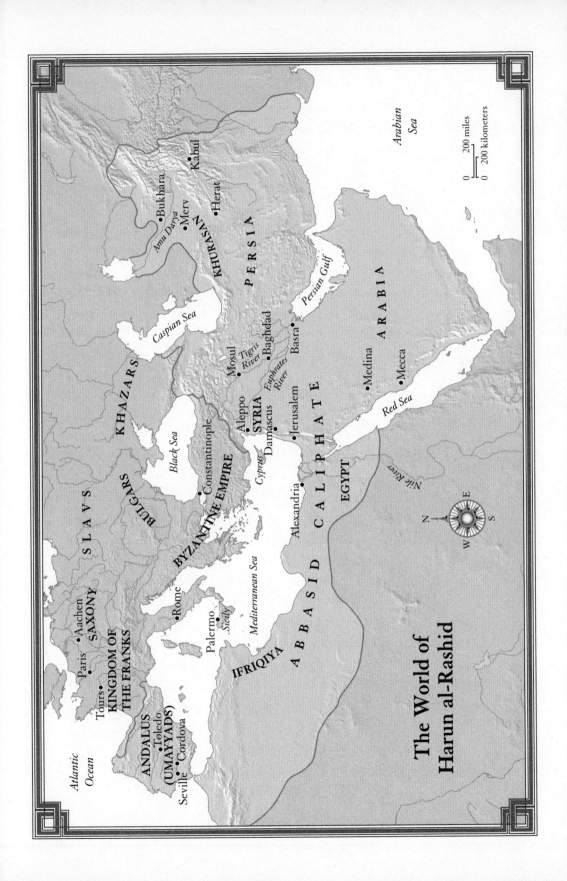

The World of Harun al-Rashid

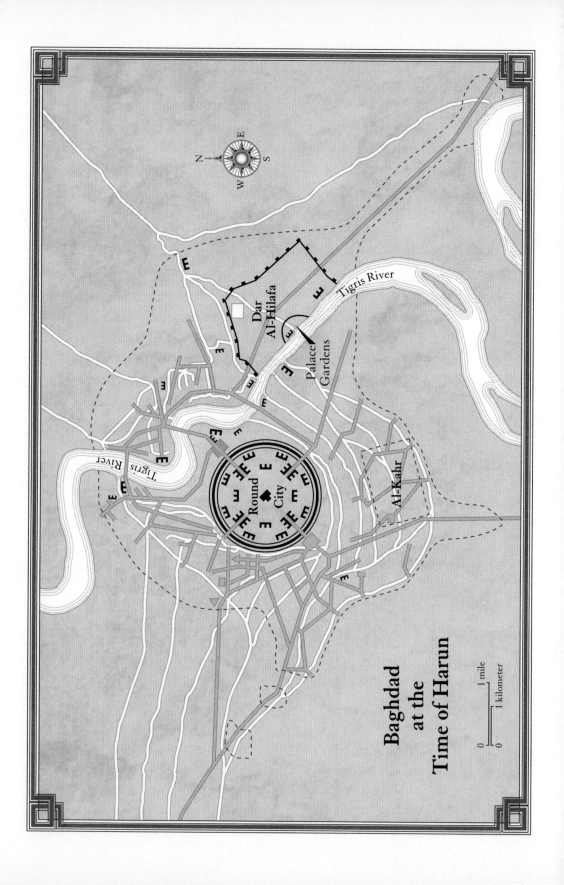

Baghdad
at the
Time of Harun

0   1 mile
0   1 kilometer

Tigris River

Tigris River

Dar
Al-Hilafa

Palace
Gardens

Round
City

Al-Kahr

N E S W

PART ONE

We can compare our course across the world
to the progress of the sun across the heavens.

—Masudi, *The Meadows of Gold*

chapter one

MINARET AND TOWER

On the twenty-first of March 630, the Byzantine Emperor Heraclius entered Jerusalem by its Golden Gate at the head of his legions to set up the True Cross of Christ, which he had just recaptured from the Persians in one of his great Persian wars. Dressed in humble garb, he dismounted not far from the Church of the Holy Sepulchre, and went the rest of the way on foot. Thousands of weeping Christians, overcome with elation, parted before him and carpets scented with aromatic herbs were strewn across his path. "An indescribable joy," wrote one Byzantine court poet, "seized the entire Universe." It was "a triumphant event for all Christendom," and is still marked today in the Church calendar as the "Feast of the Elevation of the Cross." Yet even as it was taking place, in one of the strangest coincidences of history, word came that an imperial outpost beyond the Jordan River had just been assailed by a small Arab band. The emperor paid little heed. Within a few years, however, Palestine and many other provinces would be torn forever from Roman rule, the Persian Empire shattered, and a new faith and people would arise to control the world's stage. In 636, just six years after Heraclius shrugged off this first Arab attack, his own vast legions would be crushed by the forces of Omar, second caliph from the Prophet, on the banks of the Yarmuk River in Syria.

Ever since that day, the forces of the Near and Middle East have had "a deep, silent disdain" for the thunderings of Christian power.

∽⚭∾

THE RISE OF ISLAM IS OFTEN DEPICTED AS HAVING TAKEN place in a primitive community of desert Arabs, who tended their flocks when not raiding caravans or engaged in tribal feuds. After their conversion to Islam, these tribes banded together and, upon the death of their Prophet (so the story goes), folded up their tents and swarmed out of the desert to spread his new doctrine to the world. Almost overnight they began to demonstrate a marked degree of culture and became an invincible military machine.

That strange picture, still popular in the West, is at once both too pathetic and high-flown. Islam had its cradle in an area where advanced civilizations—Egyptian, Babylonian, Persian, and Byzantine—had thrived since ancient times. Arabia lay on their outskirts, but in succession or combination all had irrigated its psychic soil. Cuneiform tablets record large Arab armies complete with infantry, cavalry, and chariots as early as 853 B.C. And the oral tradition of Arabic poetry is resplendent with heroic lays that tell of mighty battles, the dreams of love, and the oases of paradise. Empires rose and fell, and by the seventh century A.D., those large Arab armies and the kingdoms they served had long since dispersed. But the region remained in dynamic transition, where the vibrant streams of faith and culture converged.

The Prophet Muhammad sprang from its soil.

Born ca. A.D. 570 at Mecca in Arabia on the shores of the Red Sea, Muhammad was the son of a merchant and belonged to the elite Arab tribe of the Koraish. Orphaned early, he was raised by in-laws, married a wealthy merchant's widow (much older than himself), had four daughters and two sons, and embarked, in the footsteps of his father, on a business career.

Despite his worldly interests, he was a religious man, spent whole nights in contemplation on Mount Hira near Mecca, and there one day in 620, it is said, the angel Gabriel appeared to him and urged him to preach among the Arabs on behalf of the one true God. Like other Arab prophets, he spoke in rhythmic prose, but his revelation was distinctly monotheistic, which set him apart.

Most Arabs worshipped the forces of nature and at Mecca the central pagan cult revolved around a meteorite. This was the famed Black Stone, built into a cube-shaped sanctuary called the Kaaba. Muhammad fulminated against polytheistic idolatry (the Kaaba contained at least 150 idols) and such barbarous practices as burying female children alive. Though he had no direct knowledge of the Hebrew or Christian scriptures, which had not yet been translated into Arabic (the only language he knew), he had many probing encounters with Jews and Christians, both on his caravan journeys and in Mecca; and his religious understanding was deeply swayed by the ideas he had acquired of these faiths. His grasp of their doctrine and tradition, however unclear, was earnest and he cast himself as a religious reformer entrusted by God to restore the ancient cult of Abraham, which he believed the Jews and Christians had betrayed.

Muhammad, in fact, never claimed to be the founder of a new religion, but merely one whose unsought if sacred calling it was to warn his fellow man of the coming Judgment Day. He saw himself as the last of the prophets, the seal and keystone of those who had gone before. But the Meccan elite resented his attack on their beliefs and the implied threat it posed to the profits they derived from the annual pilgrimage (or Hajj) that Arabs made to the Kaaba. His teaching at first also aroused hostility and derision, from the community at large, which forced him to flee Mecca in 622 for the town of Medina to the north. This became known as the year of the Hegira, or Flight. In the Muslim calendar, it marks the year One. Everything in the Muslim calendar dates from that time just as Christians date their calendar (backward and forward) from the presumed birth of Christ. In Mecca, Muhammad had been the despised preacher of a small congregation; in Medina, he became the leader of a powerful party, which formed the basis of his rise. He began to act as lawgiver for his small community of refugees, won new converts, expelled or killed those who reviled him, and established a theocratic city-state. Between 622 and 628 various clashes occurred between his followers and Meccans, but by 630 he gained the upper hand. Mecca was taken, and Arabs from as far away as Bahrain, Oman, and southern Arabia joined his ranks. Though Arab tribes had long been a volatile force in the region,

Muhammad managed to forge them into a single confederation and persuade them to put aside their jealousies and feuds.

Their bond of union was not only Muhammad's charisma, but Islam,
their newfound faith. "Islam" means "surrender" or "resignation to the
will of God." One who professes Islam is therefore a "Muslim," meaning
"one who surrenders oneself." Islam's simple creed is "There is no God
but God, and Muhammad is His Prophet." The essence of its teaching is
a belief in God ("Allah" in Arabic) and His Angels; in the Scripture or
Koran (meaning "recitation") as revealed through Muhammad to man-
kind; and in a final Resurrection and Judgment of man according to his
works on earth. Equally plain and direct are the obligations placed upon
believers. They consist of almsgiving; prayer five times a day—at dawn,
noon, midafternoon, sunset, and dusk—facing Mecca; the observance of
the fast during the month of Ramadan, the ninth month of the Muslim
year; and the Hajj, or pilgrimage to Mecca, which Islam appropriated
from the pagan past. Muslims abstain from eating pork and drinking
wine; regard marriage as a civil ceremony; and bury their dead. Orthodox Muslims do not tolerate images of anything divine, and in the forms
of their worship no priest or cleric stands between the soul and God. The
mosque, where the faithful assemble for public devotions every Friday,
is an open courtyard surrounded by colonnades and unadorned save
for Koranic texts. It features a mihrab or niche showing the direction of
Mecca, a pulpit, and a minaret where the muezzin (as he is called) utters
the call to prayer.

Although Muhammad, like Christ, never wrote anything, over time
scattered transcriptions of his teachings were posthumously collated and
compared with oral recollections. By a lengthy editorial process (not unlike that which attended the making of the New Testament), a canonical
version of the Koran emerged. In time the sacred text was supple-
mented by a voluminous compendium of Muhammad's reported pro-
nouncements and deeds, known as the Traditions or Hadith. Hadiths,
real or spurious, served as the Muslim Talmud and "furnished the community with apostolic precepts and examples covering the minutest
detail of man's proper conduct in life." They also provided an encyclo-

pedic fund of anecdotes, parables, and sayings by which Muslims were edified.

Muhammad died in 632 while returning from a pilgrimage to Mecca and leadership at first passed by election to a series of caliphs, or "successors"—Abu Bakr, Omar, Othman, and Ali—who inherited his temporal but not theocratic crown. These first four caliphs, who ruled without founding dynasties, are sometimes known as the Orthodox caliphs, and it was under their aegis—and that of their invincible general Khalid ibn al-Walid ("the sword of Islam")—that the early conquests were made.

Yet Islam had been a "church militant" from the start. Even under Muhammad (if not at his direction), Muslim bands had carried out raids along the borders of the Byzantine Empire. Within two years of his death, victories brought the Muslims into Chaldea (southern Iraq), gave them the city of Hira, and with the Battle of Yarmuk in 634, opened Syria to their arms. Damascus fell in 635; Antioch and Jerusalem in 636; and Caesarea in 638. Seleucia-Ctesiphon, the capital of Chaldea, was taken in 637; Mesopotamia subdued; the cities of Basra and Kufa founded; and part of Persia annexed in 638–40. Egypt, then mostly Christian, was conquered in 641. The decisive Battle of Nahavand in 642 put an end to the Sassanid dynasty of Persia and placed all of Persia in Muslim hands.

Circumstance favored their advance. The Byzantine and Persian empires were both exhausted by fighting (having fought each other to a standstill in their own "Thirty Years' War"), while the Semitic inhabitants of Syria, Palestine, and Mesopotamia were more nearly akin to the Arabs than to their Byzantine and Persian lords. The latter had also overtaxed their subjects, and among Egyptian Christians there was a religious schism between Eastern Orthodox believers and the Copts. Some resistance came from centers of Greek civilization—Alexandria in Egypt, for example, and Jerusalem in Palestine; but by 660, barely thirty years after Muhammad's death, Islam had swept over an area the size of the former Roman Empire.

Still the conquest went on. Muslim troops swept through Persia to the river Oxus and began to annex Bukhara, Khujand, Farghana,

Samarkand, and other lands beyond. As the eighth century dawned, they reached the borders of China, at Kashgar, where a treaty was concluded with the Chinese. All this took place in concert with Muslim gains in the West. The Barbary Coast and its wild Berber population was occupied (if not quite subdued) up to the gates of Carthage by 647; Kairawan founded in 670; and Carthage taken in 693, as Arabs reached the Atlantic coast. From Tangier they crossed into Spain in 710; took the whole Gothic kingdom, including Toledo, by 712; and in 725 advanced into southern France. At length, they were checked by Charles Martel, then king of the Franks, at the Battle of Poitiers in 732 in the foothills of the Pyrenees, but the Muslims held on to Narbonne; raided Provence; ravaged Corsica and Sardinia; invaded Armenia; annexed Cyprus (649); and from 670 onward kept Constantinople under intermittent siege. They also continued to press eastward to Afghanistan and the westernmost part of India known as Sind.

India was not unknown. Even before the Arab conquests, Arab coastal traders found that a coasting voyage eastward from the Persian Gulf would bring them to the mouth of the Indus, and that if they ventured farther out, or were carried out at certain seasons of the year, the monsoons would drive them across to India's southwest coast. Seafaring traders on the coast were therefore familiar with India's western ports, and a number of Arab merchants had sailed to there from Shiraz and Hormuz or crossed from harbors in Oman. Upon their return, they had described "a land of wealth and luxury, of gold and diamonds, jeweled idols, and gorgeous religious rites."

One expedition, during the Caliphate of Omar, had made a failed attempt to seize territory near Bombay. Another in 644 wandered off course into the Thar desert and came to naught. Sixty years later, however, eight boats carrying Muslim women from the King of Ceylon to Al-Hajjaj ibn Yusuf, the Arab governor of Iraq, were attacked and plundered off the western coast. The caliph demanded reparations, but the local ruler refused on the ground that the pirates were not under his control.

That led to the dispatch in 711 of a third expedition, this time under Muhammad ibn Kasim, a prince of royal blood. A handsome young man of nobility and dash, he started at the head of a cavalry force 12,000 strong (6,000 on camels, 6,000 on Syrian horse) and a large baggage train. He also had the best contemporary artillery, including one huge catapult or ballista—designed for hurling great stones over battlements—that was shipped to him by sea. Reinforcements also came to him in a steady stream, until at length he had an army of 50,000 men. As one Muslim chronicler put it, he had "all he could require, including needles and thread."

Kasim besieged the Hindu port of Debal and carried the town by assault. The main Hindu army retreated up the Indus River with Kasim in pursuit. On the west bank of the Indus Kasim beheld for the first time an imposing force of Hindu chiefs, mounted on armored war elephants, led by their king, Dahir. The battle at a place called Rawar was fierce. Dahir fought bravely but was killed. From Rawar, Kasim proceeded further up the Indus. In subsequent years, two separate Muslim kingdoms in India were established—one in Mansurah or Sind proper (up to Aror on the Indus), the other at Multan. But that was the end of it for three hundred years. The Muslims settled in, made no attempt to push farther east, and on the whole remained on friendly terms with their Hindu subjects and neighboring Hindu states. In the northern Punjab the limits of Arab rule were set by the powerful Hindu kingdom of Kashmir; in the east, by a military caste known afterward as the Rajputs, who were prepared to contest every inch of ground.

By then, Islam spanned three continents in a broad swathe of conquest that stretched from the Atlantic to the Indus and from the Aral Sea to the cataracts of the Nile. Many of their great battles—Yarmuk, Yamanah, Alexandria, Nahavand, Makkah, Kadisiya, and so on—ring through Islamic history with the same power and aura as do Agincourt, Yorktown, Waterloo, and Gettysburg in the West. Wherever the Arabs went, "their intrepidity and vigor," as one writer put it, "strengthened by their proud feeling of a common nationality and their zeal for the faith," helped them to prevail. Under Islam, the Arabs had become a world-conquering nation, and within a century of Muhammad's death, the banks of the Jaxartes and the shores of the Atlantic alike resounded with the call of "Allahu Akbar," "God Is Great."

The West at the time was sunk in the Dark Ages. Who could say for sure that the muezzin's cry, as was suggested, might not one day sound over Paris, London, or Rome?

Although it is sometimes said that the Arabs lacked any military tradition beyond that pertaining to tribal raids (with no experience, for example, in besieging fortified towns), their formidable early tactics were based on "desert power"—in effect a kind of sea power, for Arabia was "a sea of sand." Adopting the same principles of attack later used by modern maritime nations (and by tank divisions in North Africa during World War II), the Arabs seemed to strike out of nowhere—east into Persia, west into Egypt, north into Syria and Iraq—with sudden force, only to disappear into the sandy wastes from which they came.

As their conquests advanced, however, their soldiers adapted, and in outfit and armor most later Muslim armies were not unlike the Persian and Byzantine. They encased themselves in iron, insofar as that was practical (in helmets, breastplates, and coats of mail); used the same weapons (the bow and arrow, lance, javelin, sword and battle axe); formed, as needed, into mobile units or lines that entrenched; fielded light and heavy artillery (powered by swing beams or twisted ropes); and used ladders, battering rams, and catapults for besieging forts and towns. By the 800s, Muslim armies also began to add companies of flame-throwing archers or "naphtha-firemen" to their battle wings. These elite troops wore fireproof suits that enabled them to rush into buildings and forts they set ablaze.

Beyond their military ingenuity and skill, Muslims were transported by worldly desire joined to religious zeal. For those who survived the carnage, there was untold spoil, captive maidens, property, and public adoration; for those who fell, the bliss of martyrdom. Then as now Muslim warriors believed that black-eyed virgins (known as Houries) impatiently awaited their embrace in Paradise.

Any army excited by such an incendiary mix of flesh and spirit, faith and plunder, heavenly devotion and "passion for sex even in the throes of death" could not readily be vanquished. No matter how ardent their opponents were (or thought themselves to be), they were often halfhearted by comparison when the fighting grew fierce. At the Battle of Yarmuk, 40,000 Arabs had crushed 140,000 Byzantines; in the conquest of Spain, 25,000 Saracens, as Muslims were called in the West, annihilated 90,000 Goths.

IN THE IMPERIAL ADMINISTRATION OF THE VAST NEW ARAB empire, general authority was placed in the hands of Arab commanders, civil rule in local hands. Most subject communities were allowed to continue under the laws that had governed them, and since Muslims were exempt from the tax imposed on the conquered, the conversion of non-Muslims was actually discouraged, as it diminished revenue. In time, of course, the social and racial barriers between Arab and non-Arab populations began to break down. Arab military outposts grew into towns; Arabs far from home acquired local land; Muslims were permitted to take non-Muslim wives. This levelling process had a leavening effect. Islam became more attractive to outsiders, due to the social stature and economic freedom it conferred. Increased diversity in turn diversified Arab knowledge, as the conquered peoples schooled their overlords. This was so in every branch of the sciences and arts. In architecture, for example, country palaces were decorated in a mixture of Greco-Syrian and Persian styles, which also affected the development of the mosque. The Dome of the Rock at Jerusalem, founded by Abd al-Malik in 691, was a shrine built for Muslim worship, but its geometric plan and elevation was based on the Church of the Ascension on the Mount of Olives and other churches of similar construction in Syria and Palestine. It was Byzantine inside and out (until Byzantine mosaics were replaced by Persian tiles), as was the Great Mosque at Damascus, founded in 708. Even the sacred fields of Muslim theology and law were affected, as Muslims expanded their legal code. Although that code was fundamentally religious, statutes relating to taxation, commerce, finance, and other areas reflected existing Byzantine practice, and sometimes Talmudic or rabbinical thought.

By its very inclusiveness and adaptation, the Caliphate went from strength to strength.

Yet a riptide cut across the current of all these gains. Within the vast tent or canopy of Islam, even at times of its utmost triumph, there was intrigue, betrayal, depravity, and violence worthy of the Roman Empire's darkest days.

Muhammad's sudden death in 632 without a surviving son to inherit his mantle had left the Muslim community in disarray. A violent breach had been averted by the selection of the Prophet's venerable father-in-law, Abu Bakr, as caliph. He died of natural causes (pneumonia, brought on by a chill). But the second caliph, Omar, after a celebrated reign of ten years, was butchered by an assassin as he led prayers at dawn in Medina. The third, Othman, was mutilated by an irate mob. An equally savage fate would befall the fourth, Ali.

Upon Othman's death in 658, the succession had been disputed—by Ali, a cousin and son-in-law of Muhammad, and by Muawiya Umayya, the governor of Syria and Othman's kin. The Muslim elders turned first to Ali, whose wife, Fatima, was the Prophet's only surviving child. To the outrage of many, in fact, Ali had been passed over in the previous three elections even though he was Muhammad's male next of kin, which seemed to give him a "divine right." Not all agreed, and the fateful contest that ensued marked the beginning of Islam's continuing divide between the Sunni and Shiite sects. The Shiites were the partisans ("shia") of Ali. They maintained that only a direct descendant of the Prophet could act as head of state. The Sunnis, beginning with Muawiya's adherents, upheld the traditional practice or custom ("sunnah") of the Muslim community in electing as caliph the man most qualified. Such a caliph, in Sunni eyes, inherited the Prophet's political and administrative authority, but not his spiritual power. The Shiite "imam," by contrast, was a divinely ordained caliph who inherited the whole of the Prophet's authority.

After two notable battles between the two camps, Muawiya's troops appealed for a truce by spiking the tips of their lances with pages of the Koran. The Caliphate was submitted to the arbitration of elders, but in the end the prize went to the Sunnis by default. On January 22, 661, as Ali entered a mosque at Kufa, a Sunni fanatic plunged a poisoned dagger into his brain. With key backing from the governor of Egypt,

Muawiya appealed for peace, won pledges of allegiance from most of the Arab elders, and assumed the Caliphate. So began the Umayyad dynasty at Damascus, which after Muawiya's own stern reign of twenty years, made the office of caliph hereditary in his House. Fourteen Umayyad caliphs were to rule in turn and dominate Islam for a hundred years. Syria became the empire's center of gravity with Damascus as its capital and military hub.

Under the Umayyads, the march of conquest continued, naval supremacy was established in the eastern Mediterranean, and some administrative innovations—including an empire-wide postal system (run as a "pony express," using horses and camels); the standardization of Arab coinage; and the establishment of Arabic as the official language of state—helped keep the empire intact. Even so, agitation by the Shiites, revolts in Mecca and Medina, unrest in Basra, festering hatred in Persia, and the recrudescence of old clan enmities bedeviled Umayyad rule.

In 681 Ali's second son, Husain, the grandson of the Prophet, led a failed revolt. His death in battle and the subsequent desecration of his corpse made him a martyr. To this day, "vengeance for Husain" rings through the back streets of Baghdad, where Shiites observe the anniversary of his death as a day of mourning and rage. The city of Karbala, where he fell on October 12, 681, became a site "almost as holy as Mecca and Medina," and his tomb, like that of Ali in Najaf, a sacred shrine.

In the end, two things undermined Umayyad power: the decay of the Arab tribal system on which their military strength depended, and disaffection toward the government arising from its Persian misrule. The Shiites, who denounced the Damascus caliphs as "ungodly usurpers," were supported by the Persians, whom the Umayyads had reduced to a near-servile state; both in turn were joined by the Abbasids, descended from Abbas, an uncle of the Prophet, and who challenged the Umayyad regime.

Four Umayyad caliphs came and went in a single year (743–44). Meanwhile, Shiites in Persia rallied to revolt "all those whose patriotism was outraged by Arab domination" and "seasoned their propaganda with tales of the turpitude of the reigning princes, to inflame the fanaticism of the Faithful with a description of their impiety and vice."

In 747, after forging a broad coalition of insurgent groups, the Abbasids raised the standard of revolt. Under Abu Muslim, a manumitted Persian slave, their troops seized southern Persia and Iraq and under a black flag (their emblem) outfought the Umayyads from Kufa to Khurasan. At length, in a climactic battle of Mosul—not far from where Alexander the Great had trounced King Darius of Persia in 331 B.C.—they prevailed. The last of the Umayyads, Marwan II, fled to Egypt, where he was captured, killed, and his tongue fed to a cat.

The ethnic character of the Caliphate began to change. Under the Umayyads, it had been a purely Arab thing, and only those of full Arab parentage on both sides had been admitted to the highest offices of state. Under the new regime, not only half Arabs but Persians and others would rise at court.

As the first Abbasid caliph, Abu al-Abbas began his rule with a horrific massacre of the whole Umayyad house. He called himself "Saffah," that is, "the Bloodshedder," and in one gruesome account held his victory feast on a field full of corpses which he covered with a heavy carpet, like a tablecloth. The tombs of the Umayyad caliphs were also ransacked and their bones burnt and scattered to the winds. (The only Umayyad to escape was a nineteen-year-old prince by the name of Abd al-Rahman, who slipped through North Africa to Spain and founded the independent kingdom of the Moors.)

Despite this dread beginning—which later good governance helped to repair—Abbasid rule would be sustained through thirty-seven caliphs over the course of five hundred years. The stage for that stability was set in 754, when Abbas was succeeded by his brother, Abu Jafar Abdullah al-Mansur ("the Victorious"), a tall, thin man with a narrow face, dark complexion, lank hair, and a thin beard.

At first it seemed there might be civil war. Mansur's uncle, encamped with Syrian troops on the edge of Asia Minor, had contested his accession and it had taken five months of fighting for Mansur to gain his throne. Abu Muslim had led the defense of his rights, but after using him to defeat this Syrian revolt against his rule, Mansur endeared the Syrians to him by executing his redoubtable commander in February 755 for pretended misdeeds. He subsequently promoted Syrian nobles to high office and selected Syrian army units to man key posts. At the same time, he took immediate steps, by means of land grants, gifts, and generous tax incentives, to reconcile Abu Muslim's leading supporters, based in Khurasan, to his reign.

Born and bred in the deserts of Edom, Mansur in time proved an exemplary ruler, thrifty, energetic, circumspect, and wise. Though he continued the baneful frontier war that had long been carried on between Islam and what remained of Byzantine rule, he improved his own outposts with new fortifications, repaired strongholds in Armenia and Cilicia, and erected defenseworks in maritime towns on the Syrian coast. After the wild Khazars from southern Russia invaded territory south of the Caucasus and took Tiflis (now Tbilisi), he vowed to prevent such marauding and seized territory as far as the sulfur springs of Baku.

Mansur's intelligence service extended to distant regions, and made note of everything from civil unrest to the price of figs, giving him the appearance of omniscience in his conduct of affairs. He rose at dawn, worked until evening prayer, and granted himself only brief periods of rest. He impressed such vigilance upon his son and heir: "Put not off the work of today until the morrow and attend in person to the affairs of state. Sleep not, for thy father has not slept since he came to the caliphate. For when sleep fell upon his eyes, his spirit remained awake." Notoriously frugal, he was surnamed Abu al-Duwaneek ("the Father of Small Change"), watched his tax collectors like a hawk, and made sure even large expenditures were carefully accounted for. "He who has no money has no men," he once said, "and he who has no men watches as his enemies grow great."

The fruits of his exertions were reaped by his successors, and the great prosperity of the realm for a long time thereafter owed much to what he achieved.

But it is the founding of Baghdad for which Mansur is remembered most.

When the Abbasids first took charge, Damascus was naturally hostile to the new regime. It was also far from Persia, the base of Abbasid power.

So almost immediately (under Abu al-Abbas) the search for a new capital had begun. During the early Muslim conquest, two garrison towns had been founded in Iraq—Basra on the Euphrates, and Kufa, where the desert caravan road to Persia entered the Mesopotamian plain. Not caring for either, and insecure even in the midst of loyal subjects, Abu al-Abbas al-Saffah had secluded himself in a palace complex north of Kufa, where he died. Upon his accession, Mansur thought of creating a new town in the same district. But the local population of fanatical Shiites gave him pause. On one occasion, a mob of zealots surged round his palace proclaiming him divine. When the caliph rejected their homage, they turned violent, attacked his guards, and in an instant he found himself in danger of being killed by those who had just revered him as a god. Mansur then went in search of a site on the lower Tigris, traveled slowly up the river to Mosul, and at length chose the Persian hamlet of Baghdad, on the west bank.

"Baghdad" in Persian meant "Founded by God," and Babylonian brickwork, stamped with the name and titles of Nebuchadrezzar, showed that it had once been the site of an ancient city, built by a monarch of immortal fame. In Muhammad's day, it had sunk to the level of a market town, and by the time Mansur came upon it, even the bazaars had vanished, with Christian monasteries appearing in their place. Mansur learned from the local monks that the area was unusually free of mosquitoes (an important consideration), the winters mild, and some of the summer nights cool and pleasant (or so he was told) even during hotter months. It was also in an area of seasonally rotating crops, shaded by palm trees, and a potential commercial hub—linked to Egypt and Syria by the caravan route, to river commerce through Mosul, with ready access to the Persian Gulf (as well as to Arabia, Syria, and Armenia) and to commodities from China and Byzantium by sea. The site appealed to him for other reasons besides. Both banks of the river were cultivable yet naturally fortified against attack: to the east, the stream was impossible to ford, and a network of canals to the south provided a moatlike means of defense.

From the beginning it also seemed a fateful place. The Muslim historian Tabari tells us that an ancient prophecy preserved by the Christian monks held that a great city would one day be built there by a lord named Miklas. When Mansur heard this he nearly jumped for joy, for, legend has it, he had been given that very nickname as a child.

After his Jewish astrologer Mashallah (the foremost expert of his time) elected a propitious time for the city's founding, the plan of the city was traced in the soil with lines of cinders then literally burned into the ground. This was done by placing balls of cotton saturated with naphtha along the outline and setting them on fire. Construction was then pushed rapidly—with one hundred thousand workmen drawn from throughout the Near and Middle East—and carried out on a magnificent scale. Vast sums were expended on palatial buildings, mosques, barracks, bridges, aqueducts, and various fortifications; baked bricks used for domes and arches; and sun-dried bricks of extraordinary size—some weighing as much as two hundred pounds—for the massive walls. Completed in 766, the "Round City," as it was called, was two miles in diameter with inner and outer battlements made up of three concentric walls and a deep, water-filled moat. The residential quarter was divided into four quadrants, which housed senior officials and the imperial guard. Flanking the inside of the city walls, arcades were built for merchants' shops and stalls. In the center stood the Palace of the Caliph (called the Golden Gate), and beside it the Great Mosque. The Palace, named for its heavily gilded great door, was made of stone and marble and had a great green dome topped by the statue of a mounted horseman that turned like a weathervane. Above the inner wall, a gallery ran the length of the crenellated rampart wide enough for the caliph to ride along on horseback as he scanned the surrounding terrain. From the city's four immense iron gates—so heavy it took a company of men to move it—four high roads, marking the four points of the compass, radiated out like the spokes of a wheel.

Each gate was named for the major city or region it faced: Damascus, Basra, Kufa, and Khurasan. In concept, the city's four quadrants also reflected the four quarters of the world. At their symbolic, intersecting center, the caliph made his home.

As formidable a citadel as the Round City was, there were some practical flaws in its design. Though it might be difficult for enemies to reach the caliph, "it was equally difficult for him to reach safety should the need arise." Because the principal mosque adjoined the palace, the heart of the caliph's domain was also swamped by the masses during Friday prayers. One day a diplomat from Constantinople was talking to the caliph when his audience was disrupted by a loud tumult from the streets below. A cow, set to be butchered, had escaped in terror, overturned some stalls, and was running about the arcades. When told of this, the diplomat advised the caliph to place the public markets outside the walls to avoid the risk of harm from mobs.

Before long, the city ramified far beyond its original plan, to cover five square miles of suburbs that grew up along the high roads and on the opposite bank. It encompassed large parks and pleasure haunts; ethnic enclaves; a Christian quarter, adorned with churches, monasteries, convents, and shrines; and a highly developed waterfront for commercial use. Three large pontoon bridges (traversed by planked walks) spanned the river— above, below, and in the middle of the city—anchored to great piles on either bank by iron chains. Some thirty thousand skiffs also ferried people to and fro. Meanwhile, on the east bank of the Tigris, the al-Rusafah palace of Mansur's son, the crown prince Muhammad al-Mahdi, arose. A suburb grew up around it opposite a second palace known as al-Khuld ("the Mansion of Paradise"), bordered by extensive gardens that lay along the west bank. In time, the city's unusual and exotic attractions would also come to include large public squares for horse racing and polo (a Persian game); a palace constructed around a solid silver tree with mechanical, singing birds; and a Wild Beast Park, with fenced-in preserves for lions, elephants, peacocks, leopards, and giraffes.

Called into existence "as if by an enchanter's wand," Baghdad became the greatest city in the world. Mansur christened it "Madinat-as-Salam," "the City of Peace," which is the name it also bore on the coins of the Abbasids. Mansur had laid the first brick with his own hands, and in doing so intoned: "In the name of the Lord! praise belongeth unto Him and the earth is His: He causeth such of His servants as He pleaseth to inherit the same. Success attend the pious!" Wars, sieges, constantly recurring riots between the Sunnis and Shiites, rebellions in Medina, Basra, and

Kufa, the removal of the government for a time to Samarra, higher up on the Tigris, even the devastation of the city by the Mongols in 1258—none would ever quite succeed in totally erasing its allure.

The empire had been built, its capital established, its ruling house secured. The stage was thereby set for Islam's Golden Age.

chapter two

THE NIGHT OF DESTINY

After a reign of twenty-two years, Mansur died at the age of sixty-five on October 21, 775, near Mecca, when he was thrown from his mighty charger as it scrambled down a steep mountainside. Some say his health had already begun to fail and that his doctor had found evidence of some mortal disease. As fearsome as he was, the insubstantiality of worldly power had also come to distress him—as it seemed to distress most caliphs, in their time. One day he was consulting with Rabi ibn Yunus, who had first served him as "hajib" or chamberlain (controlling access to his person), and then as prime minister or vizier. Mansur said to him: "How sweet would the world be, O Rabi! were it not for death." "Say, rather," replied Rabi, "that the world had not been sweet were it not for death." "How so?" asked the caliph. "Were it not for death, you would not be sitting on that throne." "True," replied the caliph; but years later, as death approached and latent horror haunted him for some misdeeds, Mansur said to him, "O Rabi! We have sacrificed the world to come for a mere dream!"

When that dream expired, he was attended by a grandson and a few top aides. To keep his death a secret, Rabi warned the women in the caliph's entourage not to openly mourn his passing, and in a stratagem designed to protect the succession rights of his son, "propped up the caliph's corpse on a couch in the royal tent behind a thin curtain" and had all the leading members of the Abbasid family renew their oaths of allegiance as they filed by. Mansur's death was then revealed, and that night he was buried in the desert, in one of a hundred graves that were dug near Mecca to baffle any attempt to find and desecrate his bones.

His grave was thus lost forever in the sand.

At Baghdad, Mansur's son and heir, Mahdi, assumed power. One of Saffah's nephews (the governor of Kufa) contested his succession, but relented upon the false promise that power would revert to him on Mahdi's death. On the face of it, that was unlikely anyway since Mahdi had two sons.

Born in 745, Mahdi had spent his childhood in Syria and served in a military capacity in Khurasan, which he also governed, taking up his residence at Rayy, not far from modern Tehran. Tall, elegant, and debonair, Mahdi "had a dark complexion, a high forehead, and curly hair." Women adored him; and he worshipped them. In his pursuit of pleasure, he spent freely, taxing his treasury's supply. He was always enamoured of someone, but his true love was a young girl "slender and graceful as a reed," named Khaizuran (meaning "bamboo"), the daughter of a rebel ruler of Herat. Mansur had told one of his officials: "Take her to my son and tell him that she is made to bear children." Khaizuran satisfied his amorous expectations, and in time would bear Mahdi three sons: Musa (Moses), born in 764; Harun (Aaron), born in 766 (both destined for power and fame), and Isa, whose life remains obscure.

Khaizuran also bore Mahdi a daughter, named Yacuta ("the Ruby"). Born in 767, she was her father's favorite as a child. He could scarcely let her out of his sight. She had her own adjunct palace in the grounds of the royal complex and used "to ride out" with him, dressed as a little cavalry soldier, complete with sword. But she died young, at age sixteen, and in his great grief, Mahdi declared a day of mourning and received the condolences of the court and people at a public audience, "as if she had been a great prince."

Beyond producing heirs, Khaizuran had considerable ambition in her own right. Politically savvy, she established herself in the palace as a power to be reckoned with by those who sought the caliph's ear. In time her sister, Salsal, became the concubine of Mahdi's half brother, Jafar, to whom she bore a daughter and a son. Mahdi had many concubines himself, including Shikla, a young black African slave captured from another prince along the southern coast of the Caspian Sea. She bore Mahdi a dark-skinned son named Ibrahim, who became a celebrated poet and singer, beloved of the Caliph Harun al-Rashid. This was entirely normal for the prodigious sex lives of caliphs with their harems, which had been a continually developing feature of court life. Among wives, concubines, and slaves, ethnic diversity was also commonplace. Mansur's first wife had been a woman from Yemen, of royal blood; his second, a descendant of a hero of the Islamic conquests; his third, a Persian slave. He also had at least three concubines: one an Arab; another, a Byzantine, nicknamed the "Restless Butterfly"; the third, a Kurd.

As above, so below. Because slavery in its various forms, including concubines, was so large a part of Islamic life, it was governed by complicated rules. A man could have four wives at the same time, an indefinite number of concubines and divorce and marry the same woman twice but not marry her again until she had been married and divorced by someone else. The children born to a concubine slave enjoyed the same right of inheritance as other freeborn offspring, provided the father acknowledged his paternity. A female slave accepted as the child of her master could also not be sold and was automatically freed upon his death. The offspring of a male slave by a free woman was also free. Although in theory any Muslim could have up to four wives, there were obvious financial and other constraints on maintaining such a household, and most Muslims had no more than one wife and did not keep concubines or slaves. Those who kept to one wife were often deemed wise. In the words of one Arab proverb: "He who has two wives has an anxious life; he who has three is embittered; he who has four might as well be dead."

Since the enslavement of Muslims was forbidden by law, slaves were acquired by various means. Some were captured in war; others were the offspring of a female slave by another slave, or by any man who was not her owner; or by her owner if he did not acknowledge himself the father. The last enjoyed no legal or property rights and were entirely subject to their masters. At the death of their master, unemancipated slaves became the property of his heirs. At the same time, the Koran demanded that slaves be well-treated, and the Prophet had urged that their families not be broken up. "A man who behaves ill to his slaves will not enter Paradise," he had said. But he had not condemned slavery itself.

The slave trade was conducted throughout southern Europe and the Near East. On the block were Slavs (hence the word "slaves") from central and eastern Europe, Nubians and Ethiopians from the Sudan, Franks, Azeris from Azerbaijan, Greeks, Tatars, Berbers, Armenians, and other peoples of the far-flung Arab world. Some were singled out to become eunuchs, while a special class of girls (often educated, much like Japanese Geishas, to serve as refined companions) became the concubines of caliphs and the well-to-do. Yet many slaves were freed, for to free them was considered a pious act. There was little incentive not to. For a freed slave became his master's "freedman," in principle liberated, but honor-bound to continue in his service, as before.

The royal "harem" (meaning "forbidden or sacred place") formally developed at this time. Among the desert Arabs in pre-Islamic days, "women," it seems, "had been remarkably free. It was in the early Abbasid period, with the advent of wealth, luxury, and Persian customs, that palace women became increasingly secluded, and the wives and concubines of the wealthy set apart. Each wife had her separate house or apartment, with her own establishment of eunuchs, servants, and maids." When a concubine bore her master a son, she was raised in rank and also received a suite of apartments (and servants) of her own.

Eunuchs, or castrated males, played an important part in the harem as trusted go-betweens and guards. The role of the eunuch, however, was not Arab in origin but Byzantine. And in the Byzantine Empire they played a larger role. Though most eunuchs were castrated against their will, some chose castration in the hope they might one day rise to a responsible position at court. In addition to serving in the harem (the word "eunuch" means "bed keeper"), they often occupied offices in the treasury and archives, handling top-secret documents and performing other delicate tasks. They were believed to be more reliable than others since their minds were less likely to be distracted by pleasure from the business of state. Within the court of Baghdad, several had considerable power. Salam al-Abrash (whose name means "the Speckled One"), for example, "began his court career as a young page, waiting on Mansur," notes one historian, and rose to the post of Commissioner of Petitions, in charge of the public sessions when petitioners could approach the caliph with their complaints. After Mansur died, he served Mahdi and two of his sons, and became a man of some learning, evidently mastering enough Greek to translate Greek works into Arabic.

Despite the seeming sexual license of the Arab world, Muslim scholars like to trace the emphasis on chaste restraint to the Prophet himself. According to tradition, he once said to his son-in-law, Ali: "O Ali, do not follow one glance [at a woman] with another, for the first is allowed you, but the second is not." With that exhortation in mind, a scholar at Mahdi's court recalled that once during his circuit of the Kaaba, he "saw a girl who was like an oryx, and I began to watch her and to fill my eyes with her lovely form. She noted this and said to me, 'What's wrong with you?' I said, 'What is it to you if I look?' But she replied, 'You cannot have everything you want,' then quoted these lines: 'When you sent your eye scouting for your heart, / You saw something over the whole of which / You did not have power.' "

THOUGH IT IS SOMETIMES SAID THAT ARABS OF THE DAY preferred women of goodly size, the typical maiden celebrated in song was as elegant "as a willow's twig," with "a face like the moon," had large, black, almond-shaped eyes; long black hair; rosy cheeks; thin, arched brows; small red lips; teeth "like pearls set in coral"; breasts "like pomegranates"; and beauty spots "like drops of ambergris."

Khaizuran, whom Mahdi married in 775, conformed well to this composite ideal. But she also accepted that he would not be true. Through it all, she remained more than a first among equals, and always lured him back. Once, when he was ailing, she sent him a soothing potion in a crystal cup inscribed with these words: "When you have recovered your health and have improved it further by this drink, then be gracious to her who sent it, by paying her a visit after dusk."

Within court circles, Khaizuran built her own network of allies. One day, when she was in her apartment surrounded by other royal women, a maidservant whispered that Muznah, the widow of Marwan II, the last

Umayyad caliph, was at the door. Muznah was destitute and her story and condition so touched Khaizuran's heart that Khaizuran arranged for her to be provided for.

That evening, when Khaizuran and Mahdi dined together, she told him what had happened. Mahdi commended her charity and accorded Muznah the rank at court of a royal princess, which she enjoyed until her death in a subsequent reign.

Accomplished as she was, Khaizuran would be remembered in the history of the Caliphate not because of her queenly character or stature, but "because of the direction she would give to the political course of the Abbasid Empire," as one writer put it, "chiefly through her energetic intrigues in the succession of her sons."

MAHDI BEGAN HIS REIGN BY FREEING A NUMBER OF POLITI-cal prisoners, enlarged and beautified the mosques of Mecca and Medina, provided the pilgrim caravanserais with more fountains and establishments, and made them commodious and secure. He developed the postal service; elaborated the intelligence service; fortified cities, including Baghdad, and especially Rusafah, its eastern suburb; and created a more vibrant court. His charitable giving to the poor and needy was considerable, and he rescued the Kaaba at Mecca from collapse. Every year for decades it had been covered with gifts of rich brocade made by the reigning caliph, one on top of another, until their cumulative weight was almost too much for it to bear. Under Mahdi, these layered coverings were removed and their place filled by a single new covering sent each year.

Mahdi had mixed success, however, in his efforts to appease the Shiites; cracked down on "schismatics"; beheaded one of his ministers as a Manichean heretic; launched a failed expedition from North Africa to win Spain for the Caliphate; and stepped up the border war with the Byzantines.

In the meantime, he had anointed his elder son, Musa, surnamed "Hadi" (meaning, "the Guide"), as his heir.

While the early Abbasid caliphs had been preoccupied with securing their own power, the Byzantines had been engaged in fighting Slavic tribes in Macedonia and Thrace and warding off attacks by the Bulgars. With

Mahdi's accession, war with the Byzantines was waged with more force. He extended his line of fortifications from Syria to the Armenian frontier and claimed the strategic town of Tarsus, near a pass that cut through the Taurus Mountains linking Anatolia, Syria, and northern Iraq.

Mahdi also launched two major expeditions (in 779 and 781–82) under his son Harun. In this Mahdi was schooling his son for command, just as his father had schooled him. At the time, the Byzantine throne was occupied by a child named Constantine VI whose mother, Irene, ruled as regent in his name. Her power was fragile and to some degree hobbled by domestic strife. Under the guidance of seasoned generals, statesmen, and aides-de-camp, Harun, not yet twenty, took the fortress of Samalu after a thirty-eight-day siege, and on February 9, 781, marched from Aleppo at the head of 100,000 men, advanced through the Taurus Mountains, met and defeated the renowned general Nicetas, Count of Opsikon, and took the major fortress of Magida at the Cilician Gates. From there he marched to Chrysopolis (now Uskudar), and on to Constantinople itself where he "leaned his lance" against its walls. He threatened to sack the city if a large annual tribute was not agreed to, and the Greeks acquiesced. According to the Muslim historian Tabari, the Greeks had lost 54,000 men in the campaign, and Harun had needed 20,000 beasts of burden to carry off the booty he obtained. There was so much of it, according to the chroniclers, that the price of a sword dropped to a single dirham (the standard silver coin) and that of a horse to a single gold Byzantine "dollar" or dinar.

Harun's expedition against the Byzantines raised his political stock and upon his return on August 31, 782, he had been anointed "al-Rashid," meaning "the Rightly-Guided One." He was proclaimed second in line to the throne and placed in charge of the empire's western dominions, from Syria to Azerbaijan.

Though Mahdi accomplished most of his domestic and foreign policy objectives in the decade of his rule, he was not as frugal as his father had been, passed most of his time at Rusafah, involved Khaizuran in state matters, and in general liked to have a good time. Former caliphs on pilgrimage to Mecca had made the long desert trek "with goatskins full of muddy water and saddlebags of dates." Mahdi saw no reason for self-denial on that scale, traveled in royal style, and even had ice wrapped in layers of sacking hauled all the way from the Persian mountains to Mecca so that his drinks could be refreshed. On the arduous pilgrim road, he thought nothing of providing himself and his princely retinue with sherbet or wine.

But he could also take a self-mocking view of the pretensions of his rank. One day, Mahdi was out hunting gazelles and, accompanied by a single aide, became separated from his retinue. Tired and hungry, the two dismounted at the tent of a poor bedouin, or desert Arab, and asked him if he had anything to eat. The man promptly set out some brown bread, butter, and oil. "You wouldn't have some wine, would you?" asked the caliph. "I do," said the Arab, who produced a bulging goatskin to Mahdi's delight. The caliph decided to humor himself a bit. "Do you know who I am?" he asked. "I have no idea," said the Arab, "and I don't really care. Eat and drink." (In those days, of course, few outside the court would have known the caliph by sight.) "Well," said the caliph, "I am one of the servants of the Prince of the Faithful." "That must be a good job," said the Arab. "I hope you appreciate your luck." Mahdi held out his cup and downed the refill at one draft. "Do you know who I am?" he asked again. "You told me," said the Arab. "No, I am one of the caliph's top army commanders." He held out his cup again. The Arab filled it but eyed him askance. The caliph tossed it off. "Now then, do you know who I really am? I am the Prince of the Faithful himself!" Once more he held out his cup. "Not another drop!" exclaimed the Arab, and tied up the goatskin. "If I give you any more, you'll claim to be the Messenger of God!"

THOUGH MAHDI HAD MADE HIS FIRSTBORN SON, HADI, HIS heir, doubts crept into his thinking as he watched his two sons mature. Thus far, Hadi had done nothing of distinction, and had even botched an expedition to pacify the turbulent province of Jurjan southeast of the Caspian Sea. One night the caliph dreamed that he had given each son the branch of a tree. Hadi's bore only a few leaves on its stem, while Harun's was covered with foliage from end to end. Mahdi interpreted this to mean that Hadi's reign would be short, while Harun's would thrive and endure. The same discrepancy turned up in their horoscopes. At length, in 785 Mahdi changed his will and made Harun his heir.

He was staunchly supported by his wife.

Hadi, however, refused to renounce his rights and at length, after a number of threats, the caliph set out for Jurjan himself at the head of an army to enforce his will. With him he took Harun and Yahya al-Barmak, his new vizier.

En route, on August 4, 785, Mahdi paused at Masabadhan, a lovely alpine resort, to hunt gazelles. One morning, he went out with his hounds, caught sight of an antelope, and chased it through a ruined estate. As he spurred his charger to a gallop, he tried to pass through the entrance to a fallen house, struck his head on the lintel, and was killed. So went one account. Another alleged that he was inadvertently poisoned by a concubine named Hasanah, who was jealous of a girl to whom the caliph had been drawn. To rid herself of her rival, she had prepared a dish of sweets, on top of which she placed a poisoned pear. The core of the pear had been extracted and replaced by a lethal paste. She sent the dish to her rival by a maid, but Mahdi happened to meet the latter on her way and said, "That looks good. May I deprive you of that juicy pear?" Without pausing, he plucked it off the top. Soon afterward, he complained of stomach cramps and died that night—aged forty-three, after a reign of ten years.

Harun was in a state of shock. After praying beside his father, he consulted with Yahya al-Barmak as to what he should do—contest the succession, or not? Some advised him to return with his father's body to Baghdad before publicly announcing his death. But Yahya argued that the death could not be kept secret and that when the troops discovered they were escorting the caliph's body, they might riot for bonus pay. He therefore advised Harun to pay off the troops, bury his father where he was, and write at once to his brother to congratulate him on his crown. He also urged Harun to send him the imperial scepter, insignia, and seal. Harun did all this promptly and later that day Mahdi was carried to his grave on a door taken from a nearby house and buried beneath a walnut tree.

Despite Yahya's precautions, there was subsequent unrest among the garrison in Baghdad and the chamberlain's house was sacked. Khai-zuran appeased them (as Harun had appeased the soldiers in his train) with a bonus; meanwhile, Hadi had abandoned his camp and advanced by forced marches back to Baghdad, arriving on August 31, 785. By then the city was calm. Harun had reached Baghdad before him and to demonstrate his loyalty had dispatched heralds to different parts of the empire to announce his father's death and Hadi's accession to the throne. Hadi spent his first day as caliph in the arms of his favorite mistress, set himself up at a suburban pleasure resort called Isabadh on Baghdad's east side, placed Yahya al-Barmak in charge of Harun's household, and made Rabi ibn Yunus his vizier.

Harun acceded to all this without a murmur. "By no single act of his brilliant career," wrote one biographer, "did Harun better vindicate his worthiness of the imperial sceptre than by renouncing it in the interests of civil peace. The army was his for the commanding, and he disbanded it. His elder brother was at his mercy, and he placed him on the throne. His mother sought to thrust greatness on him, but he preferred to abide by the verdict of Fate. Of few can it be said so truly that he was born great."

Nevertheless, it was a tense time. Until his accession, Hadi had been "a big, ill-tempered boy with a hanging lower lip which invited ridicule." Now he ruled the realm. The great Muslim historian Masudi wrote that Hadi was "hard and coarse, conceited, undignified, difficult to approach," and always flanked by a bodyguard wielding spiked clubs and swords. Though he was not unintelligent, his learning was tinged with malice, and for the most part he took a fanatical interest in religious affairs.

Accordingly, he began his reign by persecuting a sect of Manichaean dualists known as "zindiks" who had scoffed at Islamic customs, including the annual pilgrimage or Hajj. One of their leaders rashly compared the ritual circuit of pilgrims about the Kaaba to "oxen trampling round a threshing floor." Hadi caught and killed the man and hung his body on a cross. The cross, however, fell down on a pilgrim and killed him, in an early sign that Hadi's reign might go awry. Nevertheless, he threatened to hunt down others and ordered one thousand palm trees hewn into gallows for following through on his threat. Meanwhile, he also set out to extirpate the Shiites. This provoked a sharp, if short-lived, revolt in Medina, where rebels allied to Husain, the great-grandson of Ali (the saint of the Alids), routed the town garrison and took over the mosque. A few days later, Husain issued an emancipation proclamation to all slaves who joined him and set out for Mecca, in emulation of Muhammad's own famous march on the holy site. Hadi sent an army in pursuit and in a clash of forces known as the Battle of Fakhkh, near Mecca on June 11, 786, Husain was killed.

In addition to hating Manichaeans and Shiites, Hadi had a horror of lesbian liaisons. One night when he was entertaining some friends a servant entered and whispered something in his ear. According to one eyewitness, Hadi rose at once and left the room.

After a while, he returned, breathing heavily, and threw himself on a couch. He lay there panting for some time. A eunuch had come in with him carrying a tray covered with a cloth, and all the time [the man] stood there shaking. We all wondered what was going on. At length, Hadi sat up and said, ... "Lift the cover!" and there on the tray were the heads of two concubines. . . . By God, I have never in my life seen two more beautiful faces, or lovelier hair, still entwined with jewels and fragrant with their perfumed scent. We were all amazed. Then the caliph asked, "Do you know what they did?" "No," we replied. "Well," he exclaimed, "I was told they had fallen in love and were meeting for immoral purposes. So I had them watched and caught them together making love under a quilt. So I killed them." Then he said to the eunuch, "Take the heads away!" and continued on with the conversation as if nothing unusual had occurred.

Hadi's reign was inglorious and short. At the outset, he had enjoyed his mother's indispensable backing and, in deference to her stature, had included her in his official rounds. Meanwhile, Harun had accepted his secondary position with equanimity and made no effort to claim more than his share. All might have been well for both had Hadi let well enough alone. But things began to come apart after he had a falling-out with his vizier, Rabi al-Yunus, over their shared love for a girl.

A few years before, Rabi had offered the girl, named Amat al-Aziz

("Handmaiden of the Almighty"), to Mahdi. Mahdi had given her to Hadi. Hadi was smitten and by the time he became caliph, she had borne him two sons. By then he had also learned that Rabi had made love to her before giving her up. The worm of jealousy gnawed at him day and night. Rabi was demoted to head of the accounting department and one day invited to join the caliph at his midday meal. Hadi showed him every honor, then handed him a cup of honeyed wine. "I realized," Rabi told his family later that evening, "that my life was in that cup, but I knew that if I were to hand it back he would cut off my head. So I drank it, and now I am going to die. I can feel the poison working in my body as I speak." By morning, he was dead.

At about this time, Hadi had also begun to chafe at the size and imperial character of his mother's court. For the ten years of his father's reign, she had played an active role in state affairs. Officials had often consulted her on important matters, and she had continued to attract a host of wealthy retainers, nobles, and generals to her door. It seemed to Hadi that she received as much obeisance as he did. And that he could not abide. One day, he called his top officials together and said, "Who is better, you or I?" They replied, "Certainly, you are, O Commander of the Faithful!" He said, "Who is better, my mother or your mother?" They replied, "Assuredly, your mother, O Commander of the Faithful!" He said, "Which of you would like to have men talking with your mother behind your back?" They replied, "None of us would." "Then," said the caliph, "what do you think of the men who keep coming to my mother behind mine?"

Things came to a head when one day his mother asked him to oblige her in some matter having to do with an official appointment, and he refused. "You must do this for me," she said. He said he would not. "God knows," she said, "I will never ask anything of you again." "God knows also that it will not worry me," replied her son. Khaizuran rose to leave but Hadi lost control of himself and shouted, "Sit down and listen to what I have to say! . . . What is the meaning of these crowds of petitioners outside your door? Haven't you got a spinning wheel to keep you occupied or a Koran to read?" "Thereafter," according to Tabari, "she spoke no word to him, bitter or sweet, and entered not his presence until death paid him a sudden call."

That happened before long. Khaizuran was a mortal enemy to make. As tensions within the royal family grew, she had all her food tasted while within the imperial harem, and she established a subtle new web of intrigue to secure the end of her designs.

Meanwhile, Harun had also come within his brother's sights. One day, while Hadi was holding court at Isabadh, Harun entered and took his seat to Hadi's right. Hadi's new vizier, Ibrahim al-Harrani, sat to the caliph's left. Hadi stared at his brother for some time in silence, then said: "O Harun, it seems to me that you allow yourself to dwell too much on the fulfillment of our father's dream. Do not hope for that which is not now within your reach."

Harun replied that he had no desire to come to power before his time. He also said that if he ever did become caliph, he would put Hadi's sons before his own. "I will bring that to pass which is worthy of the memory of . . . our father and paradigm." Hadi seemed pleased, promised Harun an immense stipend, and to show him still more honor when Harun rose to leave, ordered that his brother's horse be brought up to the very edge of the royal carpet for him to mount.

Yet it was not long before Hadi began to think of replacing Harun with his own son as heir. He raised the subject with Yahya al-Barmak, who argued forcefully against it, pointing out that such a precedent could one day be used against his own son, Jafar. "O Prince of the Faithful," he said, "by teaching people to break their oaths, you weaken your own position. It would be better to persuade Harun voluntarily to abdicate," though he also advised him to wait at least until Jafar had come of age.

Hadi considered this advice disloyal and thought of putting Yahya to death. One night when the caliph sent for him Yahya was sure his time had come. He said farewell to his family, put on new clothes, and, we are told, in a grotesque gesture of resignation "anointed himself with the aromatic substances used in preparing" a corpse for the grave. Hadi, however, received him politely, conversed in an informal manner, then abruptly asked, "O Yahya, what is the relationship between us?" Yahya replied, "I am your obedient slave." The caliph said, "Why, then, are you coming between me and Harun?" He replied, "O Commander of the Faithful, who am I that I should presume to come between the two of you? It is merely that Mahdi enjoined me to look after him and his needs." The caliph said, "What exactly has Harun been up to?" Yahya replied, "He hasn't been up to anything, and it is not in his character to do anything untoward." That seemed to satisfy the caliph and he let Yahya go.

But Harun soon found himself stripped of his bodyguard and shunned at court. Yahya advised him to leave the capital for Syria at once on an extended hunting trip. "Keep far away," he told him, "and put off the days of your return." But scarcely had Harun done so than Hadi tried to dispose of his own mother (with a dish of poisoned rice) and clapped Yahya in chains. Khaizuran survived and moved at once to set things right.

And so it was that one day, as Hadi set out to visit an estate he owned south of Mosul, he was suddenly crippled by stomach pains. He returned to Baghdad and from there was carried on a bier to Isabadh. When a messenger brought Khaizuran the news, she said, "What difference does it make to me?" and promptly readied a circular dispatch announcing the caliph's death and the accession of Harun.

As Hadi declined, his chamberlain, Fadhl ibn al-Rabi, suggested he try a new doctor. Presently an apothecary from Syria arrived. He promised to give the caliph more effective drugs and had his assistants pound medicines within hearing. "Just keep on pounding," he told them, "so he will hear you and be calmed." Meanwhile, an order had been forged in the caliph's name by some of his advisors to put Yahya al-Barmak and Harun to death. But that night, at Khaizuran's command, his concubines smothered him in his sleep.

Upon learning that his brother was dead, Harun released Yahya from prison, sent greetings to his mother, and summoned his inner council, which included a large black African eunuch of tremendous strength named Abu Hashim Masrur. Masrur had been his companion since childhood and would serve him as bodyguard, confidant, and special executioner throughout his reign. No sooner had Masrur arrived than a messenger entered to announce that one of Harun's concubines, a Persian by the name of Marajil, had just given birth to a son. That child, whom Harun named Abdullah, would one day become the great Caliph Mamun.

It had been a momentous night. Indeed, it would go down in the annals of Islam as the "night of destiny," for it had witnessed the death of one caliph, the accession of a second, and the birth of a third.

As dawn broke, Harun set out for Isabadh, where he said the final prayers over his brother, assembled all the notables in the palace, received their oath of allegiance, and in a brief speech promised to work for the interests of the people and to preside justly over their affairs. Meanwhile, Hadi's young son Jafar had been roused at dawn and compelled to renounce his rights as crown prince. He was taken to an upstairs window and made to say to the assembled crowd, "O good Muslims! Anyone who has sworn loyalty to me in the lifetime of my father is released from his oath. The caliph is my uncle, Harun al-Rashid. I have no right to the caliphate."

chapter three

KING OF KINGS

orn on March 17, 763, Harun al-Rashid, the fifth of the Abbasid caliphs, was twenty-three years old when he came to the throne on the night of September 15, 786. The night had been clear and bright, resplendent with a million stars. Legend has it that the crescent moon itself seemed curved like a scythe above the "al-Khuld" or "Eternal" Palace, with a single star near the center of its arc, as in the later Muslim battle flag.

The following morning Harun set out from the suburb of Isabadh and made his official entry into the imperial capital of Baghdad, preceded by his praetorian or palace guard. Legions of troops followed, their arms and armor flashing in the sun. Among the men-at-arms was a troop of holy warriors known as the Ansar, or Medina, "Helpers," first recruited by his father, the Caliph Mahdi.

The banks of the Tigris River were crowded with expectant throngs—the more so because it was a Friday, the Muslim day of public prayer. Thousands also lined the great bridge of boats that the caliph would cross; "swarmed about the Khurasan Gate through which he would pass; covered the parade grounds, overflowing to the very portals of the palace; and massed about the Great Mosque," where he would soon lead the faithful in prayer. Fleets of skiffs and barges full of spectators completely jammed the river, and merchants and nobles stood upon the decks of terraced mansions that overlooked the quays. Among them the black cloaks, turbans, and flags of the Abbasids "stood out like splashes of kohl on the face of the sun-bleached city, and glistened like black onyx in the sun." Khaizuran, observing, stood on the battlements of the Green Domed Palace. From rooftops and windows, women uttered the high-pitched Muslim ululation, or trill of joy.

The imperial procession swept by slowly. Harun's palace guard was dressed in brilliant uniforms, and in their midst rode Harun himself in full body armor, regally erect on a magnificently caparisoned white steed. Slung over his shoulder, Islamic style, was the famed "Dhu al-Fakar," a two-pointed sword captured at the pivotal Battle of Badr in 624. Once wielded by the Prophet himself (and bequeathed by him to his son-in-law, Ali), it was said to have magical powers and was inscribed with the words "la yuktal Muslim bi-kafir," meaning, "no Muslim shall be slain for killing an infidel."

At noon, Harun led the prayers in the city's Great Mosque and then sat publicly in the courtyard while dignitaries and commoners alike filed past him to swear allegiance and declare their joy at his ascent. The following day at a palace audience and formal reception, the new caliph appointed Yahya al-Barmak his vizier and granted him plenary powers. As he presented him with the state seal, he addressed him in honorary fashion as his "father," saying, "My father! I owe my position to your wisdom. I place on you the responsibility for the welfare of my subjects. I take this responsibility from my own shoulders and lay it upon yours. Govern as you see best, employ whomever you wish, and dismiss whomever you will."

Hadi's evident murder was known to few that day and did nothing to cloud the festive pomp and air. Nor did its subsequent report besmirch Harun's stature in posterity's eyes. Years later, most Muslim historians would endorse the contemporary judgment of one admirer, who exclaimed: "Did you not see how the pale sun rebounded on Harun's accession and filled the world with light?" For no caliph has stood more completely for the supremacy of Islam, in its force and cultural achievements, as it embarked on its Golden Age. As a student of history, Harun himself regarded his own elevation as an instance of fated grandeur, and this was reinforced by his knowledge of Islam and its own improbable rise. As he took stock of his inherited dominions, he absorbed, at the hands of a select group of tutors, its majestic story and the glory and might now at his command.

All things considered, Harun had come to the throne in a relatively bloodless transfer of power. Khaizuran had pressed for the execution of those who had opposed his succession, but Yahya al-Barmak suggested instead that, after the fashion of King David's treatment of Uriah the Hittite, they be given risky frontier assignments on the front lines. For the most part, Harun didn't even go that far. He refrained from reprisals, and revenged himself upon only one of Hadi's retainers, by the name of Abu Ismah, who had insulted him when he was still a prince. Not long before, Ismah had been out riding with Hadi's son and happened to come upon Harun on a bridge in Isabadh. Ismah exclaimed, "Make way for the heir-apparent!" Harun had replied, "To hear is to obey, where the prince is concerned," and stood aside as they had passed. But the insult snaked its way into his heart. Before he entered Baghdad in triumph, he had Ismah's head struck off and his scalp affixed to the tip of a spear.

At the age of twenty-three, Harun was tall, handsome, and lean but strongly built, with curly hair and olive skin. In Baghdad he established himself at the palace of al-Khuld, built by his father on the banks of the Tigris and fashioned, like the Round City, of stucco-covered mud and baked brick. Its battlemented walls and large, crenellated towers, gave it the character of a mighty citadel and (much like Moscow's Kremlin of a later date) combined the royal residence and the offices of the imperial administration into a single complex "with vast audience and reception chambers, and innumerable rooms and private apartments for court dignitaries, department secretaries, and their staffs." In front of the palace was an expansive parade ground flanked by the headquarters of the chief of police. On ceremonial occasions, "reviews and parades were held there before the large crowds that came to admire the spectacle of imperial pomp and the caliph's serried ranks."

The grounds also included a number of gardens in one charming account, "with ponds and waterfalls," "little bridges of rare wood from far-off places; pavilions; yews and cypresses mirrored in still water; banks of flowers carefully grafted and arranged to reproduce the words of famous Arabic poems; and trees banded with precious jewel-studded metals, their leaves gilded and silvered with great artifice." Within the palace itself, according to Tabari, there was also "a small garden planted with pink-flowering trees surrounding a room carpeted in pink fabric, which was manned by servants dressed in pink uniforms." In one of the meeting rooms, an array of rare flowers was reflected in an alabaster pond. Some of these gardens—where the caliph would go in search of peace and quiet—were later described (with some embellishment) in the *Arabian Nights*.

The *Arabian Nights* also described a great room in the main palace furnished with a dome held up by eighty alabaster pillars, sculpted with gold birds. Inside the dome, "lines of living color repeated the designs of the wide carpets which covered the floor. Between the columns were jasper, agate, and crystal vases of exotic flowers." Some of the palace walls were painted with scenes from the lives of earlier caliphs and dramatic events pertaining to Islam's rise. In addition to the instruction he received from his tutors, Harun had all around him the storied past of Islamic history vividly pictured for his own imagination to ponder and review.

As a child, he spent part of his time in the royal harem, where he had been supervised by its staff, as was normal for a budding heir. His sojourn there had often been stirred by visits from his imposing grandfather Mansur, who stomped about in his great black boots and black turban and mixed stories of his reign with "pious advice on the virtues of thrift." But in other respects, he had undergone the typical training of a crown prince. He had studied history, geography, and rhetoric (eloquence); music and poetry; and economics in the form of finance. Religious studies encased or colored all these subjects, for Islam was a religious culture, and under the supervision of Ali ibn Hamza al-Kisai, a leading theologian, Harun's foremost energies were given to mastering the Hadith or Traditions of the Prophet and the text of the Koran. His physical training as a future warrior of God was also stressed and coupled military exercises such as swordplay, archery, and jousting with studies in the art of war.

Yet Harun, who was somewhat shy by nature, also had a genteel side. One of his tutors is said to have been Abd al-Malik ibn Quraib al-Asmai. If so, Harun could not have had a more learned or tactful guide. A native of Basra, and some twenty years Harun's senior, Asmai was, wrote the great early Muslim historian Ibn Khallikan, "a complete master of the Arabic language, an able grammarian, and the most eminent of those persons who transmitted orally historical narrations, singular anecdotes, amusing stories, and rare expressions" that keep a language alive. He knew the idiom of the desert Arabs better than anyone (by Harun's time that idiom had become a subject of almost antiquarian interest) but never pretended to know more about a subject than he really did. At the same time, according to a colleague, he always knew more than he seemed to, for "he never professed to know a branch of science without it being found that he knew it better than anyone else."

Asmai wrote on a wide variety of subjects, from zoology and meteorology to proverbs and games of chance, but was discreet in how he wielded his knowledge and declined to become involved in inflammatory public issues or religious disputes.

ONE OF HARUN'S IDOLS WAS THE ANCIENT PERSIAN KING Darius, who did much to reform his realm. The king devised an orderly tax system, uniform coinage, and standard measures and weights; built irrigation systems in Central Asia and the Syrian Desert, harbors on the Persian Gulf, a canal from the Nile to Suez, and the first road system ever constructed for wheeled vehicles, on which relays could carry a message more than sixteen hundred miles in a week. To some degree, it was in that king's image that Harun set out to rule.

At the head of the Islamic state, as perfected by Harun, stood the caliph, in theory the fountainhead of all power. He delegated his civil authority to a prime minister or vizier, his judicial power to a judge or qadi, and his military function to a general or amir. But the caliph himself remained the final arbiter of all government affairs. In their imperial conduct, the early Abbasid caliphs had exploited the popular reaction against the secular character of the Umayyads to emphasize the religious dignity of their office as that of an imam. The Umayyad caliphs—all drawn from the Arab elite—had based their patriarchal power on class; the Abbasids, on divine right. No longer was the caliph the deputy of the Prophet of Allah. He was now the Shadow of God on earth.

Since his family had "come to power on the crest of a religious movement," Harun presented himself to the people as a divine-right ruler who would initiate a new era of prosperity and justice. The Persian tradition of despotism, which influenced the Abbasids to some degree, had also begun to transform the caliph into an autocrat before whom courtiers bowed and whose hands and feet they kissed. At the same time, the influence of prominent Arab families declined. Long gone were the days of the desert Arab caliph whom anyone might approach. In his place was a nearly inaccessible monarch, hidden behind an impenetrable veil, in the heart of a battlemented palace, where he was enthroned after the fashion of the ancient Persian King of Kings.

In his palace, Harun usually received visitors and dignitaries while seated on a canopied couch, known as the sarir, screened from common sight by a curtain. No petitioner or guest was allowed to speak first, interrupt or contradict the caliph, fidget, or otherwise fail to give his complete attention to what the caliph had to say. When allowed to reply, the petitioner was expected to measure out his words with the utmost care. As a mark of the religious character of his exalted office, Harun now wore on ceremonial occasions the mantle once worn by the Prophet himself.

It was Islam, after all, that made the empire cohere. The Umayyad empire, as noted, had been mainly Arab; that of the Abbasids was increasingly made up of converted Muslims in which the Arabs formed only one of many component ethnic parts. The new caliphate was also not coterminous with Islam, since Spain, North Africa, and other areas formed independent or semi-independent domains. To replace the weakening bond of Arab ethnic cohesion, Harun therefore laid greater stress on Islamic identity, in an effort to impose on his vast and diverse empire the unity of a common culture and faith. Moreover, in basing his claim to the Caliphate on his descent from the Prophet's uncle, Harun, like the earlier Abbasids, did not subscribe to the "first among equals" principle of the early caliphs but began to adopt pre-Islamic Persian models for government and the court. Like the Persian Empire before it, the Empire of Islam sought by its high ceremonial and theocratic character to compete with the pretensions of the Roman and Byzantine empires with which it struggled for control of Central Asia and the Near and Middle East.

One ironic consequence of this imperial manner, however, was a growing Arab-Persian divide. Once the basic pattern of Arab social organization had dissolved, the new transnational spirit of Islam failed to compensate the Arabs for their sense of loss. Even the caliphs, in such matters as the choice of wives and mothers for their children, no longer set any special value on Arab blood. Concubines were unofficial wives. Since no slaves were Arabs, and all concubines were slaves, their children had non-Arab mothers who often raised them with affection for the ethnic group or nation from which they had come. The caliphs themselves, born and raised in this manner, became less and less Arab in character, culture, and ideals. Among the Abbasids only three caliphs were sons of free mothers: Abu al-Abbas (Saffah), Mahdi, and, later, Harun's son Amin, who enjoyed the unique distinction of being descended from the Prophet's family on both sides.

In short, as the pure Arab element receded into the background, non-Arabs, half Arabs, and the sons of freed women often took their place. Before long, the Arab aristocracy was superseded by a hierarchy of officials representing diverse ethnic groups. The strongest strain among them was the Persian, as the conquered became tutors to their overlords. "The Persians ruled for a thousand years and did not need us even for a day," as one Arab put it. "We have been ruling for one or two centuries, and cannot do without them for an hour."

Harun's grandfather Mansur had been underpinned by Persian troops and had advised his son to pin his faith on them without reserve. Mahdi, in turn, ably supported by Khaizuran, his Persian wife, had bequeathed to his heirs a largely Persian caliphate. With Persian trappings, Harun, in turn, did everything he could to reinforce his public image as the spiritual head of Islam, as well as its temporal lord. In his priestly role, he sought to ensure orthodox obedience and challenged heresy in all its forms. But he was not a fanatic like Hadi. In his early policy toward the Shiites or Alids, for example, he embraced the conciliatory manner of his father, released a number of Alids from prison, and even awarded them pensions from the state.

Even so, Harun was unremitting in the ceremonial observance of his faith. Every morning, he gave away a thousand dirhams to charity and made one hundred prostrations (each accompanied by many prayerful incantations) a day. He made the pilgrimage to Mecca (1,750 miles from Baghdad and back) by camel seven times, beginning with the year after he came to the throne, and an eighth pilgrimage from Rakkah (in Syria) to Mecca on foot. "When we consider the distances involved," writes one historian, "and the inhospitable nature of the arid desert through which he had to pass, this fact alone will give some idea of the indomitable energy and perseverance of his character. He was the only Caliph who ever imposed upon himself so austere a duty, and he was perhaps the only one who ever condemned himself to the performance of so many prostrations with his daily prayers."

On pilgrimage, he also dispensed large sums to the populations of Mecca and Medina, the two holiest cities of Islam, and to poor pilgrims along the route. There were always a number of ascetics whom he supported in his entourage, and when unable in any given year to go on pilgrimage himself, he sent high-ranking surrogates along with three hundred clerics at his own expense. His seal bore the device "Harun leans on God," and in his practice he seemed to incarnate the belief that "a pilgrimage is one of the five columns that support the Faith."

His reign also gave a renewed importance to the holy places, and, for political reasons, turned the pilgrimage to Mecca into an imposing propaganda event. Khaizuran followed his lead, and in 788 made her own pilgrimage as the queen mother, dispensing charity to the public on a grand scale. On one occasion after another, "she ordered a shelter, a fountain or a mosque to be built along the pilgrims' route." She seems to have been the first as well to adopt the idea of preserving buildings of historic interest. When she arrived in Mecca, where she would remain for several months, she not only funded an effort to restore the house in which the Prophet Muhammad had been born, but repaired a building known as the House of Arqam, where the first Muslim converts had convened. Both were afterward revered as shrines. In this way she exalted her own stature while giving the regime of her son a more religious stamp.

Harun paid her the respect that Hadi had refused her, and when she died at age fifty the following year, in November 789, Harun "walked barefoot through the mud" before her coffin to the grave. When he reached the cemetery on the west bank of the Tigris, he washed his feet, donned a fresh pair of boots, and in farewell "recited the famous eulogy of ibn Nuwairah, which Muhammad's wife Aisha had pronounced over the tomb of her father (and the first caliph) Abu Bakr."

BY THE TIME THE ABBASIDS HAD COME TO POWER, THE IS-lamic conquest had more or less run its course. But the Byzantine frontier remained in flux. After a series of setbacks the Abbasids sought once more to press it back. Harun's two spectacular campaigns as crown prince had whetted his appetite for the purpose, and year after year—to enhance his stature as Commander of the Faithful—he took the field. On the Abbasid western border, clashes were bound to occur often, since both sides manned a fortified line that extended through the whole of Asia Minor—also called Anatolia (roughly, modern Turkey)—from Syria to the Armenian frontier. Shortly after his accession, Harun designated the Muslim portion of this zone a separate military province, called "the Awasim," with an administration under a general or amir. Annual summer raids were launched against the Byzantines from its bases and new fortifications went up with every gain. Most raids also yielded a substantial harvest of slaves, valuables, and other goods. But some went awry. In 791, Muslim troops reached Caesarea in their usual rampage of plunder, but on their return they were caught in a blizzard in the high mountains, where they perished in the bitter cold.

Although the Caliphate never maintained a large standing army, it was sizable enough, and substantial numbers of troops could be called together in short order when needed out of general levies drawn from tribal groups. There were also contingents of regulars, who received regular pay, and a large imperial bodyguard that comprised an elite army in itself. In Roman-Byzantine fashion, troops were also organized into units of ten, fifty, a hundred, and a thousand men. A body of a hundred men formed a company or squadron; several companies, a cohort; a thousand, a battalion; and ten thousand, a corps, with an amir or general at its head. At any given time, 125,000 Muslim soldiers were stationed along the Byzantine frontier, as well as at Baghdad, Medina, Damascus, Rayy, and other strategic sites, to deal with any unrest. The Baghdad garrison was quartered, we are told, "north and west of the Round City (away from the commercial districts to the south) where prominent officers had their compounds, including the chief of police, who had a house just outside the Kufa Gate." Soldiers from different parts of the realm tended to form their own ethnic districts, creating, for example, a "little Bukhara," a "little Tabaristan," or a "little Balkh."

Formal military reviews were sometimes held in the capital, with light and heavy cavalry, infantry, and archers taking the field. The heavy cavalry was completely encased in iron, with helmets and thick plates. Like medieval knights, their only unprotected points were the tips of their noses and tiny slits opposite their eyes. The infantry, armed with spears, swords, and pikes, were just as formidable, and (in keeping with Persian tradition) trained to stand so firm that, wrote one contemporary, "you would have thought them held fast by clamps of bronze."

The Muslims had plenty of siege machinery at their disposal, such as catapults, mangonels, battering rams, ladders, grappling irons, and hooks, all managed by military engineers. But "the main Muslim siege weapon" was evidently the manjaniq, "a swing-beam engine, similar to the trebuchet used in Western medieval times. From the seventh century on, it had displaced torsion artillery (powered by twisted ropes) as used in classical times." Field hospitals and ambulances in the form of litters borne by camels accompanied the army in the field.

By Harun's time, the Arabs had also developed incendiary grenades. This is not surprising. In Iraq, petroleum had been known since ancient times. Noah's Ark, reputedly built on the site where Najaf was founded, was said to have been sealed with coal pitch, and the Greek historian Herodotus and the Roman historian Strabo both describe the use of pitch by the Babylonians in the construction of buildings and roads. Pitch was later used by the Arabs (as it had been by the Greeks and Romans) for curing their wine in earthenware casks. Naphtha subsequently went into the manufacture of incendiary devices, and according to the Roman historian Ammianus Marcellinus, the Persians had tipped their reed arrows with flammable gum.

THE CIVIL ADMINISTRATION OF THE ABBASIDS WAS AS IMpressive as their military machine. In keeping with a tradition adopted from Persian kings, Harun's vizier enjoyed next to unlimited powers. He presided over the high cabinet or council, whose membership included the various heads of the departments of state and appointed and deposed governors and judges, and he even transmitted his own office to his sons. Under Harun, a special "bureau of confiscation" was also instituted as a regular governmental department, for it was customary for the vizier to confiscate the property of any governor who fell from grace, just as it was customary for the governor himself to appropriate the estates of inferior officials and private citizens—and for the caliph in his turn to mete out the same penalty to a deposed vizier. As one later caliph put it: "[The vizier] is our representative throughout the land and amongst our subjects. Therefore he who obeys him obeys us; and he who obeys us obeys God, and God shall cause him who obeys Him to enter Paradise. As for one who, on the other hand, disobeys our vizier, he disobeys us; and he who disobeys us disobeys God, and God shall cause him to enter the fires of Hell."

Aside from the chamberlain, who, as noted, controlled access to the caliph's person, there was a large bureaucracy of clerks, subclerks, and scribes. Under Harun, the machinery of government continued to evolve. Decentralization was the unavoidable consequence of such a far-flung domain, and the empire was divided, for administrative purposes, into twenty-four provinces under delegated rule.

Greater order was also brought into the areas of justice and finance. Income flowed to the imperial treasury from a variety of taxes, including a land tax; a tax on herds, gold and silver, commercial wares, and other forms of property; a head or poll tax (levied on non-Muslims, who had to pay a stipulated tithe on all they owned); and customs dues (fixed at one-tenth of the value of all imported merchandise). Estates acquired by conquest were often leased to individuals as taxable holdings—a system widely adopted by the Byzantines. The taxes themselves were paid either in kind (according to the crop grown, sometimes up to half the yield) or in money, in proportion to the value of the land. The tax collector took a portion of the payment for himself and was given room and board by those he took the taxes from on his rounds. There was plenty of potential for extortion and corruption in all this, in the form of unwarranted fines, confiscation, and a special "protection" tax. Beyond that, the tax rates were sometimes arbitrary: while rich merchants often managed to avoid paying their due, peasants and other members of the lower classes were often driven into deep debt and even indentured servitude. Others became vagrants and joined the ranks of the landless unemployed.

From time to time, as later in medieval Europe, there were peasant revolts. From the second half of the eighth century, the divide between rich and poor grew, and the ostentatious luxuries of the court and upper classes scattered seeds of discontent. In time, a turbulent border population developed (especially in the region of Azerbaijan) of bandits and frontiersmen, not unlike that from which the Cossacks later arose along the Russian frontiers. Non-Muslims also chafed under their own special taxes and were often moved to convert to Islam to alleviate their plight. Yet under Harun's aegis, the various sources of revenue never dried up. Just as, in a later time, it was said that the sun never set on the British Empire, so Harun could say as he looked up one day at rain clouds blowing across the sky, "Rain where you like, but I will get the land tax!"

Besides the bureau of taxes, Harun had another audit or accounts office (introduced by Mahdi); a board of correspondence or chancery office that handled all official documents; and a department for the review of grievances, which served as a judicial court of appeals. Each large city also had its own special police force, which in addition to keeping order was supposed to inspect the public markets (to make sure, for example, that proper weights and measures were used); enforce the payment of legitimate debts; and crack down on forbidden activities such as gambling, usury, and the public sale of wine.

Under Harun, each provincial capital was also provided with its own post office and hundreds of routes were developed to connect the imperial capital with other cities and towns. For the delivery of mail, a system of relays covered the intervening ground. The central post office in Baghdad was even equipped with directories and maps that indicated the distances between each town. Under Harun, the imperial road system—furnished with caravanserais, hospices, and wells—ramified eastward through Rayy, Merv, Bukhara, and Samarkand, all the way to the towns of the Jaxartes and the Chinese frontier.

Public convenience was not the only goal of this service, for the post-master general also served as the caliph's intelligence chief. All postal clerks therefore doubled as secret agents who kept an eye on local affairs.

No one was more responsible for the shape of the new imperial administration than the Barmaks—or Barmakids, as they were also called. The paterfamilias of the clan had been Khalid al-Barmak, with profound ties to the Buddhist monastery complex in Balkh in northern Afghanistan. The most important of the temple monasteries was known as Nava Vihara and became a center of higher Buddhist learning for all of Central Asia. Its care had been entrusted to a line of hereditary priests known as the Barmaks, hence the family name, and Khalid had been the son of the monastery's chief priest, who in addition to his bureaucratic duties supervised the translation of a number of Sanskrit texts.

About the year 705, the family converted to Islam, and, being prominent, began to play a notable part in government affairs. Khalid al-Barmak held a command in the army of the last Umayyad caliph, served in Iraq, but deserted to Abu Muslim (the insurgent general who did so much to bring the Abbasids to power) when the latter emerged as the head of the revolt in Khurasan.

In 749, when Saffah was proclaimed caliph in Kufa, Khalid became his principal advisor. Two years later, in 751, he assumed the post of minister of finance. Among his other innovations, he was the first to use ledgers (replacing scrolls) in recording tax and other revenue. Variously described as pious, clever, resourceful, learned, and humane, Khalid wielded considerable authority for more than a quarter of a century and in so doing laid the foundations of his family's fortunes and power. Although Mansur received the credit for Baghdad, it was Khalid who largely drew up the plans and (thankfully) managed to dissuade Mansur from completely destroying the ancient Persian capital of Ctesiphon, south of Baghdad and dominated by a great brick arch that Mansur wanted to plunder for its stone. Khalid won over Mansur to the idea that it would only enhance his own dignity if it remained as "an uninhabited ruin" in contrast to the thriving new metropolis he planned to build. Mansur also honored Khalid with a number of critical assignments—as the provincial governor of Fars in Persia, for example, and later of Tabaristan.

In the meantime, his son, Yahya, born in 738, had entered the civil service, risen to occupy important posts, accompanied Mahdi (when he was still heir apparent) to Persia in 758, and, upon his return to Baghdad in 769, had begun to play a major role in the financial administration as his father's top aide. When Khalid went to Mosul, Yahya was appointed governor of Azerbaijan. He held that post until 778, when Mahdi made him tutor and guardian of his son Harun, then fifteen years old. In the following year, Yahya accompanied Harun on his first Byzantine expedition (as managed by Mahdi's vizier, Rabi ibn Yunus), and, after Khalid died at Mosul in 781, Yahya helped Harun oversee the administration of the western part of the realm.

By then the imperial family had bonded with the Barmaks almost as one. Khalid was on such intimate terms with Saffah that his daughter had been nursed by the wife of the former caliph, whose daughter was likewise nursed by Khalid's wife. Yahya's two eldest sons, Fadhl and Jafar, were both born about the same time Khaizuran had given birth to Harun, and their mothers nursed them in common, without distinction as kin. And of course Harun and Yahya had both been together with Mahdi when he died in 785 en route to Jurjan.

Not surprisingly, in the course of their service the Barmaks had accumulated fabulous fortunes and erected their own palaces, with spacious gardens by the Tigris in eastern Baghdad, where they lived in grand style. Yet they were not caliphs—and had to be reminded of that from time to time. At some point, for example, Mansur became concerned about the magnitude of Khalid's wealth. As a test of his loyalty and obedience, he suddenly demanded that Khalid contribute an enormous sum to the coffers of the realm. It turned out to be far more money than Khalid had. So he asked his son, Yahya, to approach some of their powerful associates for loans. Something like the requisite sum was rounded up, but as the deadline drew near, more money still had to be found. As it happened, the Kurds had just overrun Mosul and in the sudden crisis the caliph set aside his intemperate demand and turned to Khalid to quash the revolt.

YAHYA SHARED HIS FATHER'S SHREWDNESS, COMPETENCE, and tact. In appointing him vizier, Harun conferred on him unusual powers, including the right to appoint department heads. Things great and small came under his ken, from bureaucratic reforms to strongholds along the frontiers. He encouraged trade, secured the public safety, filled the treasury, and in general enabled the Caliphate to thrive. As a minister he was eloquent, wise, accomplished, and prudent; exuded great charm; had an affable demeanor; and commanded general respect. He proved a master at cutting deals, bridging differences between rivals; and won the allegiance of fellow officials by countless favors and endearing acts. When one department head complained that he had more petitions than he could handle, and was falling farther and farther behind, Yahya urged him to take a break, took his paperwork in hand, and with his trademark efficiency quickly brought the affairs of the office up to date. Because he was so industrious himself, he also could not abide those who were not. He upbraided desultory officials and replaced the negligent with more zealous clerks. He also acted with decision in a crisis; built dikes when the Tigris River, swollen by rains, threatened to overflow its banks; increased areas of cultivable land whose crops were used to cover army pay; arranged for wheat shipments to the holy cities of Mecca and Medina; was a great patron of learning and the arts; and developed in-depth knowledge himself of everything from astronomy and astrology to prisms, Hindu culture, and medicinal plants. He was, in fact, "in many ways the public face of Abbasid government," and sometimes worked late into the night in order to attend to the people's needs. "No one," we are told, "was refused admission" to his presence or spurned for their humble requests.

Yahya also had a shrewd way of inducing Harun to endorse his own decisions, while allowing the caliph to imagine he had made them himself. At the same time, he found it wise to oblige Harun on all contentious points. "With Caliphs," he once said, "to argue against something is the same as inciting them to do it, for if you try to prevent them from acting in a certain way, it is as if you were spurring them on." Yahya was uniformly assisted in most of his high functions by his sons Fadhl and Jafar. A number of canals, mosques, and other public works owe their existence to their joint initiative and munificence, and Fadhl is credited with having introduced the use of lamps into mosques during the month of Ramadan. Just as Khalid had been sent by Mansur to handle the crisis in Mosul when it was overrun by the Kurds, and Yahya tamed Azerbaijan, so in subsequent years his sons Fadhl and Jafar met and solved one crisis after another that threatened the state.

The two, in fact, remained close, however much their temperaments diverged. Fadhl was rather reserved, Jafar more easygoing. Both found favor in the caliph's eyes. In 799, when Yahya retired from state service, Fadhl, already known as the "Little Vizier," took his place. Yet Jafar may have wielded more power. Educated by the famous qadi or judge, Abu Yusuf, he was handsome, eloquent, well educated, and refined; an able administrator; and a connoisseur of philosophy and the arts. In Baghdad, his sartorial elegance, including high collars, set the fashion for men. Courtiers also imitated his habit of wearing a beret covered by an embroidered turban, and even the way he did his hair, which fell over his brow and curled up about his ears. The elegance of his speech had a balanced quality to it that might be compared to the euphuistic ideal of the later English Renaissance. When an official, for example, apologized for some fault, Jafar replied: "By the pardon which we have already granted you, God has relieved you from the need to excuse yourself to us; while our friendship for you is too great to permit us to entertain an unfavorable opinion of your character."

As long as the Barmaks exerted the influence they did, Jafar al-Barmak was probably closer to Harun than any other man. For a time the two even shared a cloak. The degree of this private familiarity and favor was reflected in a series of public offices and honors, even as Jafar became the caliph's "boon companion." In time, he was also married (under certain strict conditions) to Harun's own sister, Abbasah, which made him a member of the royal house.

Yet no competitive envy seems to have marred the fraternal bond between Yahya's sons. When Harun told Yahya that he wanted Fadhl to relinquish his post as keeper of the privy seal so that Jafar could have it, Yahya wrote to Fadhl: "The Prince of the Faithful—may God exalt his rule!—has ordered you to transfer the signet-ring from your right hand to your left." Fadhl understood what that meant and replied, "I have obeyed the Prince of the Faithful. No prosperity that accrues to my brother is a loss for me, and no rank that he attains is viewed by me as subtracted from my share." After Jafar took charge, Fadhl remained one of the caliph's most trusted advisors, especially in military matters; served as governor of western Persia, which he made loyal to the crown; and was so beloved of the people of Khurasan that during his tenure some twenty thousand children were named after him in recognition of the benefits they reaped.

In equal stature, Jafar had his own suite of apartments in Harun's wing of the palace of al-Khuld, shared wine with the caliph twice a week, and however soused he became, was up early the next morning executing with unimpaired intelligence and promptness his official tasks. As a troubleshooter, Jafar also did yeoman's work. He served as governor of Egypt; went to Syria as Harun's special envoy to keep rival factions from cutting each other's throats; commanded the caliph's palace guard, headed the intelligence service, controlled the royal textile factories, and directed the mint. For many years he also held the great seal of state. Today we would say by analogy to modern systems of governance that he was de facto treasury secretary, national security advisor, and secretary of state. With such hydra-headed power, it is not surprising that Jafar was sometimes called a "sultan" (meaning, the "Pearl of Rulers") suggesting an authority coequal to that of the caliph himself. Eventually Harun even put him in charge of the education of his precocious son, Mamun, when the latter became second in line to the throne. Incredibly efficient at his tasks, he once wrote out in a single night, with Harun looking on, "upwards of a thousand decisions," we are told, "on as many memorials which had been presented to the caliph, and not one of these decisions deviated in the least from what was warranted by the law."

In the course of his career, Jafar became so rich that his wealth became proverbial. When anyone got a windfall, people would say he was now "as rich as Jafar." Yet he was also a tolerant and generous man. After he had served as governor of Egypt (in 792), he became estranged from his successor, for reasons that remain unclear. One of Jafar's aides, for his own kindly reasons, decided to forge a letter to the governor that struck a note of rapprochement in Jafar's name. The governor was delighted but sent an agent to Baghdad to determine if the document was real. He met with an advisor to Jafar, who showed the letter to his master, who recognized the fraud. Jafar knew at once who the guilty party was. So he asked his officers and attendants present what should be done with a man who had taken such liberties with his name. Some said he ought to be put to death; others that he should be whipped or have his right hand cut off. Jafar listened patiently, then exclaimed, "Is there not one man among you of good will? You all know the bad feeling that has kept the governor of Egypt and myself apart. Pride prevented us from making amends. Now along comes a man who has tried to help us. And you want me to punish him for that?" Then he took a pen and wrote on the back of the letter— "To the Governor of Egypt. The sentiments herein expressed are truly mine. The man carrying them back to you is a trusted friend. Treat him well." And he handed the letter for delivery to the guilty aide.

From time to time, Jafar also helped lift the caliph's spirits by his cheerful disposition and lively wit. One night when Harun was unable to sleep, he sent for him and said, "I want you to dispel the sadness and weariness I feel." Jafar proposed they go up on the roof of the palace "and watch the myriads of stars, and the moon rising like the face of one we love." But the caliph said, "I have no mind for that." "Then," said Jafar, "open the palace window that looks out upon the garden, and take in the songs of the birds, and the sweet smell of the flowers, the hum of the water-wheel." Said Harun, "I have no mind for that, either." "Then," said Jafar, "let us go down to the stables, and look at your Arabian horses—chargers black as night, grey, chestnut, bay, pied, and cream-colored, steeds." But once more the caliph said, "I have no mind for that." "O Commander of the Faithful!" said Jafar. "You have three hundred girls who sing and dance and play; send for them, and it may be that the sadness that weighs upon your heart will cease." "Strange to say," said Harun, "I have no mind even for that." "Then cut off your servant Jafar's head, for he can't soothe his Sovereign's grief!" At that Harun laughed and his spirits revived.

AT THE AGE OF EIGHTEEN, FIVE YEARS BEFORE HE BECAME caliph, Harun had married Amat al-Aziz (nicknamed Zubaidah), the daughter of Salsal, Khaizuran's sister, and the granddaughter of Mansur. She was therefore his cousin on both her father's and her mother's side. A roly-poly little girl, she charmed the court elders. Mansur had affectionately named her Zubaidah, meaning "little Butterpat." In time she grew into a graceful, slender young woman "with marvelous out-pointing breasts and a bee's waist." The wedding banquet was held in the al-Khuld or Eternity Palace and basins of gold dinars were distributed among the guests. A coveted heirloom—a bejeweled sleeve-less jacket worn by the Umayyad queens and which had also belonged to Khaizuran—was passed on to the new bride. Zubaidah and Harun were in love, but he later had other wives (as allowed by Islamic law) including Azizah, daughter of Khaizuran's brother Ghitrif; and Ghadir, who had been Hadi's concubine—all belonging to the ruling house.

In the end, he would be married six times (though never to more than four wives at one time) and father twenty-five children—ten sons and fifteen daughters by his numerous concubines and wives.

Like Harun, Zubaidah often figures in the anecdotes and stories of the *Arabian Nights* (though the stories were compiled long after his reign); and like Mahdi's wife, Khaizuran, she became a powerful figure at court. Also like Khaizuran she had numerous harem rivals, and was by no means the first to win his heart. Before his marriage, he had been enamoured of a Christian girl named Hailana or Helena (evidently captured from the Byzantines on a summer raid), who served him as a concubine while he was in his teens. There had been real affection between them, and when she died three years later, Harun was distracted with grief. In her memory, he composed a lament that spoke touchingly of the void she had left behind and of her "inexpressibly sweet face." But it was not long before another slave girl stole his heart. Once more he took up his pen and in his serenade celebrated the "cool mountain pools of her eyes" and the "honey sweetness of her lips . . . envied of the bees." A few years after he married Zubaidah, another concubine, named Dananir, educated at one of the music schools for slave girls in Medina, also beguiled him. Zubaidah became alarmed by Harun's affection for her, but he assured her that he was simply enchanted by her voice. It may have been true. But not long afterward Zubaidah presented Harun with ten beautiful slave girls to otherwise divert his thoughts. She succeeded all too well. One of the ten was the Persian girl named Marajil, who died (on the "night of destiny") in childbirth but bore Harun a son whom Zubaidah brought up herself. Six months later, in April 787, she gave birth to her only son, Muhammad, later to become the Caliph Amin. Harun also fathered five children by another slave, Maridah, from distant Sogdian. One of these, Mutasim, would also become a caliph.

By all accounts, Harun's sexual appetite was rapacious, and despite the extent of his harem, stories about his trysts abound. In one such tale, Harun was out hunting when he met a caravan of merchants from Persia, one of whom offered him a number of gifts, including a beautiful girl. The girl had an "undulating form, full bosom, slender waist, eyes like a gazelle, and a mouth like Solomon's ring." Harun, ever susceptible to female charms, paid the merchant a princely price for her and set her up in her own apartment in Baghdad, far from Zubaidah's anxious eyes. Harun took the liberties he pleased. At his "Petronian feasts," we are told (in a somewhat fanciful account), harem girls wore red tunics and scarves "embroidered with verses, which could be read through their hanging locks of hair interwoven with hyacinths and jewels." Their eyes, according to the fashion, were "painted to the inside of the eyelids," which made them appear "very alluring and languorous in the torchlight." As they moved about "one could see through their transparent robes the undulating outlines of their lovely forms." Eunuchs and page boys, too, wore robes "drawn back at the waist to disclose the lines of their hips. They glided about with amphoras and varicolored crystal flasks, filling glasses with wine and pomegranate juice, the syrup of apples and sherbets of violet snow." When they tried to escape some unwanted caress, "they were cajoled; if they opposed blandishment with mockery, the guests laid hold of them or blocked their passage with a sprig of basil, or a jasmin wreath. Their provocative treble was a delight to jaded ears."

Yet from time to time, Harun showed some restraint. One day he was visiting the son of an official when he was smitten by a beautiful slave. He asked the man to give her up, and the man did so, but was visibly shaken at her loss. "My love for her is indelibly printed," he explained, "like ink on paper, on my heart." Harun was moved by his simple eloquence and gave her back. Harun also strove as best he could to be mindful of Zubaidah's feelings, at least within the context of his world. The caliph's sister, Ulaiyah, sometimes acted as a go-between in their disputes and used her own considerable musical and poetical talents to reconcile the pair.

Indeed, as lurid as the sex life of the caliph might seem, the quarters reserved for the royal concubines "was not," as often imagined, "a glorified brothel, but a complex of private apartments staffed by eunuchs and maidservants who created a world of imperial dignity all their own." Many of the women came from noble families wishing to ingratiate themselves with the sovereign and were drawn from throughout the realm. But their obligations were also not in doubt. Every day, we are told, "seven slave girls" came in, undressed, and put on perfumed linen tunics and sat on pierced chairs with incense wafting up from below. They were thereby made abundantly fragrant, and so readied for Harun's embrace. At the same time, most were women of accomplishment and taste. Some had been specially educated at elite schools in Baghdad and Medina in singing, music, and dance. Their cultured refinement would later be epitomized in the legendary story of Tawaddud, the beautiful and talented slave girl in the *Arabian Nights*, whom Harun consents to purchase only after she has proved her extensive learning in a rigorous oral exam. In the crowning moment of the tale, she is presented by Harun with a lute and captivates her audience with her consummate skill: "She laid her lute in her lap and, with bosom inclining over it, bent to it with the bending of a mother who suckles her child; then she played in twelve different modes, till the whole assembly was agitated with delight, like a waving sea."

Many other women passed through Harun's life and gave Zubaidah restless nights. Some of them come down to us with beguiling names, such as Dhat al-Khal ("Beauty Spot"), Diya ("Splendor"), and Sihr ("Charm"). Now and then these women quarreled among themselves. "Beauty Spot," for example, once cut off the tip of the nose of a rival. With equal malice the rival gouged out the "beauty spot" (a mole) from Dhat al-Khal's upper lip.

EVEN THE LAW BECAME IMPLICATED IN HARUN'S AMOURS. The government of a great empire required a regular system of justice, and in time a staff of paid judges had become a feature of the state apparatus. Even so, many judges remained wary of being co-opted by their salaried dependence and rightly suspected that they would be under political pressure to render verdicts favorable to those they served.

Not all judges were governed by such qualms. Notable among them was Abu Yusuf, who became the first chief justice of Baghdad under Harun. A man of ingenious learning, his gainful career took off after he accepted in return for a questionable verdict splendid gifts of gold, silver, carpets, and treasures from the wife of the Caliph Hadi. A jealous colleague asked him if he recalled that the Prophet had said, "Let a man who receives a gift share it with his companions," to which Abu Yusuf replied, "You give this tradition only its superficial meaning. The presents of those days were a dish of dates or a bowl of leben [plain yogurt]. The presents of today are gold, silver and precious objects. There is also a verse in the Koran which says, 'God gives to whom He wills, for He is the Giver of great gifts.' The objects which you see are great gifts and, therefore, have been given to me by God." That kind of opportunistic reasoning seems to have marked his career. At the same time, there is no doubt that his knowledge of Muslim law was encyclopedic, and, when asked for an opinion or a ruling, he was never at a loss for an informed reply.

He was a great favorite of Harun because he also had a gift for extracting any wanted conclusion from the law. And despite his august rank, he seems to have been at Harun's beck and call. One day, for example, he was summoned by the caliph to decide which of two dinner dishes being served was best. One was favored by Zubaidah, the other by Harun. The qadi repeatedly sampled both until there was nothing of either left. Then he said, "I never saw two claimants [i.e., the dishes] whose arguments were better matched."

Other, personal matters also brought him to court. It so happened that on one occasion when Harun and Zubaidah had a falling-out, Harun, who coveted a slave girl owned by a kinsman named Isa, sent for Yusuf to adjudicate the case. Despite threats from the caliph, Isa had refused to give her up. Isa explained that he had once sworn a solemn oath (in the middle of an ecstatic sex act) that if he ever gave the girl away, or sold her, he would divorce his wife, emancipate his slaves, and give all he possessed to the poor. Abu Yusuf was called in to figure out a legal (or legalistic) way for Isa to maintain his possessions even if Harun got the girl. Yusuf decided that if Isa "gave" or allotted half of the girl to Harun and simultaneously "sold" him the other half, it could not be said that he had either given her away or sold her, keeping the substance of his oath intact.

On another occasion, Jafar al-Barmak and Harun were drinking together when Harun similarly confessed his longing for a slave girl owned by Jafar. "Sell her to me," said Harun. "I can't do that," said Jafar. "Then give her to me." "I can't do that either," and he explained that (not unlike Isa) he had sworn a solemn oath not to let her go. "May I be divorced from my beloved Zubaidah," cried Harun, "if you will not oblige me." No sooner had he said this than he paled at the import of his oath. "This is a matter," said Harun, "which none but Abu Yusuf can decide." He was sent for (in this case, in the middle of the night), got up, saddled his mule, and told his servant to bring the mule's nosebag of oats with him, as he might be detained. When he appeared, the caliph rose to greet him and explained the difficulty he and Jafar were in. Yusuf pondered the matter a while and then proposed a way out. "I will marry her [the girl] to one of your slaves, who will instantly divorce her [by mere proclamation] and she will be lawful for you."

So a slave was brought in, married to the girl, and told to divorce her. To the caliph's amazement, he refused. He was offered a bribe but declined it, driving the caliph, who remained intent on a legal solution, almost mad. Yusuf, however, quickly worked it out. The slave was made over as a slave to his own new wife, which, according to a provision of Islamic law, rendered the marriage null and void. So Jafar could give her up, Harun could have her, and Abu Yusuf returned home with a bag full of gold.

Harun may even have turned to Abu Yusuf now and then to adjudicate points of faith. If many such stories are apocryphal, they point to a fundamental truth: that in all aspects of the caliph's life, the law was subject to his will.

Yet through it all, even as she aged, Zubaidah managed to maintain Harun's affection and esteem.

She also developed her own world. Like her imperious mother-in-law and aunt, Khaizuran, Zubaidah employed a staff of secretaries and agents to manage the many properties she owned and to act for her in the numerous enterprises she undertook, independent of Harun. Her private household was also managed on an opulent scale. Her meals were served on gold and silver plate instead of the simple Arab leathern tray, and she introduced the fashion of wearing sandals embroidered with gems. She was also the first to be carried about in palanquins (covered chairs) of silver, ebony, and sandalwood, lined with sable and silk; and in an ambiguous anecdote of choking largess, poets who pleased her were invited to fill their mouths with pearls. At times she had to be supported by two retainers as she staggered under the weight of her jewels.

Zubaidah also built herself a palace with a huge, carpeted reception hall supported by columns inlaid with ivory and gold. Verses of the Koran were inscribed on the walls in gold lettering, and the whole was surrounded by a garden full of rare animals and birds. A remarkable bodyguard of slave girls, attired as pages, attended her wherever she went. Each one knew the Koran by heart, and as conspicuous evidence of her own piety, if not theirs, their task was to intone it, with each of them reciting a tenth of the book each day. The palace in which she lived was therefore filled (in one description) with a continual humming "like a hornet's nest." In a court given to extravagance, even diversions ran to extremes. Zubaidah, for example, had a pet monkey dressed like a cavalry soldier and attended by some thirty retainers to wait upon its needs. Those who came to pay court to Zubaidah, including ranking generals, were obliged to kiss the monkey's hand.

In time, Zubaidah acquired estates all over the empire; rebuilt Tibriz in northern Persia after a devastating earthquake in 791; and subsidized public building projects, including the excavation of canals for irrigation and water supply, and the erection of hostels and mosques. The famed extensive engineering works she carried out at Mecca helped supply water for the ever-increasing number of Muslim pilgrims, and her improvements along the pilgrim road across nine hundred miles of desert from Kufa to Mecca was equally ambitious and bold. Not only was the road leveled and cleared of boulders, which were stacked along the sides, but at intervals deep wells and masonry-lined water storage cisterns (some thirty yards square and thirty feet deep) were laboriously cut through rock. These caught the discharge of heavy rain from the storms that swept across the desert and descended in such torrents that they sometimes drowned people in their path. Her five or six pilgrimages to Medina and Mecca (beginning in 790) established an exalted place for her in the hearts of those fervent in the faith. The "Spring of Zubaidah" on the Plain of Ararat, where the pilgrims gathered, would be remembered for centuries to come, and to this day the main pilgrim route from Baghdad to Mecca is named for her because her large charitable bequests did so much to help reduce the hardships of the road.

IN 796, HARUN, WEARY OF BAGHDAD AND ITS CLIMATE, DEcided to move his court to Rakkah in northern Syria, where there had been a growing palace complex since the time of Mansur. In 771–72, Mansur had rebuilt the town and established a fortified palace-city to the west "as a forward base against the Byzantines." Its horseshoe design was a modified version of his earlier circular plan for Baghdad, and its Great Mosque, with eleven archways, twenty towers, and a towering minaret, was imposingly built on a base of ancient stones. He called it "Rafika," meaning "the companion," and by Harun's time it and Rakkah had merged.

Even before 796, Harun had adopted Rakkah as his summer resort. He established a new palace for himself which he called "Kasr al-Salaam," or the "Castle of Peace," on the Euphrates River; constructed a race course and polo grounds (Harun had introduced the Persian sport of polo to the Arabs) as well as game parks and an archery range; and planted gardens along both riverbanks. His vizier and some other high officials were also centered there, along with royal glass workshops and the imperial mint.

The gates of the palace, its double walls, and street layout all recalled the Round City, but on a smaller scale. The crenellated outer wall of dried-mud brick, twelve to fifteen feet thick, was strengthened at intervals by twenty-eight towers. Harun designed and decorated his palace in Persian rather than Byzantine-Syrian style, with ovoid or elliptical domes, semicircular arches, spiral towers, indented battlements, glazed wall tiles, and metal-covered roofs, all of which became features of Abbasid art.

For the next thirteen years, it would serve as the co-capital of the empire.

Though Harun relied for the most part on the Barmaks in administrative matters, he could work the levers of power when he wished. On one occasion, for example, he wanted Ismail ibn Salih, the brother of a disgraced official, to become governor of Egypt. When the post was dangled before him, Ismail, who also happened to be a fine musician, went to see his brother, who warned him, "They only want you to drink with them and sing to them, to humiliate me. If you do so, you are no brother of mine." Ismail swore he would do neither. But when he came to court, Harun graciously received him, invited him to dine, and after dinner offered him some wine. "By Allah!" said the caliph, "I will not drink unless Ismail drinks with me." Ismail demurred but the caliph refused to take no for an answer, and in the end they drank three glasses each. A curtain was then drawn aside, some singing and dancing girls entered, Ismail began to grow merry, and Harun handed him a lute draped with a string of precious stones. "Come, sing us something, and expiate your oath out of the value of these gems." Ismail sang a clever little song about doing things he had never intended to do (thus describing his own plight), and the caliph was so pleased he called for a lance. Affixing the banner of Egypt to it, he handed it to his guest. That, by tradition, signified his appointment to the post.

In another instance, a few years after Khaizuran's death, Harun had suspected the then governor of Egypt, Musa ibn Isa, of alienating Egypt by his incompetent and corrupt rule. Harun took steps to remove Musa from office and decided to replace him with Omar ibn Mehran, who had ably served as general secretary to Khaizuran for many years. Omar agreed to undertake this new duty only on condition that once he had set the province in order, he could return to Baghdad and retire.

Omar left Baghdad in the most unassuming manner, sharing his mount with a black slave. He arrived at Fustat, Egypt's capital, and for three days went about the city in the guise of a merchant, sizing up the situation and selecting good men to help him in the task ahead. On the fourth day he attended the governor's crowded public session, and humbly taking the lowest seat, waited till the session was over and the hall had emptied out. Seeing him still sitting there, Musa ibn Isa said to him, "Is there anything you want?" "Indeed," said Omar, and presented him with Harun's directive that stripped him of his post.

Omar now set up shop; proved unbribable, a fair if diligent tax collector, and won the people's respect. Having set things right, he saddled his horse for home.

Though impatient with errant officials, Harun kept an open mind, and now and then reversed himself in some warranted case. So it was with an official named Maan ibn Zaidah, who had long been out of favor when Harun encountered him at court. Seeing that he walked slowly, and with difficulty, Harun said, "You have grown old." "Yes, O Commander of the Faithful," he replied, "in your service." "But you have still some energy left," said Harun. "What I have," said the man, "is yours to dispose of as you wish." "You are a bold fellow," said the caliph. "Only," he replied, "in opposing your foes." The caliph was pleased by these answers and made him governor of Basra to provide for his declining years.

THOUGH A MODEL CALIPH IN SOME RESPECTS, HARUN WAS A restless soul and (so story has it) was given to incognito rambles through Baghdad's streets at night. At times he was evidently accompanied by Jafar al-Barmak and his bodyguard and henchman, Abu Hashim Masrur.

These nocturnal excursions may have stemmed from "a sincere and benevolent interest in the well-being" of his subjects, for, it is said, he was "diligent . . . to alleviate their hardships and cares." Others suggest that "he suffered greatly from ennui," for he was "surrounded by pleasures too easy to command."

Some of these outings found their way into the *Arabian Nights*. He "strolled in and out of bazaars," we are told, and "frequented the populous quarters, the old-clothes shops and water-mills, explored the markets and their wares, the stands of gleaming cucumbers and melons, black raisins, saffron, and peppers; taverns where legs of mutton were roasting on spits, and talked with mule-drivers, trinket-vendors, and sailors about their voyages to distant lands." In such tales, Harun is almost always shown in a genial light. But he was never a lighthearted soul.

Not long after he came to power, Harun asked his chamberlain to bring him a famous ascetic, Ibn al-Sammak, from whom he hoped to obtain some pearl of wisdom to guide him in life. "What would you like to tell me?" the caliph asked him frankly. Answered Sammak: "I would like you always to remember that one day you will stand alone before your God. You will then be consigned either to Heaven or to Hell." This was too stark for Harun's taste and he was visibly distressed. His chamberlain exclaimed: "Good God! Can anyone doubt that the Prince of the Faithful will go to heaven, after having ruled justly on earth?" But Sammak ignored the chamberlain and looking hard at Harun, said, "You will not have this man with you to defend you on that day."

There is no doubt that from time to time Harun feared for his soul. He was said to be "quickly in tears when he remembered God," and when he read poems about the transience of life, "the tears ran down his cheeks."

Some years later, Sammak was summoned to court again. After he had talked with the caliph for a while, Harun asked a page for some water to drink. A pitcher was brought in, and as he tipped it up to his lips Sammak asked him, "Tell me, by your kinship with the Messenger of God, if this drink of water were withheld from you, how much would you give for it?" Harun replied, "Half my kingdom." Sammak said, "Drink, and may God refresh you." When Harun had drunk his full,

Sammak asked him, "In the name of your kinship to the Messenger of God, if you were prevented from eliminating that water from your body, what would you give to do so?" "Oh," said Harun, "my whole kingdom." "A kingdom worth no more than a drink of water," said Sammak, "isn't worth striving for."

chapter four

BAGHDAD

Whatever the wisdom of his worldly ambitions, Harun's empire had continued to grow and thrive. Baghdad in particular had developed into a vast emporium of trade linking Asia and the Mediterranean. By the end of his reign, it would surpass even Constantinople in prosperity and size. Its administration managed to harness the Tigris and Euphrates rivers for the cultivation of grain, and a brilliant system of canals, dikes, and reservoirs drained the surrounding swamps. Immigrants of all kinds—Christians, Hindus, Persians, Zoroastrians, and so on—came from all over the Muslim world, and from lands as far away as India and Spain. For the most part, they were welcomed in an ecumenical spirit, and there was much to entice them to stay. There were many rich bazaars and covered shops along the embankments, where all sorts of artisans and craftsmen—marble workers from Antioch, papyrus makers from Cairo, potters from Basra, calligraphers from Peking—plied their trades. In some cases, whole streets, with little recessed shops set on stone slabs, were devoted to a particular trade. Food stalls sold lemon chicken, "lamb cooked over a spit with cardamom," small rolls dipped in honey, or slices of pita bread "smeared with fat." There was a large sanitation department, many fountains and public baths, and, unlike the European towns and cities of the day, streets that were regularly washed free of refuse and swept clean. Most households had water supplied by aqueducts, and some had subterranean rooms cooled by screens of wet reeds. Wet drapes were also hung over the windows to help cool the house with any breeze, and in some homes flues for venting hot air extended from inner apartments to ventilators on the roof. Footpaths flanked the Tigris, and "marble steps led down to the water's edge," where, along the wide-stretching quay, river craft of all kinds lay at anchor—from Chinese junks to Assyrian rafts resting on inflated skins. "Thousands of gondolas, decked with little flags," also carried the people to and fro.

On the outskirts of the city were numerous suburbs with parks, gardens, and villas, some adorned with varnished frescoes of lapis lazuli and vermilion, or faience panels and ceramic mural tiles. An immense square in front of the central palace was used for tournaments and races, military inspections and reviews. A forest of minarets dominated the skyline and a hundred and fifty bridges spanned the canals. The hub of government, once confined, now also extended to a wide tract of land on both sides of the Tigris and included, in addition to the Round City, numerous official residences, the military cantonments of the northern suburbs, and an entirely new palace complex on the river's east side. Together these areas represented the government sector. Before Harun's reign drew to a close, some twenty-three palaces would magnify the majestic center of his realm.

Like any big city, Baghdad had its many classes, its independent shopkeepers and itinerant workers, traders and merchants, doctors, bankers, jewelers, commodity dealers, teachers, poets, and craftsmen, its commercial districts, pleasure haunts, alleys, markets, and slums. The rich lived in great luxury, possessed large household staffs, and were often wealthy enough to loan money to caliphs and viziers. Not infrequently, such magnates helped to finance the building of mosques and public fountains, maintained charitable institutions, and were conspicuous as patrons of the arts. Many writers, poets, musicians, and singers were sustained by emoluments received from their hands. In flattering ways, these artists also formed part of a prosperous merchant's private court.

Most houses were built of sun-dried or kiln-fired brick. Poorer dwellings were of pounded earth cemented with mortar or clay. "Due to the scarcity of wood," as one history notes, "furniture (in the form of beds, chests, tables and chairs) was largely unknown in the Arab world." Except for the divan, or sofa, which often extended along three sides of a room, most people sat on cushions on the carpeted floor.

Large private houses had rooms for bathing and ablutions, and by Harun's time Baghdad had thousands of hammams, or public baths. The typical hammam was made up of several tiled rooms grouped around a large central chamber. The chamber was crowned by a dome studded with small round, glazed apertures for admitting light, and was heated by steam from a central jet of water, caught in a large basin, that rose from beneath the floor. After their cleansing, bathers usually retired to outer rooms set aside for lounging, where they enjoyed refreshments and drinks. There was usually a barber and/or masseur on staff to give them a rubdown, and at the end of every day the baths were purified with incense and thoroughly scrubbed.

These baths were not only a boon to public hygiene but served a religious purpose, since daily ablutions were prescribed by Islam. Moreover, entrance fees to the baths were normally so low that everyone could afford them. "I leave it to the bather," remarked a caliph in the *Arabian Nights*, "to pay according to his rank." Under Harun, the hammam was publicly adopted into the religious culture of Islam and became an annex to the mosque.

Yet it had taken time for Muslims to fully embrace it, reflecting the ambivalence of Muhammad himself. On the one hand, he had commended the heat of the hammam (which in Arabic means "spreader of warmth") as enhancing fertility; on the other, he looked upon baths as places of potential iniquity and vice. "Whenever a woman enters a bath, the devil is with her," he reputedly said, and he suspected that evil spirits were also drawn to such abodes.

A bustling city by day, Baghdad had many attractions in its lamplit nights. There were cabarets and taverns, game rooms for backgammon and chess, shadow-theater productions, concerts in rooms cooled by punkahs, and acrobats to entertain strollers by the quays. On street corners, storytellers regaled occasional crowds with tales such as those that later inspired the *Arabian Nights*.

In those glory days of Baghdad's ordered splendor, London and Paris were still grimy and chaotic little towns made up of a maze of twisting streets and lanes crammed with timbered or wattle-and-daub houses whitewashed with lime. Most of the dwellings were shabby, and a fifth of the populations lived and died in the streets. There was no real paving of any kind, and for drainage only a ditch in the middle of the road. That ditch was usually clogged with refuse—including the welter from slaughterhouses as well as human waste—and in wet weather the streets were like marshes, awash in a depth of mud. Footpaths along the main streets were marked by posts and chains. There were some shops, of course, but most of the real commerce took place at trading stations (like the famed Six Dials in Southampton, England) where livestock and crafts were purchased or exchanged. In Paris, all that remained from its commercial development under the Romans were the vast catacombs under Montparnasse.

In Baghdad, there were ethnic quarters where minorities—Greeks, East Indians, Chinese, Armenians, and so on—tended to coalesce. Jews and Christians also had their own suburbs, though most of Baghdad's Jews had been assimilated into the Arab community and considered Arabic their native tongue. Even so, some Jews studied Hebrew in their own schools and Jewish religious scholarship thrived. "The unification of the Muslim empire," it is said, "had enabled Jews to restore links between their scattered communities throughout the Near and Middle East." The city's Talmudic institute helped disseminate the rabbinical tradition into southern Europe, and the Jewish colony in Baghdad eventually boasted ten rabbinical schools and twenty-three synagogues. Fittingly enough, the city contained not only the tombs of Muslim saints and martyrs, but the tomb of the Hebrew patriarch Joshua, whose remains had been brought to Iraq during the first flight of the Jews from Palestine.

Baghdad also had two principal Christian sects—the Jacobites and the Nestorians—with their own churches. The Nestorians, who taught that the human and divine natures of Christ were distinct, not one, was by far the larger. They owned a number of monasteries, figured prominently in medical circles, and stood in the forefront of every branch of learning, including translation work. The views of Nestorians had led the Syrian

Church to break from Rome, and its missionaries eventually ventured as far as China, Mongolia, Korea, and Japan.

At the center of the Christian quarter was a large monastery known as the Dayr al-Rums (the monastery of the Romans, i.e., Christians) where the patriarch-elect, who received his investiture from the caliph, made his home. He was generally recognized as the official head of all Christians in the empire, with metropolitans and bishops of his own designation in such cities as Basra, Mosul, and Tikrit. All told, Christianity had an energetic life under the caliphs, which made possible the evangelical zeal of the East Syrian Church.

Baghdad was also home to various other sects, such as the Mandeans (followers of John the Baptist); the Sabians of Harran, who worshipped the stars; Manichaean dualists; and various mystical societies, like the Sufis, who eventually became part of the fabric of Islam. Sufis relied on intuition, emotion, and the "inner light" rather than on intellect or tradition, and in time absorbed elements from Gnosticism, Neo-Platonism, and Buddhism, as well as Christian ascetic ideals.

Some holy men went naked or in rags. Now and then, even a highborn prince forsook the world. One of Harun's own grandsons adopted the life and habits of a recluse, and when Harun reproved him for "disgracing him among the kings," the youth replied that his father was "disgracing him among the saints." He left the palace confines to work as a day laborer in Basra, fasted and prayed, survived on almost nothing, and gave most of his meager income away in alms. He died in abject poverty, but when his corpse was brought back to the capital, it was royally anointed with camphor and musk and wrapped for burial in fine Egyptian cloth.

TO MANAGE ITS BASIC SERVICES, BAGHDAD HAD A LARGE staff of civil service personnel. These included night watchmen, lamplighters, town criers, food inspectors, market inspectors (who checked "weights and measures as well as the quality of goods"), debt collectors, and the like. It also had a regular police force with a police chief who had his headquarters within the compound of the caliph himself.

In public parks could be found all sorts of entertainers—snake charmers, contortionists, jugglers, men with dancing apes and bears, conjurors, tricksters, sword swallowers, self-mutilators, wonder-working monks, acrobats, martial artists, professional wrestlers, fire walkers (who coated their feet with fat, orange peel, and talc), and yogis who could walk on ropes in air.

Among Baghdad's criminal element, there were gangsters, cat burglars, "criminal brotherhoods" (as in "Ali Baba and the Forty Thieves"), beggars who feigned blindness, drug addicts, and alcoholics who descended into dives. Prostitutes plied the back streets "in red leather trousers with little daggers in their belts." By discreet coughing, they called clients to their dens.

In more reputable settings, the people of Baghdad were devoted to sport and play. Horse racing and polo, introduced to the Arabs from Persia by Harun, were among the equestrian contests popular among the elite. Fencing was a familiar sport, along with swimming contests and boat racing on the Tigris. Dog, camel, and pigeon racing were common to every class.

Harun himself was a keen and proficient horseman, was fond of hunting (with salukis, falcons, and hawks), and liked military exercises such as charging dummy figures with his sword. Harun was also the first Abbasid caliph to have played and encouraged chess.

There was also much general feasting in the everyday life of Muslims, who celebrated Christian holidays as well as their own. There were two main Muslim feasts: one marked the end of Ramadan; the other, "the Feast of Sacrifice." The former was particularly festive, when "children would make collections in the street," so one historian tells us, "to buy decorations and sweetmeats; food would be prepared and new clothes acquired. On the day itself, mid-morning the caliph would lead officials, escorted by armed troops, in procession to the Great Mosque, where he would put on the Prophet's cloak and lead the prayers. The devotions over, everyone would exchange good wishes and embrace their loved ones and friends." It had an Easter-like character, with festivities lasting for three days. In the evenings, "with the palaces illuminated and vessels on the Tigris strung with lights," Baghdad "glittered 'like a bride.' " In the

Feast of Sacrifice, sheep were slaughtered in the public squares and the caliph would attend a large-scale sacrifice in one of the palace courtyards. Then meat would be distributed to the poor.

In addition to these two celebrations, Shiites marked the birthdays of Fatima and Ali, while marriages and births in the imperial family were observed by all. The announcement that one of the caliph's sons could read the Koran fluently was greeted by public rejoicing. When Harun officially acquired this holy skill, the people lit torches and decked the streets with garlands. His father, Mahdi, freed five hundred slaves.

Of all the feasts imported from foreign calendars, the one most celebrated in Baghdad (many of whose inhabitants were of Persian stock) was Naurouz, heralding the arrival of spring. In a kind of ritual cleansing originally introduced by Persian troops, people splashed themselves with water from rivers and wells and ate special almond cakes. For six days the palaces of the royal family were lit with lamps burning scented oils. Other Persian feasts were Mihraj, marking the onset of winter (signified by a good deal of pounding on drums), and Sadar, when houses were fumigated and "crowds would gather along the banks of the Tigris to see the glittering barges of princes and viziers."

Although alcohol was prohibited by the Koran, a slightly fermented, pungent wine made from dried grapes, raisins, or dates was allowed. Muslim jurisprudence sometimes went to great lengths to determine how much fermentation was permitted, but stronger stuff was also widely enjoyed. Most caliphs, viziers, princes, judges, scholars, poets, singers, and musicians paid little heed to the religious stricture, and many dignitaries seem to have had a "drinking companion," in keeping with a court tradition adopted from the Persian shahs. At royal drinking bouts, rooms were rendered fragrant by incense; men perfumed their beards with civet or rose water; wore special, bright-colored robes; and were entertained by singing girls. The palaces and pleasure haunts of Baghdad were sometimes littered with wine jars, and the delights of drink were celebrated in poetry and song.

Wine was also in ample supply. Christian monks served as the "bootleggers of Baghdad," dispensing liquor from their cloisters, where it was also brewed. "On a rainy day, what a pleasure it is to drink wine with a priest," wrote one grateful chronicler who happily ignored the religious ban.

Most Muslims—like most Jews and Christians—also believed in angels, demons, and other creatures of the spirit world. The *Arabian Nights* is full of such figures, and as that collection serves to remind us, the imaginative literature of the Near and Middle East is large. Fairy stories were just as common there as in Europe (the Persian "Peri" and English *fairy* have the same root); and most Muslims believed that sorcery derived from two fallen angels who were suspended by their heels somewhere over a pit in Babylon. In Arab folklore the typical magical agent was either a "jinn" or an "afreet." Jinn or genies (or the spirits they embodied) were made of flame, pervaded heaven and earth, assumed the forms of people or creatures, and could often be found locally in public baths, wells, ruined houses, bazaars, and at the junctures of roads. When Arabs entered a bath or let down a bucket into a well, they often exclaimed, "Permission Please!" The "afreet," on the other hand, was a queer figure with a wicked sense of fun, like the English Puck. Other popular figures of Arab enchantment were the "sada" and the ghoul. The sada was the unquiet ghost of a murdered man that issued, crying for vengeance, from his head; the ghoul, a cannibal-vampire, familiar to the West.

Some jinn or genies were incredibly large (or small), handsome, comely, or grotesque. They could expand or make themselves invisible at will, and might manifest themselves as whirling pillars of sand or whirlpools at sea. They could be evil or good, and quite as beguiling as any fantasized figure of romance. Evil genies were widely feared. They carried off beautiful women, bombarded pedestrians from rooftops with stones, stole goods, and so on. To protect themselves, Arabs would sometimes exclaim, "In the name of God, the Compassionate, the Merciful!" when locking the doors of their homes at night. For the same reason, women sprinkled salt on the floor. Many of the jinn encountered in the *Arabian Nights* had originally been imprisoned in flasks or columns of stone by King Solomon, who was said to have controlled them with his fabled ring.

The ghoul was considered a lesser demon but like a genie it could appear in human or animal form, haunted gravesites and other gloomy and sequestered spots, fed upon the dead, and cannibal-like on people who got in its way. Most Muslims also feared the Evil Eye and to ward it off wore amulets, talismans (from the Arabic word "talsam"), or written charms. They considered some days of the week more fortunate than others, pondered dreams ("Good dreams are from God; false dreams from the Devil," Muhammad had said), and believed in Fate. As one figure in the *Arabian Nights* put it: "Know that what Allah hath writ upon the forehead, be it good fortune or ill, none may efface."

IN SUCH A COSMOPOLITAN CITY, NATIONAL COSTUMES abounded. Since the time of Mansur, it had been the custom of court officials to wear black honorific robes for ceremonial occasions (black being the official color of the Abbasids), and high, round Persian hats with a scarf that hung down behind and covered the back of the neck. Harun himself wore a long black robe with the name of God (or a short verse from the Koran) stitched in gold thread on the sleeves or chest. When walking about in the palace or in his gardens, he usually carried a bamboo cane, but otherwise he wore a sword. The only jewelry he donned was the official ring of the caliphs, which was engraved with the words "There is no god but God."

In general attire, the common folk of Baghdad wore trousers held up by a cord, shirts with wide sleeves that could be used as pockets, and plain or embroidered robes. The head was always covered, either by a skullcap or fez (with a turban wound round it) or a scarf. Fashionable men wore clothes perfumed with scents such as rose water or powdered musk; shoes and sandals of different colored leather; and oilcloth rain cloaks. Elegant women wore saris perfumed with sandalwood or hyacinth.

In general, the rich decked themselves out. As one lady tells us in the *Arabian Nights*, "I bathed and perfumed myself, chose the fairest of my ten new gowns and, dressing myself in it, put on my noble pearl necklace, my bracelets, my pendants, and all my jewels. I wound my brocaded belt round my waist, threw my large veil of blue silk and gold over my head, and, after elongating my eyes with kohl [a black powder used as an eyeliner, made of stibnite or antinomy sulfide], put on my little face veil and was ready to go out." In another of the tales, a woman at the baths is plucked free of unwanted body hair by servants, rubbed down, perfumed, and dressed in a cloth-of-gold robe, with a pearl headdress, ruby earrings, and long, black braided hair. The new fashionable headdress for women, introduced by Harun's half sister, Ulaiyah, was a dome-shaped cap with a circlet adorned with glass beads or jewels.

All this reflected the varied commerce of the city. And indeed, the trade of the Islamic empire, centered at Baghdad, was of vast extent. Under Harun, seaborne trade through the Persian Gulf flourished, with Muslim ships trading as far south as Madagascar and as far east as China, Korea, and Japan. The growing ease of life in the capital and other urban centers inevitably stimulated the demand for luxury merchandise and created a class of entrepreneurs who organized long-distance caravans for the distribution of their goods. At the Chinese bazaar in East Baghdad, one could find furs such as sable, ermine, and marten; leather and wax; arrows, silk, and iron implements; and fine porcelain. There was a considerable trade with the Baltic and even some contact with the British Isles. Muslims exported to northern Europe woven materials, jewelry, metal mirrors, glass beads, spices, fine brocade and linen, flowered perfumes (prepared from roses, water-lilies, orange blossoms, and musk), and even harpoons for whaling. Sugar and metal objects came from Persia, enameled and drawn glass from Syria and Iraq. In exchange, the Arabs received raw materials from the north. Tens of thousands of Arab coins found in different parts of Russia and even on the Swedish coast bear witness to this far-flung trade. Gold coins struck by King Offa of Mercia (in England) in the eighth century were modeled on the Arab dinar; in one archaeological dig, a gilt-bronze cross found in an Irish bog bore the Arabic inscription "bismillah" ("in the name of God").

From the Persian Gulf ports of Siraf and Basra and, to a lesser extent, from Aden and the Red Sea ports, Muslim merchants traveled to India, Ceylon, the East Indies, and China, trading goods. Other routes ran overland through Central Asia. Navigators were quite at home in Eastern seas, and Arab traders were established in China as early as the eighth century. Trade to the east was centered on the area around the

Caspian Sea, with commerce up the Volga and major depots at Bukhara and Samarkand.

With Africa, too, the Arabs carried on an extensive overland trade, largely for gold and slaves. Trade with Western Europe, at first broken off by the Arab conquests, was to some extent facilitated by Jews who served as a link between the two hostile worlds. One early ninth-century geographer was understandably impressed by some Jewish merchants he met from the south of France who spoke Arabic, Persian, Greek, Frankish (Old High German), Spanish, and various Slavonic dialects. He gave a brief synopsis of the extent of their trade:

> They travel from west to east and from east to west, by land and by sea. From the west they bring eunuchs, slave-girls and boys, brocade, beaver-skins, sable and other furs, and swords. They take ship from Frank-land in the western Mediterranean sea. Once they land, they take their merchandise on camel-back to [Red Sea ports]. . . . Then they sail on the Red Sea to Jedda, and onward to India and China. From China they bring back musk, aloes, camphor, cinnamon, and other products. . . . Some sail with their goods to Constantinople, and sell them to the Greeks. Some take them to the king of the Franks. Others unload them at Antioch, haul them overland to the Euphrates, then take them to Baghdad downstream.

Many cargoes never made it to their ports. Some Chinese exports perished in fires that plagued their major ports of call, where both Arab and Chinese goods were stored. Other ships foundered. It was said that anyone who made it to China and back unscathed considered it a grace of God's. The seas were also plagued by pirates who haunted the coves of the north Indian coast and who built and manned galleys that could outrace most merchant ships. It is said that the many seafaring perils and adventures evoked in the Sinbad tales were but "a fictional re-working of mariners' yarns about the wonders to be found in the Indian Ocean and the China Sea."

One of the most prized commodities was silk. The Koran had declared that the virtuous would be clothed in silk in Paradise. Though the Arabs had long since acquired the secret of its manufacture from the Greeks (who got it from the Chinese), Harun also developed a large China trade with relays of goods along "the great silk way" through Chinese Turkestan. This overland route wound its serpentine way all the way to Baghdad through the hills and valleys of Afghanistan and Iran.

As merchandise circulated from town to town, urban centers prospered from Spain to western India, or Sind. Many were long-established ports, but inland cities were also linked by caravan tracks, with enclosed camp sites or caravanserais dotting the major routes.

A bountiful agricultural production facilitated their growth, thanks to an extensive network of irrigation channels and canals. Harun had inherited a fully developed system, but also dug new, transverse canals in the neighborhoods of Baghdad, Samarra, and Rakkah. He also considered a canal (a thousand years before Western engineers pursued it) from the Gulf of Suez to the Mediterranean Sea. But he was dissuaded from doing so by an advisor who thought it might provide an attack route for hostile forces from the West.

Some major industries, such as shipbuilding and arms manufacture, as well as textiles, were monopolized by the state. But cottage industries also thrived, including metalworking, glass blowing, pottery, lacquered wood, leatherwork, ceramics, and enameled glass. Workshops turned out soap, copper lamps, pewter ware, scissors, needles, knives, lamps, vases, earthenware, and kitchen utensils. Syrian glass, with its special "luster" or shiny metallic surface sheen, became the inspiration for the stained glass of European cathedrals after samples were later brought back from the Crusades.

The emphasis on commerce had the blessing of the Prophet: "The trustworthy merchant," he said, "shall be seated at the foot of God's throne." Abu Bakr, the first caliph, had been a cloth merchant, and the Caliph Othman an importer of grain.

Commercial enterprise in time led to the development of banking. Frequent fluctuations in the value of coinage (principally, the silver dirham and the gold dinar) made the money-changer a key figure wherever trading took place. Money-changers were transformed into bankers as soon as they could establish an office where credit was extended and maintained. Branch offices in turn sprang up in other cities, and bank checks (from the Persian word "sakk") and letters of credit made it possible, for example, "to draw a check in Baghdad and cash it in Samarkand." This enabled traders to avoid having to transport large sums of money over land or sea.

FOR ALL ITS PALACES AND PUBLIC BATHS, BRIDGES AND BAzaars, Baghdad was the capital of a religious empire, and its signature feature was the mosque. The city, in fact, seethed with fervor, and there were at least as many mosques as baths. The Great Mosque (which Harun rebuilt in 807) was used not only for Friday prayers but also for government proclamations, and other state events. There were also countless small, congregational mosques—analogous to the local church or chapel —where the local inhabitants gathered for prayer five times a day. Connected to every mosque was a religious establishment of Islamic scholars, jurists, qadis or judges (who helped settle local disputes), preachers and muezzins, and spiritual leaders or imams. All law was religious, so judges often held court in mosques with the plaintiffs and defendants seated at their feet.

The evolution of the mosque (from the Arabic "masjid," "a place of prostration") had followed the progress of the faith. As with most other creeds, nothing in the fundamental tenets of Islam prescribed what a house of worship should look like, so in the early days, Muslims made sacred as their place of devotion any open space large enough to accommodate a congregation. (Muhammad himself had so worshipped in an open courtyard in Medina.) In time the space was walled off as a central courtyard surrounded by a columned porch.

Subsequent mosques, as well as their mosaic decoration, were inspired by late antique and Byzantine architecture in Syria and Palestine. The most celebrated was the Umayyad mosque in Damascus. Built on the site of a former Christian basilica dedicated to St. John the Baptist, it was architecturally grand with three naves and a transept surmounted by a dome. It was equally resplendent within, with glittering mosaics, picturesque murals, colored marble carvings, and decoratively styled inscriptions from the Koran. Its square, stone minaret (among the earliest known) had been adapted from the watch-tower that had belonged to the Christian church. Finally, its oratory for the first time indicated the direction of Mecca. By the end of the Umayyad period, every mosque included a semicircular recessed niche known as a mihrab, indicating the direction of Mecca, a broad courtyard surrounded by arcades, and a large prayer hall.

Under the Abbasids but particularly Harun, the most distinctive feature of the mosque was a soaring tower joined to the mosque by a bridge. A spiral ramp wound round it from the base to the summit with intermediate balconies or galleries and a cone or open pavilion at the top. These minarets, which climbed heavenward, like the stepped ziggurat of the Chaldean past, enhanced the stature of mosques and were an imperial development linked to the exalted, self-appointed religious stature of the caliph himself.

Under Islam, education was also fundamentally religious and the first schools were adjuncts of the mosque. The curriculum centered on the Koran as a teaching text. Muhammad himself was said to have singled out scholarship as the highest calling, saying, "The ink of a scholar is more sacred than a martyr's blood." Study groups or "circles" formed around teachers who lectured on the Koran, the Traditions, literature, and so on, and higher education revolved around sacred theology and religious jurisprudence, as developed by various schools.

Above all, Muslims, like the English later with their King James Bible, were "a people of the Book." The Koran's 114 chapters (or "sura," in Arabic) were divided for recitation into thirty parts of about equal length—a division corresponding to the number of days in the month of Ramadan, when the entire Koran was read in the mosque.

Under Harun, Baghdad was also famous for its bookshops, which proliferated after the production of paper was introduced. Chinese craftsmen, skilled in making paper, had been among those captured by the Arabs at the Battle of Talas in 751. As prisoners of war they were sent to Samarkand, where the first Arab paper mill was set up. In time paper replaced parchment as the common medium for writing, and the production of books exponentially increased. All this had an intellectual and cultural impact that might be loosely compared to the introduction

of printing in the West. By facilitating and indeed encouraging correspondence and record keeping, it also brought a new sophistication and
complexity to commerce, banking, and administrative work. In 794–95,
Jafar al-Barmak established the first paper mill in Baghdad, and from
there the technology spread. Harun insisted that paper be used in government transactions, since something written on paper could not so easily be
altered or erased, and an entire street in the city's commercial district was
soon devoted to the sale of paper and books.

chapter five

THE CULTURE OF PROSPERITY

The material prosperity of the Caliphate under Harun, opulently reflected in the *Arabian Nights*, was accompanied by a growing interest in intellectual pursuits: in botany, chemistry, mathematics, architecture, navigation, geography, astronomy, and the literature of India, Persia, and Greece. In Baghdad, as in the heyday of Alexandria, Jews, Manichaeans, Christians, Zoroastrians, Buddhists, and Hindus met and exchanged ideas. Translation work abounded, and was so organized that the study and translation of Greek works could be energetically pursued. Over time, much of Aristotle and Plato, Hippocrates, Galen, Ptolemy, and others were rendered into Arabic. Some coveted astrological texts were also made known, including those of Antiochus of Athens and Dorotheus of Sidon. Nestorian Christians were among the most industrious scholars engaged in this effort and translated over a hundred works from Syriac and Greek. In this way, almost the whole scientific legacy of Greece was transmitted to the Islamic world.

Meanwhile, Indian culture had also become an integral part of Muslim life. Vishnu temples helped to inspire cathedral mosques; Indian towers of victory, minarets; the domes of Hindu shrines became the domes of Muslim tombs. Even the pointed arch of the prayer carpet and mihrab may have been taken from the symbolic arch of Hindu gates. Brahman scholars and Buddhist sages also helped to educate the Arab elite—in literature, philosophy, astronomy, mathematics, medicine, and other fields. So-called Arabic numerals, including the "all-important zero" (which enabled higher calculations), were acquired from the Hindus, and some Arab scholars went all the way to Benares to study astronomy and Sanskrit. Conversely, Arab settlements made Islam a part of Indian life. A contemporary list of Muslim texts contained an Arabic version of the Buddha's previous lives.

Once their eyes were opened, there was much at hand for the Muslims to take in. Outposts of Hellenic culture, for example, had long existed in the Middle East, and the task of translating ancient Greek texts had been vigorously pursued at Gundeshapur in western Persia, where a king had established a great academy modeled on that founded in Alexandria by Alexander the Great. Its curriculum included logic, medicine, mathematics, astronomy, history, and other disciplines (taught in both Syriac and Persian), with selected readings from classical Greek, Sanskrit, and Chinese texts. The academy also had a teaching hospital attached to it, and it was there that the hospital system as we know it first took shape. Medical knowledge and treatment were systematized, and medical students were obliged as modern interns are to train under the faculty and pass qualifying exams. The academy and hospital were still thriving when Harun became caliph, and some of its students and teachers found a home in Baghdad, where honor and wealth attended the learning they possessed. Harun's own doctor, Jibril [Gabriel] Bakhtishou, was a Nestorian Christian and the grandson of Jerjees, one of the most illustrious medical men of the time. Jerjees had taught at Gundeshapur and had served for a time as private physician to Mansur.

As Muslims looked beyond the Koran and the Prophetic Traditions to foreign learning, they also sought to harmonize it with their faith for guidance in their lives. Notably, the Arabs considered astronomy a religious science because it was also used to find the direction of Mecca and determine times for prayer. Harun himself commissioned translations of Euclid's *Elements* and Ptolemy's *Almagest* when "told that his astronomers did not know enough geometry to understand" Sanskrit guides, and under the influence of the Barmaks, astronomical and medical studies were expanded, observatories built, and tables of planetary movements compiled. Similarly, the study of geography grew under Islam not only by the extent of its conquests, but because of the obligation imposed upon the faithful to make the pilgrimage to Mecca (if possible) at some time in their lives. To help pilgrims find their way, nearly every part of the empire, however remote, was mapped. In other fields, everything from encyclopedias to the Bible were rendered into Arabic. At a fledgling translation bureau in Baghdad, hundreds of copyists transcribed the new works by hand. Many of these works eventually reached the general public by way of booksellers' stalls set up along the Tigris, in the public markets, or along the quays. In 791, Harun made education a matter of national (i.e., imperial) purpose when he wrote to all provincial governors exhorting them to encourage learning, and even to hold state examinations with financial prizes for students who excelled.

The Arabs had come a long way from that sorry moment in 642, when at the height of their mighty conquests they had heated the Roman baths in Alexandria for six straight months with seven hundred thousand papyri from the city's great library and institute.

In tandem with this true renaissance or revival of learning, Arabic literature also developed and thrived. The earliest known literary work in Arabic is the *Fables of Bidpai*, a translation from Pahlavi (Middle Persian) of a Sanskrit work. An Aesop-like collection of animal fables for the instruction of princes in the laws of governance, the book had been rendered into Arabic by a Zoroastrian convert to Islam who was subsequently burned alive in 757 by Muslim fanatics as a heretic. Most subsequent scholars shared a better fate. With Harun's encouragement, the oral poetry of pre-Islamic Arabia was transcribed, preserved, and studied even as Arabic itself was evolving under Persian influence to include new imagery, diction, and themes. The qasida or "ode of nostalgic longing for the free life of the desert" and the ghazal or love lyric—marked by "the roughness of old Bedouin chants"—were replaced by lyric, bacchic, erotic, and satiric verse. Such conscious literary endeavors gave rise, in turn, to rhetorical handbooks, manuals of style, and guides to urbane discourse.

Harun was a worthy patron of this flowering in the sciences and arts. He was learned himself, known for his eloquence, succinct in speech, and, when it came to poetry, a connoisseur. He also had a prodigious memory for everything he read, and "even famous men of letters," it was said, "had to be careful in his presence. If they made the slightest slip, he would always notice it." When poets recited before him, he was not unknown to "interrupt them to suggest some improvement in their lines."

As a religious scholar, he also had an exquisite ear for nuance and an exegetical command of the language of the Koran. At a palace audience on one occasion, a woman was announced to Harun when he was attended by the chief officials of his court. She addressed him in apparently fulsome terms: "O Commander of the Faithful! may Allah give repose to thine eye, and make thee rejoice in what He has given thee, for thou hast judged, and hast been just." Harun abruptly turned to his courtiers and asked, "Do you understand what this woman said?" "Nought but good," they replied. "Not so," said Harun, "I do not think you quite understand her. When she said, 'May Allah give repose to thine eye,' she meant, literally, 'may it cease from motion'—that is, in blindness or death. When she said, 'May He make thee rejoice in what He has given thee,' she alluded to the words of the Koran—'And when they rejoiced in what was given them, we punished them!' And when she said, 'Thou hast judged, and been just,' she used the last word in the sense of trespassing, as in another passage, 'and as for the trespassers, they are fuel for hell!' " Harun then turned back to the woman and said: "Who are you?" She replied, "I belong to a house whose wealth you seized and whose men you slew." The caliph dismissed her, saying, "The men suffered what Allah decreed, and their wealth was restored to the treasury, from which it came."

Incredibly quick and learned as he was, even Harun could be bested. Once at Mecca, when he was about to begin the prescribed circuit of the Kaaba, "an Arab of the desert," or Bedouin, ran before him and began to make the circuit first. The Arab was stopped by one of Harun's aides. "How dare you!" the aide exclaimed. Replied the Arab: "God made everyone equal in this place, for He said, 'The Sacred Mosque was made for all men alike' " (Koran xxii.25). Harun accepted that and let the man go. But when the caliph wished to kiss the celebrated black stone and perform his prayers before it, once more the lowly Arab kissed it first. The caliph went over to him and said, sarcastically, "I will sit down here, with your permission." The Arab replied, "The house is not mine. If you like, sit down; if not, not." Harun sat down and said, "I should like to ask you about your religious duties: for if you are right in those, you will be right in all things." The Arab replied, "Are you asking for your own benefit, or to trick me?" Harun said, "To learn." "Then," said the Arab, "sit in the position proper for a pupil."

Harun did so at once, sitting down upon his heels with his knees on the ground. "Now," said the Arab, "ask what you like." "I wish you to tell me," said the caliph, "what duty God has imposed upon you." "By that do you mean one duty, or five, or seventeen, or thirty-four, or eighty-five. Or a duty for the whole of life?" Harun was amused at that and said, "I asked you about your duties, and you give me an account!" But the man remained solemn: "O Harun! if religion did not involve an account, God would not call men to account on the Judgment Day." The caliph was abashed at his ready wit but displeased to hear himself addressed in such a familiar way. "Explain yourself," he said, "or I will have your head." "I beseech your Majesty," interposed his chamberlain, "pardon him, and make a gift of his life to this holy place." But the Arab himself now laughed and said, "I know not which of you two is the greater fool, he who would remit a doom which is due, or he who would hasten a doom that is not due yet! As for your question concerning my duties, I was not being merely statistical. When I spoke to you of one, I meant the religion of Islam; when I spoke of five, I meant the five daily prayers; when I spoke of seventeen, I meant the seventeen prostrations; when I spoke of thirty-four, I meant the thirty-four adorations; when I spoke of the eighty-five, I meant the eighty-five utterances of the formula, 'God is great!' and when I spoke of the one that lasts a whole life long, I meant the duty of the Hajj."

Harun was so impressed by this exposition that his anger abated and he offered the man ten thousand dirhams. When these were refused, Harun asked, "Would you like me to provide for you in some way?" The Arab replied, "He who provides for you will provide for me." And off he went. Harun later discovered to his dismay that the outspoken man was a Bedouin sheikh and a direct lineal descendant of the Prophet.

From time to time, Harun held poetic sessions or readings, often on feast days or other occasions for rejoicing, such as when he returned from a campaign or a pilgrimage. Poets of standing mingled at these events with anonymous declaimers, such as another lowly Arab, dressed in ragged clothes, who was admitted to the caliph and recited a long poem he said was his own. Harun admired his performance but thought the poem too good for the man to have composed it himself. The caliph's two sons, Amin (Muhammad) and Mamun (Abdullah), happened to be present, and to test the bedouin's poetic powers, Harun said: "Now improvise some lines on these two boys."

The man at once held forth:

They are the tent ropes, may God bless them,
And you, Prince of the Faithful, are the tent pole.
You are held up by Muhammad and Abdullah,
The dome of Islam, covering the whole.

That was nicely done and earned him a reward.

Poets, scholars, musicians, and wits were drawn to Harun's court by his reputation and munificence, and it says something of interest about him that they considered him their peer.

The eminent scholar and Harun's own tutor Asmai was one of his favorites and sometimes appeared at the palace with Abu Obeidah, another polymath. When a colleague was told that the two scholars would be dining together with the caliph and some of his companions, he remarked, "Abu Obeidah, in his usual pedantic fashion, will recite the whole of ancient and modern history. But Asmai is a nightingale who will enchant them by his songs." It was said, in fact, that Asmai knew thousands of poems by heart. Asmai didn't care much, in fact, for Obeidah's learning and considered it purely bookish and unreal. They engaged in an ongoing duel for favor, and this came out one day in an incident at court. As Asmai told it: "It so happened that we had both written books on horses. One day we went together to see the minister, Fadhl ibn al-Rabi, who asked me how many volumes my work was composed of. I told him, 'One.' He asked Obeidah the same. 'Fifty,' Obeidah said. 'Fifty?' said the minister. 'Go over to that horse and name its parts.' 'I am no farrier,' Obeidah objected. 'All that I have compiled was gleaned from desert lore.' The minister looked at him with scorn. Then I walked up to the horse, and laying my hand on each part of the animal, named it in turn. As I did so, I recited an appropriate verse from an old Arab poet, and when I had finished, I was given the horse as a prize. In after years, I used to get on Obeidah's nerves whenever I would ride that horse to his house."

Asmai was primarily a scholar, of course. More prominent among the court poets were Abu al-Atahiyah and Abu Nuwas.

Born in Kufa, Abu al-Atahiyah had gone to Baghdad as a youth to seek his fortune, sold china and porcelain wares, found a tutor for his poetic training, and in his mature writing displayed virtuosity in a number of meters and poetic forms. Eventually he became a fixture at the court of Harun's father, Mahdi, but his desperate love for a slave girl named Otbah, who belonged to Khaizuran, proved the ruin of his life. Atahiyah got Harun to intercede for him but it did no good.

Atahiyah was dependent on court patronage, but flattering the caliph would only go so far. At one feast given by Harun, he was invited to tell him, in a celebratory fashion, what he might hope for from his royal life. The poet began: "May you live long in royal splendor!" "Well said!" exclaimed Harun. "What next?" "May all your desires be fulfilled, from morning to night!" "Well said again! What next?" "May your subjects ever adore and obey you!" "Nicely put! And then?" The poet now paused and cast upon the caliph a mournful eye: "In time, O Commander of the Faithful, your health will fail, your breath will rattle in your throat, and you will know you have passed your whole life in a dream."

The caliph was so distressed that Fadhl al-Barmak turned fiercely on the poet and said: "The Prince of the Faithful asked you to divert him. Instead, you have plunged him into grief." Fadhl moved to strike him but Harun came to himself and exclaimed, "Forbear! for he has said nothing that is not true. He found us reveling in our own self-importance and sought only to wake us from out that sleep-walking state." Not long afterward, the lovesick poet gave up on all worldly pleasures himself and embarked on an ascetic life.

Abu Nuwas was a different sort. Whereas Atahiyah was revered for a philosophical kind of verse that struck somber themes, Nuwas was the foremost poet of trysts, gardens, the chase, and urban life. Born as Abu Ali al-Hasan in southwest Persia to a Persian seamstress and an Arab guard, he had been known from an early age as "Abu Nuwas," "he of the Dangling Locks." He was a pretty boy of sorts, and with all his poetic learning and achievement retained the attitude and character of a pretty boy all his life. When he was still young, his mother sold him to a grocer from Basra, where he met a well-known poet, Walibah ibn al-Hubab, who took him under his wing. In Basra, he participated in youthful Bacchanals; developed a great gift for improvisation; sang (in the words of Masudi) "of wine, its taste, its fragrance, its beauty and glitter," and especially of the pleasures of love. Altogether, he wrote some fifteen hundred poems and was the first to develop an independent genre for poems about the hunt.

Famed above all for his homoerotic verse—homosexuality was fashionable in some circles, and high prices were paid for beautiful boys in the slave markets of Baghdad, Basra, Kufa, and Karkh—a typical love poem of his begins:

> My body is racked with sickness, worn out by exhaustion,
> My heart smarts with pain searing like a blazing fire!
> For I have fallen in love with a darling whom I cannot mention without
> The waters of my eyes bursting out in streams.
> The full moon is in his face and the sun in his brow,
> To the gazelle belong his eyes and breast.

Yet appearances may deceive. Though "the poems of Atahiyah," noted a fellow poet, "were noted for their spirit of piety, he was an atheist. On the other hand, those of Abu Nuwas dwelt on boy-love, yet he was more passionate for females than a baboon." Some of his poems lament the passing of worldly pleasures, others fear for his soul:

> Stunned by my sin in its enormity,
> I took heart, Lord, and laid it side by side
> With that great mercy which is Thine alone,
> And measured both with yardstick up and down.

My sin is great; but now I know, O Lord,
That even greater is Thy clemency.

It was a clemency he banked on. As a young man, he had written, "He who bears the weight of love is soon fatigued." Toward the end of his life, he wondered if he had allowed himself to be fatigued enough. "Multiply your sins to the utmost," he wrote, "for you will meet an indulgent Lord. When you come before Him, and His infinite mercy, you will gnaw your hands with regret for having missed out on all the pleasures you avoided for fear of Hell."

Though Abu al-Atahiyah and Abu Nuwas are often mentioned together, Nuwas despised his colleague and their paths crossed only once. On that occasion, Atahiyah asked Nuwas how many lines he composed in a day. Nuwas replied: "One or two." Atahiyah exclaimed, "I can write a hundred!" "Yes," replied Nuwas, "because your lines are fluff. I could write a thousand like them if I wished. But if you tried to write lines like mine, your time would run out."

Harun's relationship to Abu Nuwas was an ambivalent one. On the one hand, Abu Nuwas was said to be the caliph's favorite poet and tablemate: "For you must know," Scheherazade remarks as an aside in the *Arabian Nights*, "that Harun al-Rashid was always wont to send for the poet when he was in an evil humor, in order to distract himself with the improvised poems and rhymed adventures of that remarkable man." On the other hand, at moments of guilt or remorse, the caliph preferred to think that others (like Nuwas) led him astray. One day, Harun threatened to behead the poet for his infractions and moral crimes. "You're really going to kill me," asked the poet, "out of mere caprice?" "No," said Harun, "because you deserve it." "But does not God first call sinners to account, and then pardon them?" he said. "For how have I deserved to die?" Harun cited a number of his blasphemous lines. But the poet parried his interpretation of each, based on alternate readings, with pious quotations from the Koran. In the end, Harun said to his attendants, "Let the fellow go. There's no catching him anyway."

Legend has it that on another occasion, Abu Nuwas ended up on Zubaidah's wrong side. Zubaidah liked to sing the praises of her own

son, Amin, at the expense of his half-brother Mamun whom she envied
for his brilliant gifts. This led her to promote Amin as a budding poet,
and at her prompting he submitted verses to Abu Nuwas to assess. The
latter had the courage of his convictions and as a result of his candid cri-
tique found himself in jail. Some time later, Harun summoned the poet
and was surprised to learn of his plight. When told the cause, he freed
him and rebuked Amin. Amin asked to be allowed to read some other
verses to the poet with his father present. The caliph agreed. But as soon
as Nuwas heard the first few lines, he started up to leave. "Where are you
going?" asked Harun. "Back to jail!" he cried.

The manner and circumstance of the poet's death are uncertain. It
was variously reported to have come at the hands of Harun's librarian
(whom he had lampooned in verse); in jail, while serving a sentence for
blasphemy; or in a lover's bed. After he died, his friends went through
his belongings expecting to find a treasure trove of books. Instead, recalled one, "we searched his whole house and could find only a single
quire of paper containing a collection of rare expressions and grammati-
cal notes."

OF ALL THE ARTS THAT FLOURISHED UNDER COURTLY PA-
tronage at Baghdad, none was more widely prized than music, which
before the development of instrumental ensembles meant mainly accompanied song. Elite schools for voice training were established in Kufa,
Basra, and Medina, though most students also seem to have apprenticed
themselves on an individual basis to some musician of note. The dour
Mansur had not cared for music much; but Harun's father, Mahdi, had
been an enthusiastic patron, and during his reign a number of talented
musicians, some destined for fame, had been drawn to his court. One was
Ibrahim al-Mausili, whose professional fame was later eclipsed only by
that of his son, Ishaq, perhaps the finest Islamic musician of his time.

Kidnapped from Persia as a child, Ibrahim al-Mausili had been
brought to Mosul, where he had begun his career learning brigands'
songs. In time he developed a wider range, found patronage and employ-
ment, "discovered several new musical modes," and was the first Muslim
musician "to beat the rhythm with a wand." Story has it that his ear was

so sharp that he once detected the ill-tuned instrument of one lute-player among thirty and asked him to tighten the second string. Much like other palace wits, Ibrahim was also a convivial man, known in court circles as "al-Nadim al-Mausili," "the social companion from Mosul," and was a regular guest at Harun's feasts.

Ibrahim's son, Ishaq, inherited his father's disposition and talent, was "a constant companion of the caliphs in their parties of pleasure," and "bore a high reputation for refined taste." Like Harun, he had studied under Asmai, was "thoroughly schooled in pure Arabic diction, ancient Arabic poetry, the history of the poets, and the adventures of the desert tribes," played the lute to perfection, and sang "like a nightingale." Some of his melodies were said to be so bewitching that, in the judgment of one Arab historian, they must have been "prompted by Jinn."

WHEREVER THERE IS CULTURAL REFINEMENT, THERE IS also fine cuisine. Throughout Baghdad, there was much to delight the palate of gourmets. Desert Arabs had once considered scorpions and beetles choice tidbits in a limited diet centered on dairy products, barley, and dates. By the time Harun came to power, Muslims had come to relish complex Persian dishes such as roast chicken stuffed with nuts, milk, and almonds, and delicate, dessert-like drinks such as liquid sherbet flavored with fruit.

In late eighth-century Baghdad, even relatively lowly citizens could eat well. Common dishes were sliced lamb or mutton roasted on skewers (kebab) or stewed with various fruits; chicken fried in sesame oil, and flavored with rose jam, mulberry jelly, parsley, or orange sauce; fish pickled in vinegar or fried and made into soup; meat loaf (made of ground lamb, onion, and cracked wheat); meatballs in yogurt sauce; and duck stuffed with raisins, parsley, and pistachio nuts. Eggplant had been recently introduced from India, and though considered too bitter at first, it soon became a staple of Arab meals. Today it is "the lord of vegetables" in Arab cuisine.

In the marts of Baghdad, every kind of spice and aromatic plant could be had: parsley, mint, and poppy; salt, pepper, nutmeg, cinnamon, and musk; cardamom, saffron, and clove. Then as today, meats were salted, smoked, or pickled; grains stored in silos; melons packed in ice in lead boxes; fruits and vegetables in airtight containers underground.

Almost everyone seemed to know that a well-balanced diet was a good thing. "A table without vegetables," went one Arab proverb, "is like an old man without wise thoughts." Few meals lacked vegetables, fruits, and nuts—such as peas, kidney beans, carrots, onions, and leeks; bananas, pomegranates, apples, and pears; almonds and hazelnuts. As for watermelon: "Whoso eateth a mouthful of watermelon," the Prophet had declared in a moment of gustatory zeal, "God writeth for him a thousand good works, and cancelleth a thousand evil works, and raiseth him a thousand degrees; for it came from Paradise." Who then could resist it?

The cultivation of sugarcane, native to India, had also reached the Arabs and there were many sugar confections and desserts, such as heldweh (a sweetmeat made of honey and sesame meal); fried crepes folded around a filling of ground nuts; puddings thickened with eggs and flour; and various kinds of cookies or sweet biscuits, including an almond paste like marzipan, soaked in syrup and rolled into finger-length tubes.

Cooking was usually done in open courtyards, with a tannur, or baking oven that resembled a large overturned pot and a hearthlike stove. The tannur, used to prepare casseroles and pies as well as bread, was heated by charcoal fed through a hole in its side, and the temperature regulated by opening or closing a vent on top. The stove, on the other hand, was a fireplace built to accommodate several cooking pots (made of stone, copper, or iron) at various heights.

Persian cuisine was favored in court circles, where Persian taste and culture reigned supreme. Harun's half brother, Ibrahim al-Mahdi, was a noted gourmet whose facility in the kitchen seems to have matched his musical gift. A dark-skinned man whose mother had been the black African daughter of a Persian prince, he had great wealth at his command, lived in style, and was a frequent guest at parties thrown by Baghdad's elite. Some thirty-five of his own recipes survive and were recorded in cookbook style, with an ingredients list, in a tenth-century guide. The guide also contained some twenty recipes that Harun passed on to his son, the Caliph Mamun.

The royal menu, with a Persian savor, typically featured rich and complex stews; chicken fattened on hemp seed; or meat with lentils or turnips drenched in pomegranate juice. Harun had a particular love of ground sumac as a spice. One of his favorite stews was topped with an egg sliced and arranged to look like a narcissus flower. Other popular spices seldom used in the Arab world today were caraway, asafetida, and the ginger-like galangal. Herbs such as basil, tarragon, mint, parsley, cilantro, and rue were also favored, and many dishes seasoned with a soy-like sauce called murri, made from a fermented paste.

One dish Harun greatly enjoyed was "Bazmaawurd" (from the Persian word for "banquet"), a large canapé flatbread appetizer stuffed with chopped, roasted chicken and walnuts, seasoned with lemon, minced tarragon, basil, and mint. Another was "Mulahwajah" (meaning "hasty"), a fried lamb dish, sweetened with honey, seasoned with coriander, and garnished with sprigs of cilantro and galangal. As a dessert, Harun was always happy to have "Judhaab," a sweet apricot pudding flavored with saffron, rose water, and sugar and set at the bottom of a tannur oven to catch the juices of roasting meat.

If we can believe the *Arabian Nights*, Harun was a pretty good cook himself. In one tale we find him expertly frying a fish: "Harun took the pan, put it on the fire, placed butter in it and waited. When the butter was bubbling well he took the fish, which he had first thoroughly scaled, cleaned, salted, and covered lightly with flour, and put it in the pan. When it was well cooked on one side he skillfully turned it over, and when the fish was cooked to perfection, withdrew it from the pan and laid it on broad green banana leaves. Then he went into the garden to gather lemons, which he cut and arranged on the leaves, before taking the finished dish to the guests in the hall."

Harun disliked eating alone, and if not dining with court intimates, courtiers, or important officials, he insisted on the company of wives and concubines. While he ate, he often liked to have poems read to him aloud, and when some poem struck him as particularly good, he was known to push away his food and say, "This is even better than eating."

YET IN THE RECURRENT FATE OF KINGDOMS, LUXURY AND learning can lead to a process of decline. Among the upper classes, the

material wealth of empire induced a measure of sybaritic indolence, combined with intellectual speculation of an aimless kind. As the great Ibn
Khaldun later expressed it: "The Arabs found themselves in possession of
a glory and a prosperity which had never been the lot of any other people.
Surrounded by the goods of this world and given over to pleasure, they
extended themselves on the couch of softness and, enjoying the delights of
this life, they fell into a long sleep in the shade of their glory and peace."

That process had not yet taken hold under Harun, who joined culture
and commercial progress to military might. But not long after him the
long shadow of indolence began to creep across the throne.

chapter six

AL-ANDALUS

The rule of Islam was not all one. Though Harun claimed the largest realm on earth, the rival Umayyads had established an independent kingdom in Spain. That kingdom was as grand as Harun's. It would also last for 750 years, transform Spain, and have a residual impact on the whole Christian West.

When the Muslims first crossed the Strait of Gibraltar (then known as the Pillars of Hercules), Spain had been under the Goths. The Goths were not then the "barbarians" their name conjures up, but the Christianized inheritors of Roman rule. The Romans had built highways, theaters, circuses, lordly bridges, aqueducts with granite arches, mighty dams, and majestic monuments and temples to their heroes and their gods. They had introduced highly developed political and judicial institutions, new concepts of social and family life; and Latin as the common language of learning and law. Spain had also contributed its share to Latin literature's Golden Age. The Stoic philosopher Seneca had come from Cordova; the orator Quintilian from Calahorra, a town on the Ebro River near Navarre; the epigrammatic poet Martial from Aragon. Toward the end of his life, Martial had returned from Rome to his native land to revel in the idyllic pleasures of an Andalusian farm. He wrote his fellow poet and satirist Juvenal: "My land has fresh water springs, a grove, trellised vines, a rose garden, a dovecote, and a vegetable patch. Most nights I sleep like a top, get up at nine, don a simple tunic (instead of a toga), and saunter into the kitchen, where the farmer's wife is busy cooking me a capital breakfast in a well-scrubbed pot over a blazing fire: '*Sic me vivere, sic juvat perire.*' " ("So I live, so I hope to die.")

Some of Rome's greatest and wisest emperors were also Spanish, including Marcus Aurelius, Hadrian, Theodosius I, and Trajan, whose triumphal arch adorned the Alcantara Bridge.

The Goths took over from the Romans, extended some of their achievements, but were never able to consolidate their rule. Differences of ethnicity, tradition, and faith were never bridged; native peoples scorned; the Jews harassed; and a general discontent allowed to fester from the mountains in the north to the Andalusian plains. Over the course of two hundred years, corrupt Gothic nobles had promulgated a host of inequities, taken the best land for themselves, overtaxed the middle class, and luxuriated in wealth based on the toil of a wretched and hopeless race of serfs. Among their squabbling nobles, struggles at the helm ensued. When Roderick, the last king of the Goths, claimed the throne, his rivals were prepared to go to any lengths to oust him. His own unbridled passion—and the rape of a beautiful young countess named Florinda—ultimately did him in. Florinda's father was outraged and invited the Moors (North African Muslims) to cross over into Spain and help him take the throne.

The Arab governor of North Africa at the time was a man named Musa ibn Nasyr. Based at Tangier, he had gazed longingly across the Strait of Gibraltar at the Spanish coast. On a clear day, it was said, he could count the houses, observe the ships at port, and "when the wind blew hard, sniff the sweet orange scent of Spanish citrus fruits." He consulted Damascus (at this time an Umayyad city) and decided on a reconnoitering expedition to test the resistance an invasion might meet. He placed an aide named Tarif at the head of it, and Tarif had no trouble carrying off plunder from a small Andalusian port. In July 711, Musa dispatched an expeditionary force of seven thousand Berbers commanded by Tarik ibn Ziyad, a Berber general, who landed on the Rock of Gibraltar (from "Gebel al-Tarik," meaning, "Tarik's mountain"), where he established a bridgehead for his advance. Another five thousand men soon followed and the two armies converged on Algeciras. Roderick hastily assembled his legions and met the invaders on July 19 near the banks of the Guadalete, south of Cadiz. Roderick appeared on the scene wearing a purple mantle, a gold crown, and silver boots. The Goths fought with courage but could not hold out against the Arab onslaught as wave after wave of "screaming Berber horsemen, mounted on small, long-tailed steeds, swooped down from every direction, their scimitars whirling above their turbaned heads." The Goths scattered and the only trace of their king that remained was a silver boot. Had he fled? Or been killed? No one knew. One hundred and fifty years after the battle, a tombstone was discovered at Viseu, in Portugal, inscribed: HIC REQUIESCIT RODERICUS REX ULTIMUS GOTHORUM ("HERE LIES RODERICK THE LAST KING OF THE GOTHS").

In the aftermath of the king's defeat, more Muslims crossed the strait. Their various columns swept up from the south, united, and with a vast wheeling maneuver, gained mastery of Saragossa and the entire Tarragona region. From there they pushed into Asturias and Galicia in the northwest. Within a few weeks the southern cities fell. One contingent captured Cordova with relative ease; another raced to Malaga, skirting well-fortified Seville. Meanwhile, still more Arabs effected a landing, crossed the Sierra Morena, and took Merida. After gaining a victory at Salamanca, they joined the siege of Toledo, the seat of Gothic power.

Toledo fell in turn, and Tarik claimed all the riches its treasury contained. These included twenty-five gold crowns adorned with precious stones and a marble table, edged with gold and silver, engraved with the twelve signs of the zodiac. Three hundred and sixty emeralds, each representing a degree of the ecliptic, richly embellished the top. He exclaimed, "This is Solomon's Table," which, according to tradition, had been brought from Jerusalem to Rome by the Emperor Titus and from there carried off by the Goths.

Jealous of the unexpected and phenomenal success of his Berber lieutenant, Musa ibn Nasyr crossed into Spain himself in June 712 with eighteen thousand Arab and Syrian troops. After landing at Algeciras, he took towns and strongholds—Medina Sidonia, Carmona, and Seville—that were not yet claimed. At Toledo he caught up with Tarik, who submitted to his will.

The fall of Spain proved so sudden and grand that it naturally acquired a mythic cast. An enduring Spanish legend tells us that near the city of Toledo stood an enchanted tower that in some fabled time had been built by Hercules. It was believed that some dread evil would befall anyone who entered in, and a long line of Gothic kings had each affixed a new lock to the gate. Roderick, however, had defied that custom, forced the gate, and rummaged about for imagined treasure within. Instead, in a central chamber, he found a painted cloth depicting dark-visaged men on horseback, wearing turbans and armed with swords dangling at their necks. Underneath, the legend read: "SUCH MEN SHALL CONQUER SPAIN!"

MUSA SOON DISCARDED THE SPANISH FACTION THAT HAD INvited him in and proclaimed Arab sovereignty over the conquered land. In the course of his victorious return to Damascus that fall, he disembarked at Tangier and advanced in stately fashion overland toward Syria with four hundred Gothic nobles in his train. Behind them came a seemingly endless cortege of slaves and prisoners loaded with plunder. The triumphal progress of this captive princely train through North Africa justly conjured up the ancient victorious Roman marches during the Punic wars.

In February 715, the delighted caliph received him in the courtyard of the Great Mosque, was presented with King Solomon's Table, among other trophies, and in gratitude made Musa's son, Abd al-Aziz, governor of Spain. Al-Aziz set up court at Seville and married Roderick's widow, Egilona, who persuaded her new husband to wear a Gothic crown. In a clever double gesture to the nuptial union of their faiths, she made the doorway to his audience chamber so low that all who entered had to do so bowing, yet made the door to the palace chapel lower still, so that the emir himself had to bend on entering as if in worship to a higher throne.

Spain was now a province of the Caliphate. The Arabic name it assumed was "al-Andalus," meaning, "land of the Vandals," who had occupied the country before the Goths. From this the region of Andalusia gets its name. The Muslims who came and stayed were broadly known as "Saracens" (meaning "Easterns") or Moors due to the preponderance of Berbers in their mix.

In subsequent years, the Muslims sought to enlarge their conquest and prepared to cross the Pyrenees toward France. In 720 they captured Narbonne, converted it into a huge depot for arms and provisions, and, lured on by the treasures of the convents and churches of Gaul, attempted to cross in the spring of 732. Having vanquished the Duke of Aquitaine on the banks of the Garonne, they stormed Bordeaux, setting its churches on fire. After burning a basilica outside the walls of Poitiers they pushed northward toward Tours. But between Tours and Poitiers they were met (as noted) by the Franks under Charles Martel.

For seven days the Arab army stood staring at the Franks, who had formidably massed on a hill to their front. Some were mailed and mounted warriors; others, clad in wolfskins and wearing long matted hair, looked like savage beasts. On October 11 the Muslims attacked, but the incline slowed their steeds. The Franks at once formed a hollow square and "stood shoulder to shoulder, firm as a wall, inflexible as a block of ice." Without breaking ranks, they repelled the Arab light cavalry charges, until at length the fighting died down as darkness fell. At dawn it was discovered that the Muslims had withdrawn.

Historians dispute the importance of the clash. Some regard it as one of the decisive battles of history—one that saved the West. But to Arab eyes, it was a minor if predictable defeat. "The Arab-Berber wave," notes one historian, "was already almost a thousand miles from its starting-place in Gibraltar and had reached a natural standstill. It had lost its momentum and spent itself." Moreover, though the Muslims had been checked, their raids continued elsewhere. In 734, for example, they seized Avignon; nine years later they pillaged Lyons; and held on to Narbonne until 759.

Meanwhile, the Arabs turned to the work of consolidating the kingdom they had gained. They had almost three hundred years in which to do this without much challenge. Although fugitive Christians took refuge in the mountainous districts of the north, the Arabs decided it would cost more blood to dislodge them than it was worth. Leaving the dreary wastes and rocky defiles of Galicia, Leon, and Castile to their foes, they contented themselves with the warm and fertile provinces of the east and south. Between the north and south, a great range of mountains also formed a natural divide.

On the other hand, the Muslims had to contend with divisions among themselves. Their army of conquest was made up of a number of hostile tribes, and long-standing blood feuds animated their disputes. As soon as the conquest gave way to a life of occupation, these dissensions flared. And of course they had to do with the spoils of war. Although the Berbers had done the lion's share of the fighting, they were settled on arid wastes while the Arabs claimed the fertile valleys of Andalusia and Aragon for themselves. Every ripple of discord in North Africa also brought new immigrants, who struggled with those who had already put down roots. Meanwhile, sparse centers of Christian resistance maintained themselves in the outermost regions of Galicia, Cantabria, and Asturias.

The result of these tensions was that a stable Muslim kingdom proved elusive until the throne was finally claimed by a prince of royal blood. That prince was Abd al-Rahman I, a young nephew of the last Umayyad caliph, whose House had been slaughtered by Abu al-Abbas (Saffah). Pursued for five years through North Africa by Abbasid agents, he at length set foot on Spanish soil in 755. By then he had made contact with various factions, and with the support of Syrian legions established himself as emir.

A fortuitous mix of Arab Berber stock, he had a long, thin face, long hair, and one eye. The early Arab historian, Ibn Hayyan, described him as

kind-hearted, disposed to mercy, eloquent in speech, endowed with a quick perception, slow in his determinations, but constant and persevering in carrying them into effect. He was active and stirring; never abandoned himself to indulgence; took complete charge of the affairs of government, yet never failed to consult men of wisdom and experience when a difficult problem arose. A brave and intrepid warrior, he was foremost in battle, terrible in his anger, and intolerant of contradiction. His countenance inspired awe, yet he visited the sick, mixed with the people in their rejoicings, was wont to follow biers and pray over the dead, and in the mosque on Fridays would address the crowd.

For thirty years Abd al-Rahman I struggled to unite the diverse population under his rule. Regarded with awe (even by his Abbasid foes), he brought one tribe after another under his jurisdiction; repelled invasions by the Abbasids and Franks; and for many years thereafter enjoyed in comparative peace the fruits of his realm. In his public works, he was also a great builder—of aqueducts, gardens, fountains, bridges, and baths. Two years before his death in 788, he began work on the Great Mosque of Cordova—"the Kabbah of Western Islam"—which rose above the banks of the Guadalquivir. A battlemented wall of brick and stone, it had eleven naves, fifty-one arcades, twenty-one portals surmounted by carved horseshoe arches, gilded ceilings, over twelve hundred columns, a soaring minaret, and numerous towers. Its rectangular Court of Ablutions, paved with colored tiles, was furnished with marble fountains and hundreds of brass lanterns, made out of inverted Christian bells, lit the mosque at night.

AS ESTABLISHED BY ABD AL-RAHMAN I, THE ORGANIZATION of the Emirate closely resembled that of the Eastern Caliphate in Abbasid hands. The office of emir (made hereditary in the ruling House) projected its power through a chamberlain, a vizier, state secretaries, department heads, and a prodigious assortment of agents and clerical staff. Spain was divided into seven provinces, each ruled by a civil and military governor, with a judicial system that included a chief justice in Cordova, a special judge for police and criminal cases, and an independent prosecutor to handle complaints against public officials for corrupt or unjust acts. There was also a public control officer in every town and city who checked weights and measures, and a related official who addressed issues of gambling, sexual immorality, and improper public dress.

The system was rational enough, and when things settled down after the conquest, the subject peoples found their condition no worse and arguably better than before. On the whole, Christian and Jewish communities were left unmolested, and though their members had to pay a poll tax, women and children, the aged and destitute, as well as monks and people afflicted with chronic diseases were exempt. The land tax was reduced for those converting to Islam; the overgrown estates of the great nobles broken up; state land, some of it confiscated from the Church, parceled out; and the serfs who tilled it allowed to hold on to a larger portion of their yield. Under certain conditions, non-Muslim slaves could also emancipate themselves—they had merely to go to the nearest Muslim of repute and utter the standard declaration of faith, "There is no god but God, and Muhammad is His Prophet." The Spanish economy thrived. Thanks to a well-planned system of irrigation, new crops were introduced, including cotton, sugarcane, date palms and rice; new industries developed; and precious metals and minerals mined. An extensive foreign trade was carried on with Mediterranean countries, Christian and Muslim alike, and with the help of intermediaries and a large merchant marine, Spanish Muslims made contact with Central Asia and the Far East.

Meanwhile, both Arabs and Berbers intermarried with the native population; many Christians converted—called by the Arabs "Muwalladin" ("the adopted ones") and by the Spaniards "Renegades"—though others adhered to their Christian beliefs. The latter were known as "Mozarabes" (from the Arabic word "mustarib," meaning "would-be Arab") or "arabized" Christians and remained outside Islam if not its cultural milieu. By the end of the first century after the conquest, the "adopted ones" had become the majority in many cities, where they proved a restive, and potentially insurgent force.

Conversely, in many towns and cities the Mozarabes or arabized Christians lived in their own quarters but were otherwise virtually indistinguishable from the Arabs themselves. Often they had both Arab and Christian names, spoke Arabic as well as "high" and "low" Latin (the latter a precursor of Spanish), and thought of themselves as Arab in all but the ethnic sense. Even among committed Christians, this arabization went quite far. One Christian inhabitant of Cordova bitterly complained that within his community the culture of Latin Christianity seemed to have been lost. "My fellow-Christians," he wrote, "delight in the poems and romances of the Arabs; study the works of Muhammedan thinkers— not in order to refute them, but to acquire a correct and elegant Arabic style . . . Among young Christians especially, the Latin Commentaries on Scripture are neglected and Arabic literature is all the vogue. They spend all their money on Arab books, avidly and everywhere sing the praises of Arabian lore." Worse still, he added, they were more fluent in Arabic than their native tongues.

∞|∞

EXALTED (AND ACCOMPLISHED) AS HE WAS, ABD AL-RAHMAN I was not a happy man. Distracted by bloody memories and absorbed by morbid thoughts, he had grown ever more wary and suspicious. To secure his own safety, he assembled a private army of forty thousand black Africans "whose devotion to their paymaster was equalled by their hatred of the population they repressed." As the days of his reign waned, he yearned for his Syrian homeland, which he poignantly serenaded in melancholy verse. In a vain attempt to recapture the ambience of his youth, he planted a date tree imported from Syria in the garden attached to his villa in Cordova, which was laid out like the estate in Damascus where he had played as a child.

Yet in no public purpose had he failed. The dynasty he established would endure for almost three hundred years; and in 788—just two years after Harun came to power in Baghdad—his son, Hisham, acquired a firmly established throne.

chapter seven

GREEK FIRE

Although Baghdad jockeyed with Cordova for commercial hegemony in the Mediterranean, it was not a contest that drew much blood. Another rivalry was far more fierce, for throughout his reign, Harun's great geopolitical adversary was the Byzantine Empire. Though at one time or another, he had to beat back an invasion of Armenia (then divided) by the Khazars, who took one hundred thousand people captive; contend with a rising new independent emirate in North Africa centered at Fez; and sound out the growing might of the Slavs; his chief personal antagonist was always the emperor or basileus, as he (or she) was called, who sat on the Byzantine throne. That gilded, bejeweled, and theocratic throne was in Constantinople, Baghdad's only true rival among the great cities of the world.

Perched on a triangular peninsula of land, with a spectacular bluff controlling the passage between the Black and Aegean seas, the city had been founded by the first Christian Roman emperor, Constantine the Great, in 330 A.D. Washed on one side by the Sea of Marmara, and on the other by the Bosporus, it formed the virtual end of the eastern Mediterranean and in time developed into an unrivaled port. An arm of the Bosporus, known as the Golden Horn (both from its shape and the bounty it brought) flowed into the heart of the city, providing anchorage for over a thousand ships. The Arabs had wanted to take the city for a long time, but time and ingenuity had made it nearly impregnable to attack.

Unlike Baghdad, which seemed to spring up overnight, Constantinople had ramified into the sprawling metropolis it was over the course of four hundred years. Constantine had come to power in triumph at the end of one of Rome's recurrent civil wars. He restored the unity of the empire and made Christianity its official faith, but regarded Rome itself as an unsafe place from which to manage state affairs. Those affairs had shifted to the east. Rome therefore lay too far from where most of the legions were posted and was vulnerable to its foes. Much as Mansur had transferred the Arab base of power from Damascus to Baghdad, Constantine had looked eastward for a new imperial home.

He found it in a town called Byzantion on the Bosporus, which had proved ideal for seaborne commerce and caravan trade. He expanded the town into a city, divided it into fourteen districts, and furnished it with great public works. Other towns and temples throughout the empire were ransacked for materials with which to adorn it and notable works of Greek and Roman art soon embellished its streets and squares. By means of land grants he also promoted private building, and to attract and sustain a growing population offered free distributions of food. Even so, during the first century of its existence, Constantinople, as the city was now called, was outshone by other centers of imperial rule. It wasn't until the sixth century that Constantinople became the seat of Roman imperial government throughout the Eastern Mediterranean world.

NO CITY OUTSIDE BAGHDAD WAS MORE COSMOPOLITAN OR diverse. Roughly speaking, the entire eastern Mediterranean world was represented in its population—Syrians, Armenians, North Africans, Goths, Coptic Christians, and Jews.

The rich lived well, occupied lavish apartments on colonnaded streets, built terraced houses with balconies overlooking the Sea of Marmara, or lived in gated communities—"set back from the street behind high walls of brick or stone." There they enjoyed a privileged world of inner gardens and courtyards, splashing fountains, and private pools. Overall, the sanitation system was advanced. Most public and private latrines "drained into underground sewers that emptied into the sea," and some were flushed directly by roof drains, where water accumulated from the rain. In other dwellings, "waste was collected from time to time in recessed pits and hauled off to fertilize nearby gardens and fields." Soap was made by boiling animal or vegetable fat with caustic lye; nitron (a form of sodium carbonate) was made into a paste for cleaning teeth.

The abject poor, who lived in squalid slums, enjoyed few of these luxuries or comforts. Yet for those who could afford even a little of its bounty, there was not much the city lacked. Its confluence of land and sea routes linking Europe and Asia brought a vast array of goods to its markets and bazaars: furs, amber, gold, and garnets from the north; silks, jewels, and porcelain from China; wine, fine pottery, and lamps from western Mediterranean lands. But the famed spice market was a magnet for all. An exotic array of spices—aloe, hyssop, asafetida, ginger, cardamom, musk, spikenard, and so on—were imported from Central Asia, India, the Near East, and the Black Sea coast.

Roughly speaking, the entire Eastern Mediterranean world was represented in its population—Syrians, Armenians, North Africans, Goths, Coptic Christians, and Jews. In an effort to regulate the potential chaos of this abundant commerce, municipal affairs were supervised by an eparch or prefect, whose job was to keep tradesmen honest and protect the public good. Taverns, for example, had to close at reasonable hours to keep public drunkenness in check.

Yet, as in Baghdad, there were relatively few restraints. Regulations were only intermittently enforced. Tradesmen cheated buyers, shoddy buildings went up, drunken brawls were common in the streets. Although the sexual habits of Byzantines were also provisionally governed by religious stricture, they were often quite free. Aphrodisiacs, amulets, and magical spells were sought after "to stimulate affection, maintain potency, or suppress desire." In low life and high, prostitutes thrived, concubines occupied an accepted place at court, homosexual relationships were not uncommon, and, as ever, there was passion and romance. Many a Muslim poet would have identified with the amorous pleadings of one

Byzantine scribe, who wrote: "Let us throw off these cloaks, my pretty one, and lie naked, knotted in each other's embrace. Let nothing be between us; even that thin tissue you wear seems as thick to me as the walls of Babylon."

Though Byzantine Church ritual was more opulent than that in the West, its ascetic traditions were more severe. For sincere monastics, life was often hard. Monks and monasteries were to be found throughout the Byzantine world, but there were no monastic orders (along the lines of the later Benedictines, Dominicans, or Cistercians in Western Europe) since most Byzantine monks followed the rule of St. Basil, who stressed a contemplative if communal life. Some worked the land in agricultural cooperatives; others sequestered themselves in barren, secluded locations, such as rocky cliffs and peninsulas where they excavated hermitlike cells. Many, driven by "the solitary temperament that underlies the monastic impulse," tended to wander from place to place. Especially renowned were those "spiritual athletes" who performed extraordinary feats of self-denial, such as the stylites, inspired by St. Simeon Stylites (ca. 386–459), a Syrian monk who spent the last forty-seven years of his life standing on top of a pillar near Antioch. His life became a kind of template for those who "despised all worldly things." After his death, scores of imitators mounted columns to brave the sun and rain, indulged in excruciating fasts, lived as hermits on wild fruits and herbs, and trudged with bare and bleeding feet through deep mountain snows.

AS THE CAPITAL EXPANDED, EACH NEW EMPEROR ADDED monuments, statues, and public works to its numerous thoroughfares and squares. But at its heart stood a great central square, christened the Augusteum (to honor Constantine's mother), which contained the Cathedral Church of Hagia Sophia; the new Senate House; the imperial palace, with its great bronze gate; and a vaulted, domed monument known as the Golden Milestone on which distances to the major cities of the empire were inscribed. Nearby stood a column topped by a colossal bronze equestrian statue of Justinian—clad in armor like Achilles (as Homer described him) and holding the orb of empire in his hand. There was also a large mechanical clock furnished with twenty-four shutterlike doors that opened, by turns, at each revolving hour; and a monument to the winds, decorated with images of naked women "pelting each other" with fruit.

Not far from the palace stood the vast Hippodrome, seating eighty thousand, where horse and chariot races were held. Four gilded bronze steeds from Chios surmounted the entrance; on the central strip of land that divided the tracks within stood a statue of Hercules by Lysippos, a twisted serpent column from Delphi, and a granite Egyptian obelisk on a marble plinth. In time the Hippodrome also became the site of victory parades and public assemblies, where new emperors were acclaimed. As in ancient Rome, senators sat on marble seats and the emperor had a large imperial box. A covered way connected the Hippodrome to the palace, enabling the royal family to retire unseen between events. Another private way linked the imperial palace to the cathedral church.

Nearby stood the public baths of Zeuxippus (on the site of a former temple to Zeus), adorned with more than eighty statues of famous literary and political figures, including Homer, Plato, Virgil, Julius Caesar, and Demosthenes.

Branching out from the square was an immense central boulevard, known as the Mese, lined with colonnades. As it wound its way up and down three of the city's seven hills (which conveniently recalled the Seven Hills of Rome), it passed the Praetorium or Law Court and led to the Forum of Constantine. In its midst, Constantine had erected a statue to himself in the image of Apollo, with a rayed crown facing the rising sun. Around the Forum, a number of ancient Greek statues of pagan goddesses had accumulated over time.

All this tended to give the Christian city a rather classical cast.

However, it was also a city of churches, as Baghdad was a city of mosques. Hagia Sophia, built on the orders of Emperor Justinian I, was the largest church in the world. Its columns, drawn from Ephesus and Athens, were studded with porphyry, lapis lazuli, and pearl. Its vast dome, lit by patterned windows and bathed in soft light, glistened with gilded ornaments and rose to a stupendous height. From within, the dome, made out of pumice-stone for lightness, seemed suspended in air. Scattered throughout Constantinople and its suburbs were some twenty other churches, including the city's other great house of worship, the five-domed Church of the Holy Apostles, which housed the mausoleum where the emperors were interred. The city could also boast at least one hundred monasteries, as well as almshouses, hostels, orphanages, homes for the elderly, and Christian burial grounds.

Altogether, the city's public buildings were designed on an imperial scale and skillfully joined to the heights and contours of a landscape with sweeping views of the coast.

Constantinople was also said to possess an unrivalled collection of some 3,000 holy relics, which made it "the envy of the Christian world." Visitors to its various churches, chapels, and monastic crypts could behold an icon of the Virgin "painted from life" by St. Luke; the tomb of St. Andrew the apostle; various blood-stained objects from Christ's passion; gruesomely preserved body parts of several saints; and "the Mandylion of Edessa," a cloth miraculously imprinted (like the later Shroud of Turin) with the image of Christ's face.

Byzantines believed that their "God-guarded city," as it was sometimes called, was also under the special protection of the Virgin and would survive until the end of time.

Constantinople, as one scholar notes, "did have an extraordinary record of survival." Rome, he points out, had been sacked by the Goths in 410 and by the Vandals in 455; Antioch (in Syria) had been captured and largely destroyed by the Persians in 540 and again by the Arabs in 636; Jerusalem had been taken by the Persians in 614 and again by the Arabs in 638; Alexandria and Carthage by the Arabs in 642 and 697 respectively; and Ravenna by the Lombards in 751. Thus, "of all the great cities of the ancient world, Constantinople alone" had escaped capture or demise.

As a citadel Constantinople was even more formidable than Baghdad. It had a triple line of fortifications, forming a massive protective ring, and coastal defense works along the shores of the Sea of Marmara and the Golden Horn that were seamlessly joined to land walls encompassing the city itself. These walls, punctuated at intervals by ninety-six jutting towers, were fifteen feet high, six feet thick, constructed of great blocks of stone, and fronted by a great moat. Surmounting the ramparts were tabled emplacements for the support of heavy artillery, such as catapults. Some of the city harbors could be blocked at will by mammoth metal chains that were riveted to battlements on either shore. Huge granaries and underground cisterns with vaulted roofs were established within the city proper, which was also linked to the forests of the north by a network of aqueducts that brought water in from the rivers of Thrace. A "chain of hilltop beacons built across Asia Minor was also established to give warning of Arab raids."

In short, its strategic location and natural and man-made defenses had made Constantinople extremely hard to assail. Over time, the city had repelled assaults by the Persians, Avars, Slavs, and Arabs, sometimes in coordinated campaigns and attacks. One of the greatest threats had come in the spring of 674, when a large Arab fleet slipped through the Dardanelles and linked up with a heavily equipped land army said to be one hundred thousand strong. The siege went on for four years before the Byzantines, in near despair, devised a means to drive the Arabs back. This was a new and frightful weapon, afterwards known as "Greek fire." Invented by a Syrian Christian, it was a napalm-like liquid compound of quicklime, saltpeter, bitumen, sulfur, and pitch. When it erupted with explosive force—from pressurized bronze siphons often in the shape of beasts—it made a disconcerting sound like a lion's roar, was ignited by a flame, and adhered to almost any surface, including the waves of the sea. Once lit, it was nearly impossible to extinguish except (it was said) with sand, vinegar, urine, or salt.

Faced with this fearful weapon, which the Byzantines mounted on their ships and city walls, the Arabs, disheartened, dispersed. But in 717, they returned to mount an even more ardent siege. Once more dozens of Arab vessels were set alight with Greek fire. That undid the blockade and allowed the Byzantines to bring in supplies by sea. At the same time, the Arabs, having destroyed most of the local crops so as to deny them to the defenders, found themselves short of food as the winter set in. An exceptionally harsh winter then wore them out.

No viable assault by the Arabs on Constantinople would ever be mounted again. Ultimately, the city would fall, in turn, to Roman Christian armies in the course of the Crusades, then in 1453 to the Turks.

If the Byzantines and Arabs could not defeat each other by arms, they could at least pretend to prevail in the political sphere. If the caliph claimed to be the King of Kings and the Shadow of God, the Byzantine emperor claimed to be God's regent on earth. All Byzantine court ceremonial was calculated to exalt him, and in the words of the Byzantine *Book of Ceremonies*, reproduce the perfect image of majesty and power of the Creator Himself. The emperor received all visitors on a raised throne, and even important dignitaries were obliged to bow down before him, touching their foreheads to the ground. As they did so, two bronze lions that flanked the throne would roar and the emperor's throne itself was reported to levitate, "so that he could gaze down on his grovelling visitors on the floor below."

Beneath its pious pretensions and dazzling splendor, however, the political world of the Byzantines was, like that of the Muslims, notoriously vicious and corrupt. The court at Constantinople was a viper's nest of sacrilege and crime, and the labyrinthine nature of its intrigues eventually made the word *Byzantine* itself synonymous with involuted schemes. Of the seventy or so emperors who reigned in Constantinople between 330 and 1204, fewer than half died in their beds. Of those deposed in the endless round of plots and coups, a number were butchered or had their eyes gouged out.

In part, that was because they ruled an ever-embattled realm.

At its height, the East Roman Empire had extended east to the Tigris, south to Egypt, across Anatolia (modern Turkey) through Greece, to southern Italy, the Balkans, and the Aegean Islands. But after the Persian Empire had fallen, it had yielded territory on its flanks to the Arabs, the Bulgars, and the Slavs. Slavic tribes had advanced into the Balkans and northern Greece; the Arabs had taken Syria, Egypt, North Africa, part of Armenia, and Palestine. Civil and military reforms were implemented to prevent further losses, and Christian beliefs that would become characteristic of the Eastern Orthodox Church were energetically promoted in the regions the Byzantines controlled. But in the process of competing with its rivals (not only Islam but the pagan traditions of Slavic and other tribes), the Church became enmeshed in the whole issue of image worship, which concerned not only Christians but Muslims and Jews.

That issue would tear the Christian world apart.

Jewish objections to icon worship were based on the Second Commandment, which condemned the worship of graven images. Muslim objections were guided in part by that commandment, which they accepted, as well as by the Koran, which taught that "images are an abomination and the work of Satan" (verse 92). In the Muslim view, that abomination was akin to the idolatry Muhammad had denounced at Mecca at the outset of his rise. Many Christians had their own misgivings about image worship as well, and as the Muslims made military headway against them, some Byzantines began to wonder if divine displeasure at their own idolatry might be the cause. The question was not just theological, but inscribed in blood. For a horror of icon worship had helped to inflame the passions of Muslim armies as they engaged the Byzantines in their holy wars.

Enter Leo the Isaurian, a Byzantine general and Syrian Christian, afterward enthroned as Leo III. At the Arab siege of 717, Leo had mounted its brilliant defense. It was he who first stretched a great chain across the port entry, barring the way into the Golden Horn; bombarded the Arab fleet with "Greek fire" flung from catapults; and coordinated rear guard attacks against the Arabs with the Bulgars, then in alliance with the Byzantines, who fought the Arabs throughout Thrace. It was especially galling to the Muslims, ruled at the time by the Syrian Umayyads, to be defeated by a Syrian Christian. And there is no doubt that Leo saved the Byzantine Empire by his stand. After their defeat, Arab military action against the Empire was more or less suspended and Arab attention directed northward to a new menace—engineered in part by Leo—posed by the Khazars. For in his expansive diplomatic outreach, Leo had joined his son in marriage to the daughter of their khan.

Meanwhile, Leo sought to firm up the loyalty of his own diverse population by eliminating inequities in the legal code. His reforms did much to "Christianize the spirit of Roman Law," addressed judicial corruption, restrained the development of great estates, and ensured better living conditions for the peasant class.

The issue of image-worship, however, continued to fester, so in 730, he boldly issued an edict that prohibited the worship of all icons (now deemed "idols"), including images of Old Testament figures, the holy family, saints, martyrs, and Christ. Leo met resistance from his own patriarch (whom he replaced) and vociferous condemnation from the pope. But others embraced this new "iconoclasm," as it was called, with zeal.

With his Syrian roots, Leo identified with the iconoclastic culture into which he had been born. Upon ascending the Byzantine throne he had brought these views to the capital and made them the basis of his church reform. He was neither an infidel nor a secular rationalist, as his enemies claimed; insofar as his motives were devout, he sought to purge the faith of those errors into which he thought it had strayed. "I am emperor and priest," he wrote to the pope, and in that dual role (sanctioned by Byzantine tradition) considered himself the ultimate authority in spiritual as well as temporal affairs.

The pope would have none of it and denounced him at a synod held the following year in Rome. Leo retaliated by claiming a vast region, nominally under the pope, that included much of the Balkans, Sicily, and Calabria as his own.

Despite the tremendous furor that followed, Leo's reform prevailed because the army on the whole was for it. The Byzantines were fighting the Arabs, who by faith were iconoclasts. By becoming iconoclasts themselves, they hoped to undercut some of the fervor of the Muslim war machine. At the same time, the Byzantines had Jews, Arabs, and other non-image-worshipping people under their jurisdiction and even in their ranks. To recruit them for military service—at the very least, to gain their tacit cooperation in military ventures—was a security issue of the first import.

Leo's son and successor, Constantine V, followed resolutely in his path. He achieved a number of military victories (helping to prove the value of his policy in the field), built confidence among the Byzantine provincial forces, and "enshrined the principles of iconoclasm in a developed theology, which stressed that the only true image of Christ was the Eucharist."

These declarations were endorsed by hierarchs at their self-described Seventh Ecumenical Council of Hieria (boycotted by the pope) in 754. The assembled Eastern bishops declared iconoclasm orthodox; "cursed out of the Christian Church every likeness which is made" (in the words of their own decree), and denounced iconodules, or lovers of icons, as impugning the spiritual nature of the faith.

There now followed a wholesale destruction of images, relics, and illuminated manuscripts that can be compared only to the later devastation of images and monasteries during the English Reformation under Henry VIII. Image worshippers were stripped of their property, tortured, imprisoned, banished, and killed. Constantine V initiated a crusade against monks as "idolaters and lovers of darkness" and forced many to marry and wear secular garb. As many as fifty thousand people fled to Italy to escape this persecution; others went to lands under Muslim rule. Many of the monasteries were transformed into army barracks, and monastic lands expropriated by the state. A new type of religious art arose. Human representation was replaced by symbolic and floral decoration; geometrical designs; and pictures of animals, birds, and trees. Episodes from the life of Christ were now rendered by classical analogues, such as the feats of Orpheus and Prometheus and the Labors of Hercules.

Meanwhile, the unanimous verdict of the Church Council seemed to endow it with complete authority and helped sway the public mind. Eventually, iconoclasm was widely adopted and even accepted as orthodox. Once the shock of it wore off, most Eastern monastics seemed willing to embrace it, and few bishops or lesser clergy saw the need to resign.

While Constantine V achieved his victories over the Arabs, he also brought about a renaissance within Constantinople itself, which had recently been devastated by an earthquake as well as plague. To restore the population, people were lured to the city from all over the empire; a major aqueduct was repaired; churches were refurbished and markets connected to the harbors; and artisans of all kinds engaged to repair the widespread and considerable damage many public buildings had sustained. The bustling economic life of the reinvigorated city in turn attracted artists, merchants, scholars, and those seeking a new life.

But as the Byzantines secured their dominions in the East, they faltered in the West, where Ravenna fell to the Lombards. The loss of Ravenna was also a loss for Rome, which once more found itself with "barbarians" at its gates. Rome rued the East-West theological divide that had grown up within the Church and appealed to the Byzantine emperor for help.

Constantine V, however, was just then frantically trying to contend with a powerful new confederation of Bulgar tribes that seemed intent on claiming the Balkans for their own.

Rome therefore turned to the Franks.

This enforced realignment of Christian power gave new and definitive shape to the West. For it knit Italy together with northwestern Europe in a new military and political affiliation that divorced it from the Byzantines. Ultimately, it also made the king of the Franks protector of the pope. As if to stress the full import of this change, papal documents were no longer inscribed with the year of the Byzantine emperor's rule.

All of this happened just before Harun had come to power and it is linked to the rise of Charlemagne.

chapter eight

LOMBARDS, SAXONS, AND
A POISONED CROWN

Under Charlemagne, the West was about to emerge from its Dark Ages and recover some of its former light and strength. The eldest son of Pepin the Short, and the grandson of Charles Martel, who had checked the Saracens at Poitiers, Charlemagne had succeeded his father as king and in 771 became sole ruler of the Franks. In 773 his authority was confirmed in Rome by Pope Hadrian, and he subsequently enlarged his kingdom to include the Pyrenees, northern and central Italy, parts of Bavaria, and territory along the northern Rhine.

It was a tremendous feat. Upon his accession, Charlemagne had found his kingdom hemmed in by a belt of hostile, Germanic tribes—the Visigoths in northern Spain, the Lombards in the Po valley, the Bavarians of the upper Danube, and the Saxons between the Elbe and the Rhine. He set out to bring all of them under Frankish rule and so to build up a great European state. Most of the king's time during the first thirty years of his reign was devoted to this task. Charlemagne subdued the Lombards in 774; annexed Bavaria in 787; and in 788 an expedition across the Pyrenees gained the Spanish March. Relatively little blood was shed in these conquests, as the different peoples soon recognized the advantage of being under Frankish rule.

The Saxons, however—entrenched along the Rhine, Ems, Weser, and Elbe, and inland as far as the mountains of Thuringia and Hesse—put up a tremendous fight. It took Charlemagne some eighteen campaigns marked by ruthless tactics and wholesale forcible conversions over twenty-five years to subdue them, in a contest that assumed the character of a holy war. In 782, in one notorious act of carnage, 4,500 Saxons were beheaded in a single day. Ten thousand others were deported with their wives and children from the banks of the Elbe to different parts of Germany and Gaul. Their ancient Saxon gods were condemned, Christian practice established, and anyone who refused baptism, ate meat during Lent, or even cremated their dead was apt to be accused of showing "contempt for Christianity" and put to death. Alcuin, a scholar and teacher at Charlemagne's court, later assured him that it was all "holy work." Charlemagne probably believed this, since his campaigns were accompanied by "military almoners" and bishops who fought with the troops. Before every battle, military chaplains would chant "three masses and three psalms": one for the king, one for the army, and a third for outcome of the fight.

At the outset of one campaign against the Avars, Charlemagne "ordered his army to fast and pray for three days in barefoot procession," and compared his legions to Old Testament armies made up of warriors like "the Maccabees." God, however, was not always on his side. In 778 he had crossed into Spain, seizing the area around Pamplona, Barcelona, and Navarre. In pressing his gains, he failed to take Zaragoza and enraged the Christian Basques (who had done well under Muslim rule) when he attacked them for resisting his advance. During his retreat, his entire rear guard was massacred by the Basques in the defile of Roncevalles. It was the worst military defeat of his career and chastened his estimate of the strength of Muslim Spain.

Meanwhile, his former triumph over the Lombards had secured his bond with Rome. In the fight for control of Italian land, the Lombards had been driven into Pavia, and there for six months lay under siege. This was the situation when Charlemagne, leaving part of his army to reduce it, visited Rome in state at Easter in 774. Against a background of the decayed magnificence of the papal court, he was received with theatrical pomp just south of Lake Bracciano, where civic magistrates and guards of honor waited to escort him into Rome. At the city limits, he was met by bands of schoolchildren carrying palm and olive branches, and the route was lined with applauding throngs. Charlemagne dismounted, walked with his nobles to the atrium of St. Peter's Basilica, and there was greeted by Hadrian himself as the massed clergy intoned "Blessed is he who cometh in the name of the Lord." The king climbed the steps of St. Peter's on his knees. When he reached the top he embraced the pope and together they entered the church. After praying at the apostle's tomb, they descended into the crypt, where they bound themselves to one another by mutual oaths. Three days of elaborate ceremony and devotion followed, as the army of the Franks remained encamped outside the walls. For the most part, the terms of their alliance had been worked out in advance: papal sovereignty and jurisdiction was restored to all the territory that the Lombards had seized, while Charlemagne adopted the title of "King of the Franks and Lombards, Patrician and Defender of the Romans," which gave him control of the whole of Italy except for the Byzantine districts to the south.

For the next seven years, various Italian dukes tried to chip away at the pope's hegemony until Charlemagne once more came to Rome in 781 at Easter, cowed Hadrian's antagonists, and made sure the boundaries stood firm.

THE BYZANTINES TRIED TO ADJUST TO THE SHIFTING WINDS of power.

In Constantinople, Constantine V had been succeeded in 775 by his son, Leo IV "the Khazar," who helped to quiet the Bulgars by arranging a marriage between his family and the khan; made overtures to the pope; and in 777 sent a large army into northern Syria, where the Arabs were trounced. Yet on the issue of image worship, he would not yield. In 780, it is said, he nearly went berserk when he found two icons under his wife's pillow during Lent. The inner circle of his wife, Irene, was largely made up of palace eunuchs who managed her affairs and shared her enthusiasm for image worship. Leo decided she had become the hub of a sinister cabal of heretics. In a fury (the story goes), he confronted her about it, denounced her for idolatry, and swore that he would never share her bed again. He was still a young man at the time and in good health, a few months later he was dead. All indications are that he died of a ferocious fever after donning a poisoned crown. (Though in some sense, all crowns are poisoned, this one, studded with tainted jewels, was literally so, and created a ring of ulcers on his head.) With Leo gone, Irene, then about twenty-five years old, stepped into the breach as regent for her ten-year-old son.

Born in 755, Irene had come to Constantinople at the age of fourteen as a child bride. Daughter of a prominent Athenian family, with several relatives in high government posts, she qualified for a "bride-show" of beautiful, talented girls who were paraded as candidates for marriage before her future husband, then crown prince. Once chosen, Irene had made her formal entrance into Constantinople on November 1, 769, escorted by warships through the Dardanelles. From Hieria, she had crossed the Sea of Marmara to Constantinople, was met by dignitaries, pledged to Leo in a palace chapel with elaborate and exalted rites, and crowned empress on December 17. Just over one year later, on January 14, 771, she gave birth to a child, Constantine VI.

As empress, her stature had never been assailed; as regent, Irene had to fight to hold on to power.

During the first several years, she was concerned with domestic challenges to her authority and with suppressing a revolt among the Slavs in central Greece. Though a convinced iconodule, she maintained a practical reserve toward the restoration of icon worship, in part because of army sentiment, in part because the proclamations of the Church Council of 754 still obtained. At the same time, to strengthen her own royal title, increase her influence in the West, and maintain Byzantine control of Sicily and southern Italy, then coveted by the Franks, Irene sought to join her family to that of Charlemagne.

Dynastic marriage was the linchpin of medieval diplomacy. Leo IV the Khazar had been the child of such a union, when his father had married a young Khazar princess named Cicek (meaning "flower"). That had strengthened Byzantine ties to the Khazars and helped bring them within the Byzantine fold. Irene in turn had come from a turbulent area, central

Greece, where Slavic tribes had taken hold. Her marriage to Leo had been designed to appeal to the Slavs (especially those who had recently increased the population of the capital) and encourage their adoption of the Eastern Orthodox faith.

By the marriage of her son, Irene now hoped to win over the Franks.

In 781, her envoys met with Charlemagne in Rome, and in the following year they traveled by sea to Venice, then over the Alps to his court. The negotiations culminated in an agreement to wed her son, then twelve years old, to one of Charlemagne's daughters, known as Rotrud (or "Red"), then six. A palace eunuch was dispatched from Constantinople to teach Rotrud Greek and to familiarize her with the rites and rituals of the Byzantine court. Meanwhile, to improve her hand, Irene had crushed an army revolt, struck coins featuring a portrait of herself on the front holding the orb of empire, and reorganized the secretariats by which she ruled. In the process, eunuchs of her household (trusted aides, personally bound to her for their standing) moved to the fore. Her treasurer, John Sakellarios, was made commander in chief of the armed forces, and her confidant, known only by the name Staurakios, head of civil affairs. That created considerable consternation among Byzantine nobles—not, by the way, because the men were eunuchs, but because they owed their power entirely to Irene. Indeed, whereas in Baghdad eunuchs were largely custodians of the harem, in Constantinople they not only ran the ceremonial life of the court (especially the affairs of the women's quarters) but often the machinery of state. Some pivotal positions, in fact, were reserved for eunuchs, including that of chamberlain. In both cultures, but for different reasons, their inability to procreate was thought to make them more loyal and reliable, since they were free of many of the normal ties that bind. Since castration under Byzantine (as well as Islamic) law was illegal, in deference to the empire's manpower needs, eunuchs were almost always drawn from among captured populations of enslaved males.

It was just at this time (in 782) that Harun had made his famous march, as crown prince, to the Bosporus and defeated Irene's forces. Though Arab generalship had been skilled, the campaign also coincided with treason in Byzantine ranks. In the course of the fighting, the military commander of Sicily went over to the Arabs, as did an Armenian general in charge of Anatolia, due to some intractable antipathy, it is said, toward the eunuchs who ran the empire for Irene. The latter defection proved especially costly, for most of his troops went over to the Muslims, too. That exposed Anatolia to wholesale predations and spoiled a Byzantine attempt to encircle and trap Harun. Harun triumphed, and to forestall a Muslim onslaught, Irene, in exchange for a three-year truce, concluded a humiliating treaty involving the payment of an annual tribute of ninety thousand dinars.

The wholesale defection of a Christian legion to the Muslims might seem strange, but the reason is not hard to find. Irene had been trying to purge the armed forces of generals of doubtful allegiance, and the army—in particular the eastern army—was still strongly iconoclast. But Irene weathered these setbacks, assembled new forces, and in the following year gained ground in northern Greece, pushing as far as Thessalonika against the Slavs. To celebrate the success of this campaign, she went to Thrace in May 784, named a new city after herself (Irenopolis), and fortified the Black Sea port of Anchialos along the Bulgarian frontier.

Irene's hold on the government now seemed secure and she took other steps to strengthen her grip. To improve her relationship with Church hierarchs, she refurbished over a dozen chapels and churches; founded the Convent of the Mother of God on the island of Prinkipo in the Sea of Marmara; richly endowed the Church of the Virgin with mosaics and other adornments; and allowed monastics to thrive. One exhilarated Church chronicler wrote that, thanks to Irene, "the pious began once more to speak freely. God's word spread about, those who sought salvation were able to renounce the world without hindrance, God's praises rose up to heaven, and all good things were manifest."

In the sixth year of her reign—that is, in 786, the year Harun came to power—an ecumenical council was convened to give image worship new sanction. To prepare the way, the patriarch, Paul, resigned and an iconodule took his place. With Irene he moved to make iconoclasm a thing of the past. To help legitimize the change, the former patriarch, Paul, was forced to declare that he had always revered icons and was "ashamed to have governed the church of Constantinople" when it was estranged from other Christian sees. The pope endorsed the council and sent high-level representatives to attend.

The Seventh Ecumenical Council opened in the Church of the Holy Apostles in 786. But no sooner did its members take their seats than army officers drew their swords and denounced the new patriarch as a heretic. As he cowered in the apse, they seemed ready to march down the nave, even in the face of Irene's own shouted commands. The council dissolved in chaos; Irene and her son, Constantine, returned to the palace; and chants of "Nika!" or "Victory!" reverberated through the church where only iconoclasts remained.

In the aftermath of this debacle, the imperial guard was purged and its renegade members replaced by loyal troops (many of them mercenary Slavs) brought in from Bithynia and Thrace. A portion of the suspect guard was also sent to Malagina on the pretext that an expedition against the Arabs was in the offing. But once the guardsmen arrived, they were peaceably dispersed.

In the civil administration, too, iconoclasts were replaced with loyalists wherever possible, and in 787, the Church Council was reconvened—this time at the provincial city of Nicaea, which had tremendous resonance in the history of the Church. It was there in 325, at the First Ecumenical Council, that the basic declaration of Christian faith, the Nicene Creed, had been affirmed. Nicaea was also a secure location, so to speak, with formidable defense works and battlemented walls. The delegates who gathered included 365 bishops, 132 abbots and monks, and a number of papal legates. With the legates taking part in such a large convocation, "the Council could claim to represent the entire Christian world."

Meanwhile, combing through early Christian writings, the patriarch and his coterie of scholars found ample evidence for the veneration of icons in the hallowed traditions of the Church. After several sessions, the council members—ready to issue their definitive decree—were conveyed by land and sea across the Bosporus to Constantinople, where they reconvened in the imperial palace on November 14, 787. Icon worship was affirmed, its opponents denounced, and all who disagreed with the council condemned.

⊰◦⫯◦⊱

DURING ALL THIS TIME, IRENE HAD RULED IN THE NAME OF her son. When Constantine turned seventeen, however, and came of age, Irene declined to yield her place. Undercutting his desires, she also annulled his engagement to Charlemagne's daughter (in conjunction with a policy shift), and in November 788 forced him to marry an Armenian girl he did not like. This action coincided with her decision to oppose Charlemagne's expansion into southern Italy, in a misguided hope, based on her iconodule rulings, that the pope would take her side.

Her attempt to secure southern Italy, however, failed and occurred just at the time both the Bulgars and the Arabs chose to renew their hostilities on separate fronts. As a result, her forces in eastern Asia Minor were outflanked. These reversals tempted her son to attempt a coup. Since most of the provincial armies took his side, Irene was deposed and her close advisors demoted, imprisoned, or banished. Constantine was enthroned as Constantine VI, and Irene placed under arrest.

But Constantine lacked the wit and ability to govern alone. In 790, Harun's navy successfully attacked Crete and Cyprus; in 791, the Byzantines were humiliated on the Bulgar front. On January 15, 792, Constantine was obliged to recall his mother as his "co-ruler," and for all practical purposes his power was eclipsed. Irene's bust appeared on the face of the new imperial coinage with the title "Irene Augusta," and that of her son on the back "as a beardless youth." Although mother and son appeared to rule together, within governing circles she industriously sowed the seeds of his demise. He inadvertently did all he could to help. In defiance of the Church, he dismissed his Armenian wife; married his mistress, a former lady-in-waiting at court; and in September 795 crowned her empress, with the wedding and coronation festivities taking up much of the fall. By his second, uncanonical marriage, Constantine created the prospect that his wife might give birth to an illegitimate heir. Meanwhile, in 796, Harun had led an army as far as Ephesus and Ancyra, both Byzantine territories, and Byzantine troops under Constantine, harried on several fronts, surrendered all claims to the territories of Beneventum and Istria, which they had previously disputed with the Franks. To make matters worse, Constantine stirred up new trouble with the Bulgars, when, in a pointless insult, he sent a bundle of horse shit to their khan.

His fall was only a matter of time.

On August 15, 797, being told his life was in danger, he fled the capital but was caught and blinded at his mother's command. The cruelty of the act shocked even those otherwise inured to such horrors, for red-hot irons had been driven into his eyes. One chronicler tells us that heaven itself was aghast and displayed its displeasure by a solar eclipse that descended like a curtain of night upon the capital for seventeen days.

Irene showed no remorse. Empress at last—the first, in fact, to rule the Byzantine Empire in her own right—she felt nothing if not triumphant and to commemorate the occasion issued handsomely embellished gold coins stamped with her image on both sides. Before long she would even begin to contemplate a dynastic marriage for herself that would surpass any such union—outside that of Antony with Cleopatra—the world had ever known.

The groom she had in view was Charlemagne.

chapter nine

"IRON CHARLES"

ccording to Einhard, Charlemagne's longtime private secretary, Charles was a tall, somewhat stout man with a large, round head, lively eyes, a long nose, and a bright, cheerful face. He had a bit of a paunch, but was "always stately and dignified, whether standing or sitting," with a "manly carriage," a "firm gait," and a quiet, clear voice. He drank little—abhorring drunkenness—but liked to eat well, and "often complained that fasts injured his health." In fact, he had a great weakness for roast meat, which he refused to give up, despite attempts by his doctors to get him to eat it boiled.

Despite his hearty appetite, he exercised regularly, and was a superb horseman and a swimmer of exceptional strength. Partial to the therapeutic effect of the vapors of warm sulfur springs, he built his palace at Aachen (Aix-la-Chapelle), famed for such springs since Roman times. Next to the palace he built in 805 a magnificent church (modeled on the Byzantine basilica of San Vitale in Ravenna), which he adorned with gold and silver lamps, solid brass rails and doors, and marble columns and mosaics from Ravenna and Rome. At Aachen and elsewhere (at his numerous country homes) Charles also had splendid orchards, vineyards, and gardens, which yielded a rich harvest in cherries, apples, pears, prunes, peaches, figs, chestnuts, and grapes. It is said that all the vegetables later raised in central Europe, together with many herbs subsequently found only in botanical gardens, first bloomed about his villas and estates.

In spite of his wealth and power, Charles had relatively simple tastes. On most days "his dress differed little from that of ordinary people," we are told, and consisted of the national garb of the Franks—a linen shirt and breeches under a tunic fringed with silk. In winter months, he wore a close-fitting coat of otter or marten skins. Over these he flung a blue cloak. His sword had a gold or silver hilt, but he only sheathed it in a jeweled scabbard on great feast days or when receiving ambassadors from foreign lands. On such occasions, he also (reluctantly) donned embroidered clothes, a cloak with a gold clasp, shoes studded with gems, and a jeweled diadem or crown.

While dining, Charlemagne often listened to music or to "the stories and deeds of olden time"; and was fond of St. Augustine's books, especially *The City of God*, which was read to him aloud. In his speech, he had a natural eloquence, marked by a clarity of phrase; spoke Latin "as well as his native tongue" (Old High German); and understood Greek. In Alcuin, a man of Saxon birth and arguably the foremost Western scholar of the day, he had a great tutor in all branches of learning, but he gave himself up to astrology more than all the liberal arts. He had a tablet in his palace representing the earth, the planets, and the stars and (with Alcuin's expert guidance) consulted the heavens before he undertook any expedition or campaign. He was especially interested in getting a clear read on Mars and eclipses of the sun (Mars, of course, because it pertained to war, and the sun because it pertained to kingship and the sovereign's health and strength). During one campaign against the Saxons, for example, he dispatched an urgent courier to ask Alcuin if the fact that Mars had accelerated into the constellation of Cancer was a matter of concern.

Surprisingly, given his dedicated study, Charlemagne never learned to write, however hard he tried. Einhard tells us that he "used to keep tablets and blanks under his pillow, that at leisure hours he might accustom his hand to form the letters. However, as he began his efforts late in life, they met with little success."

A devout Christian, he prayed morning and evening, even after nightfall, besides attending Mass; was "well-skilled" in "both church reading and singing"; opposed image worship (after all, he had spent much of his life in a thirty-years war against polytheistic tribes); but believed in the miraculous power of relics, which he had first witnessed as a seven-year-old child. On the same day he lost a tooth (which was one reason he remembered it so clearly), he had been present at the relocation of the relics of St. Germain. At first "it had been impossible to lift the coffin," he recalled. "Later the coffin moved of its own accord into the new tomb and exuded a sweet smell."

In his charitable giving, he was generous, "very active in aiding the poor," and helped not only those in his own country and kingdom, but Christians living in poverty in Syria, Egypt, Africa, and Palestine. One of the paramount objectives of his foreign policy, according to Einhard, was to "get help and relief to Christians living under alien rule." He also showered the pope with gifts; richly endowed the old Church of St. Peter the Apostle at Rome (built in the 4th century); and throughout his reign of forty-seven years sought "to reestablish the ancient authority of the city of Rome under his influence and care."

Yet any notion that he excelled Harun in generosity, charitable giving, religious devotion, or moral authority would be hard to sustain. He could be and at times was a savage butcher in his wars, and though he did not maintain a harem in the institutional sense, he was as promiscuous as any lusty caliph and had from eighteen to twenty-five children by ten wives and concubines. In that respect, his court was something of a law unto itself. He was inordinately attached to the company of his daughters and discouraged them from marriage. In response, they indulged in wild and scandalous affairs that produced a swarm of bastards. Yet it was also part of his singular charm that he eschewed the usual stiff ceremonial distance associated with his majesty and rank. As one historian tells us, "There is no evidence that Charles ever withdrew from the people around him," for he liked the company of people of all kinds, "even of his menial retinue." He not only invited to his banquets everybody who happened to be about; he also gathered people for the hunt and "even insisted that his magnates, his learned friends and his bodyguard were to be present when he was having a bath."

∽◦|◦∽

UNDER CHARLEMAGNE, THE EMPIRE WAS DIVIDED INTO counties, each governed in spiritual matters by a bishop or archbishop, and in secular matters by a "comes" (companion of the king) or count. A local assembly of landholders convened two or three times a year in each district capital, where they decided matters of governance and served as a court of appeals. Their conduct and judgments, however, were subject to constant imperial review. Some of Charlemagne's directives had the character of laws; others were more like moral counsels, laced with pious precepts. One, for example, advised "every man to seek to serve God to the best of his strength and ability and to walk in the way of His laws; for the Lord Emperor cannot watch over every man in the personal conduct of his life."

Though bishops were prominent in his councils, he made them subordinate to himself even in Church affairs. He also kept a close eye on corruption among monastics, priests, and nuns. He fulminated against instances of "whoring" and "drunkenness" among them, and asked the clergy "what they meant by professing to renounce the world, when we see some of them laboring day by day, by all sorts of means, to augment their possessions . . . despoiling simple-minded people of their property in the name of God or some saint, to the infinite prejudice of their lawful heirs."

The drinking and feasting at episcopal banquets was prodigious (so much so it had to be curbed by law), and in many of their habits and ways, hierarchs were indistinguishable from some of the more profligate secular magnates who kept concubines (slave or free) and "rode about in silk and purple gowns, decorated with ermine and the feathers of exotic birds." Nevertheless, Charlemagne granted the clergy their own courts, the generous bounty of a land tax, and control of marriages and wills.

But the king's patience was sometimes tried. One day at a service a young man gave a beautiful rendition of the Alleluia. Charlemagne turned to the local bishop and said: "That fellow sang well!" The bishop took this to be a joke and said, "Country bumpkins drone on just like that when they are following their oxen at the plough." The king was so furious he struck the bishop and knocked him to the ground.

Lower down on the scale, promiscuity was rampant; clerical pieties lax; and male bonding among ascetic scholars and monastics at times got out of hand. Alcuin himself perhaps tempted temptation when he wrote to a friend that he longed for the time when he could clasp him round the neck "with the fingers of his desires. Alas, if only it were granted to me, as it was to Habbakuk, to be transported to you, how would I sink into your embraces . . . , how would I cover, with tightly pressed lips, not only your eyes, ears and mouth but also every one of your fingers and toes: not once, but many a time."

Sexual deviation (as it was defined at the time) was also common enough for Theodulf, Bishop of Orleans, to want to stop his ears. However, he warned priests not to explore instances of it in their confessionals too closely lest they make matters worse. "Many crimes are enumerated in the penitentials," he wrote, "which it is not proper to make known to men. Therefore the priest should not ask too many questions, for fear the penitent will fall yet further, on the instigation of the devil, into vices whose existence he formerly knew nothing about." Oddly for a Christian realm, herbal potions for contraception and abortion seem to have been more widely sought after than almost any other drug.

Things were more orderly in the military sphere. As a warrior-king, Charlemagne tried to foster a Spartan military culture throughout his kingdom in the image of his own Spartan ways. He encouraged hunting forays under harsh conditions in wild weather and self-reliance in trackless woods and swamps. He urged his nobles to bring up their children for rough service in the field. "Today we see in the houses of the great," wrote one contemporary, "that children and adolescents are raised to support hardship and adversity, hunger, cold, and the heat of the sun." By puberty they were expected to be ready to fight as knights, and were warned countless times throughout childhood that if they didn't develop good fighting skills, they might never become a real man. Once able to wield arms, a youth was presented with a sword by his father and, in a secular counterpart to the religious ceremony of confirmation, judged an adult. The sword thereby acquired an almost occult value, received a special name, served as the young man's "constant companion" and was kept by him "even to the grave." In frescoes of the day, the Carolingian knight is sometimes pictured holding his sword like a cross between his hands. Carolingian swords, prized even in the East, were, in fact, one thing the Franks made well. The village blacksmith, "fusing his metal in a shower of sparks to produce elaborate weapons," was widely held in awe, and the longswords that issued from his forge had exceptional "solidity and bite." The knight's other inseparable companion was his horse. "Kill my mother, I don't care," one noble screamed at an enemy soldier. "Never will I give up my horse!"

Carolingian steeds, such as the destrier, were great, stout, warhorses, with powerful thighs, "well-muscled loins," short backs, and well-arched necks. Trained for battle from foalhood, they were used for jousting as well as heavy cavalry charges, and despite their size, could "coil and spring to stop, spin, turn, or sprint." Charlemagne had a special stable of such stallions that he banned from export and mated only with select mares. Another coveted warhorse was the courser, which was often "preferred for hard battle," since they were light, fast, and strong.

In accord with this knightly culture and the feudal system then emerging, the ranks of Carolingian armies were furnished from the land. Charlemagne made military service a condition of land tenure, and anyone who owned even a small estate had to report, at the call to arms, in full battle gear to the local count. The count in turn had to present himself in full gear and armor while also being responsible for the military fitness of those in his domain. The structure of the state, according to one historian, "rested on this organized force." Every summer, usually in June, Charlemagne assembled his vassals and magnates, reviewed their contribution to his forces, and tested the mettle of fresh recruits. Each knight was expected to have a buckler, lance, longsword, short sword, a bow with a quiver of arrows, a helmet and a padded jacket lined with metal plates. They were also to bring three months' worth of provisions for the field. Any man who failed to arrive on time was denied full rations, and any one who tried to evade the service faced extremely heavy fines.

Charlemagne put up with no excuse. Once in camp, there was no escape and captured deserters were beheaded on the spot. Yet many, raised to fight as they were, were not at all reluctant to appear. They came with a high heart, religious zeal, and an unapologetic thirst for blood. Charlemagne's campaigns had other palpable allures. Once in enemy territory, men could give themselves up without restraint to their appetite for spoil. As one eyewitness recalled, the Franks "flooded over the province like the serried ranks of thrushed birds who strip a vineyard in the fall." They despoiled the land of every bit of its wealth, led away the livestock, torched all else, and "ferreted out everyone alive hiding in the marshes and woods" to kill or lead away as slaves.

Their coming on was a frightful sight. During the subjugation of the Lombards, one eyewitness, hidden in a tower, watched them advance. After waves of auxiliary forces with their baggage trains appeared, the fields suddenly "bristled with ears of iron corn." Then Charlemagne himself came into view

> topped with his iron helm, his fists in iron gloves, his iron chest and his Platonic shoulders clad in an iron cuirass. An iron spear raised high against the sky he gripped in his left hand, while in his right he held his still unconquered sword. For greater ease of riding other men kept their thighs bare of armor; Charlemagne's were bound in iron plates. As for his greaves, like those of all his army, they, too, were made of iron. His shield was all of iron. His horse gleamed iron-colored. All those who rode before him, those who kept him company on either flank, those who followed after, wore the same. . . . Iron filled the fields and all the open spaces. The rays of the sun were thrown back by the wall of iron of his lines.

Over the course of his career, Charlemagne led some fifty-three campaigns in person and was known by friend and foe alike as "Iron Charles." Christians as well as pagans feared him, and in forging his evanescent dream of a united kingdom of Europe he did not exempt Christian regions from his sword. His war of aggression, for example, against the Basques of Navarre "literally forced them into the arms of the Moors." As a result of all his conquests, the traffic in slaves in Europe increased immensely, since the Franks sold their captives as part of their spoils. Charlemagne was apparently indifferent to their plight. "There are only free men and slaves," he once said, as he brushed aside the appeal of an abbot on their behalf.

Long after he was gone, Charlemagne's ruthless imprint on the martial nature of the Franks would remain. During the Christian "liberation" of Jerusalem during the Crusades, "the Franks arrived and killed everybody in the city," one Jewish pilgrim recalled, "whether of Ishmael or of Israel [Arab or Jew]; and the few who survived the slaughter were made prisoners. Some of those have been ransomed since, while others are still in captivity in all parts of the world. Now all of us had anticipated that our sultan—may God bestow glory upon his victories—would set out against the Franks with his troops and chase them away. But time after time our hope failed. Yet to this very present moment we do hope that God will give the sultan's enemies into his hands."

It is hard to know if Charlemagne would have been perturbed by this legacy or not. Nevertheless, his greatest religious desire, we are told, "was to be counted among the Just." For him that seems to have meant partly, or mainly, to be one who had Christianized as many lands as he could win.

Despite the control he sought over his subjects, Charlemagne was less of an autocrat than the caliph or the emperor of the Byzantines. Though he promulgated a host of imperial edicts (none of which were subject to appeal), he encouraged public involvement in governance and in that respect his administration was relatively enlightened and advanced. Twice a year, armed property owners assembled in the open air at Worms, Valenciennes, Aachen, Geneva, Paderborn, and elsewhere, where the king's legislative proposals were aired. After he received their advice and counsel, he often re-presented his proposals, in the form of capitula or legislative chapters, for public assent.

At such gatherings, Charlemagne was both lordly and at ease, "saluting the men of most note, conversing with those whom he seldom saw, showing a tender interest toward the elders, and disporting himself with the young." Yet before departing, he also required provincial officials to report to him about any significant developments in their locales. Typically, wrote Hincmar, Archbishop of Reims, "The King wished to know whether in any part or corner of the Kingdom the people were restless, and the cause thereof." Leading citizens were also summoned to testify under oath about the crime rate, taxable wealth, state of public order, and so on in their districts. Since these "sworn groups of inquirers," or "jurata," as they were called, were also occasionally empowered to decide issues of local innocence or guilt, they served as a jury, and it is from their name and service that the modern jury system derives.

All in all, insofar as it lay within his power, Charlemagne endeavored to foster prosperity within his kingdom. He encouraged commerce; regulated weights, measures, and prices; adjusted tolls; checked speculation; built or repaired roads and bridges; cleared waterways; and threw a great span over the Rhine at Mainz. Just as Harun contemplated a canal linking the Gulf of Suez to the Mediterranean, so Charlemagne drew up comparably ambitious plans to connect the Danube and the Rhine.

Another parallel may be drawn. Just as Harun and his son, Mamun, presided over Islam's Golden Age, so Charlemagne initiated the so-called Carolingian renaissance. Until about the middle of the eighth century, education in Western Europe, except in parts of Ireland and Britain, had been at a very low ebb. Though Charlemagne himself was not a scholar, he appreciated scholarly work and was determined to support it in a number of ways. One of his great educational measures was to enlarge and strengthen the Palace School. This school was made up of a group of scholars who had been brought together at court to advance their own studies, educate the royal household, and stimulate learning in the realm. It formed what we might call an imperial academy of sciences today. Under Charlemagne's care, it came to include such men of distinction (drawn from throughout his new empire) as Paul the Deacon, historian of the Lombards; Paulinus of Aquileia, a theologian; Peter of Pisa, an Italian grammarian; Theodulf, a Visigoth; Einhard, a Frank; and above all Alcuin, a skilled teacher and writer from England's famed School of York.

Under Charlemagne, scriptoria, where manuscripts were copied, were subsidized by the state, and a regular education system—made up of village, monastic, and cathedral schools for elementary, middle, and higher learning—began to take shape. Its general program was classical and included grammar, rhetoric, and dialectic (or philosophy), geometry, arithmetic, astronomy, and music. At the summit of this structure stood the Palace School.

To some extent, the academic standards were set by Charlemagne himself. His own court library, in one survey, included a number of St. Augustine's works, Pliny's *Natural History,* a compendium of church law, the decisions of the Council of Nicaea, the Rule of St. Benedict, and classical authors such as Horace, Cato, Lucan, and Cicero. In 787, he exhorted every cathedral and monastery to establish schools "to cultivate learning in boys from every station in life." Two years later, he reminded the directors of these schools not to discriminate against the sons of serfs but allow them "to come and sit on the same benches with free men to study grammar, music, and arithmetic." In response, schools were founded at Tours, Auxerre, Pavia, St. Gall, Fulda, and Ghent. And in what has been called "the first instance in history of free and general education," Theodulf, Bishop of Orleans, set up free schools in every parish of his diocese.

Charlemagne followed through. When he returned to Gaul after a series of victorious campaigns, he went straight to a school run by a scholar by the name of Clement and ordered the students to present examples of their work. Those from poor or moderate income families

> proved accomplished, "but the children of noble parents presented work which was . . . full of stupidity." Charlemagne commended the former and promised them honor and advancement. But to the others he scornfully thundered out: "You, the pleasure-loving and dandified sons of my leaders, who trust in your high birth and your wealth. . . . By the King of Heaven, I think nothing of your nobility and fine looks! . . . Know this for certain, unless you immediately make up for your previous idleness by diligent study, you will never receive anything worth having from me!"

As for Alcuin himself, the king's exemplar as a teacher, "there was not one of all his pupils," we are told, "who did not distinguish himself by becoming a devout abbot or a famous bishop," including two millers' sons.

In a sense, all of Charlemagne's aspirations were bound up with the images he sought to project of his majesty and power. At Aachen, for example, he enlarged his modest residence into a palace complex made up of four groups of buildings laid out in a great square. There was a large audience or reception hall (grand enough for assemblies) adorned with frescoes of heroic figures of the past; a tower that housed the king's personal archives and treasure; the king's own battlemented and palatial quarters; and chapels and rectories arranged in the form of a Latin cross. In the center of the cross stood the main octagonal chapel (inspired by Byzantine and Syrian exemplars) with a double colonnade supported by groined arches and surmounted by a gallery where the royal family presided at ecclesiastical and secular events. The chapel was crowned with a circular dome adorned with mosaics depicting Christ enthroned. Adding to the chapel's grandeur, its west wing had a three-storied annex and "a vast atrium of exedras like that of St. Peter's at Rome." Yet nearly as important to the king as his chapel were his private baths, which lay a little to the southeast and encompassed several pools fed by a warm spring. The great, enclosed central pool could accommodate up to a hundred bathers and consisted of a restored Roman bath.

Overall, the palace complex excelled anything then known in the West outside of Rome. When completed, it promised to be a brilliant achievement and gave heft to the king's aspirations as he made contact with Harun in Baghdad and renewed contact with the Empress Irene.

AFTER DEPOSING AND BLINDING HER SON, IRENE PAID PARticular attention to her political base in the capital, restoring churches and monasteries and engaging in a large philanthropic effort of social programs and public works. She refurbished the churches of St. Eustathios and St. Luke; the Church of the Virgin of the Spring, built by Justinian I outside the city walls; restored the icon of Christ on the bronze Chalke Gate of the Palace, which had sparked a riot when it had been removed in 726; and founded the monastery of the Virgin, on the island of Prinkipo. In a general program of poor relief, she also reduced the tax burden on broad segments of the population (in measures that evidently made the Finance Ministry irate), established several homes for the aged, hostels for travelers, and a cemetery for the poor.

After celebrating the Easter service in 798, she coursed through Constantinople in a chariot drawn by white steeds and threw money to the crowds of people lining the street.

From warfare, however, there was seldom rest. The long-term aims of Byzantine foreign policy—to subdue the Bulgars in the Balkans and beat back Arab attempts to extend their conquests in the East—remained firm. But Irene's three-year-truce with Harun had long since expired, and despite the pleas of her envoys, he declined to suspend hostilities. Harun overran Cappadocia, Galatia, and Malagina, and gave every indication of stepping up his campaigns.

Meanwhile, following the Council of the Church at Nicaea which had condemned iconoclasm, Charlemagne convened his own great synod in Frankfurt in 794, which endorsed most of the council's conclusions but warned against the literal adoration of images as tending to heretical belief. This led to a dispute between the pope and Charles, but not an outright break. Meanwhile, Rome itself had entered a period of relative peace and security, which allowed for the restoration of damaged churches and the reconstruction of the city's aqueducts, embankments, and fortified walls. Poorhouses were also established and monastic communities revived. When Pope Hadrian died on Christmas Day in 795, he was buried in the crypt of St. Peter's Basilica and Charlemagne, it was said, grieved "as if he had lost a brother or a child."

Hadrian was succeeded by Pope Leo III, a Greek from southern Italy who was notoriously corrupt. A movement was begun at once to remove him, and one day while riding in procession to Mass, he was ambushed, knocked from his horse, and beaten as he lay on the ground. Not long afterward, he was deposed and bound into a dungeon, but escaped and made his way across the Alps to Charlemagne's field camp at Paderborn. In December of the following year, with Charlemagne's help, he regained his throne. He was escorted to St. Peter's by Charlemagne himself and a guard of imperial troops. The whole army of the Franks lay encamped nearby. Then the pope "took the gospel of our Lord Jesus Christ, held it above his head," and in the hearing of Charlemagne, his soldiers, and those who had accused him, swore that he was guiltless, and so absolved himself.

Leo III thereafter owed Charlemagne both his title and his life.

The king now cast his eyes to the East.

THE GEOPOLITICAL TENSIONS OF THE TIME TENDED TO align Charlemagne and the pope with the Abbasids against the Byzantines and the Umayyads of Spain. Yet this picture of relations was crosshatched. Ever since the first Arab conquests, the Mediterranean world had been a vast battleground between Islam and Christianity. That religious hostility was too pronounced to make it possible for Muslim and Christian states to become true allies against members of their own faiths. At the same time, shared interests encouraged a complicated minuet of diplomatic and military ties.

The Franks and Abbasids had been in diplomatic contact since 765–68 when missions had been exchanged between Pepin (Charlemagne's father) and Mansur. Mansur's envoys had been respectfully received by Pepin at Metz. But Pepin had also played a double game, for while he supported the pope in his feud at the time over image worship with the Byzantines, in 757 he had also sent a goodwill mission to Constantine V. That emperor, delighted, had sent an envoy in return to Pepin's court. So ties also existed between the Byzantines and Franks.

Displeased by Byzantine intrigue in Italy, however, Charlemagne sought Harun's friendship, even as he viewed the emperor of Byzantium as his only great rival among the sovereigns of Christian states. That enabled Charlemagne and Harun to regard the "international situation" around the Mediterranean in a similar light. Harun had a vested interest in a weakened Byzantine empire, and of course in preventing any collaborative action by Charlemagne and Irene. He had also grown wary (as had the Franks) of the growing power and prosperity of Muslim Spain.

TOWARD THE END OF 797, CHARLEMAGNE SENT TWO ENVOYS, Lantfried and Sigismond, to Baghdad with a bilingual Jewish scholar named Isaac to serve as an interpreter. They set out from Aachen, sailed to Antioch, the principal port for overland trade with the East, then proceeded through Aleppo, Rakkah, and down the Euphrates to Baghdad. Their embassy had a twofold aim: to forge an alliance with Harun against the Byzantines and Spain; and to establish Charles as the official protector of pilgrims visiting Jerusalem and other holy sites in Palestine.

The idea of such a protectorate could mean little more than allowing Charlemagne to subsidize such establishments. For he could hardly enforce it by military means. Harun's power, after all, was unrivaled, and naval command of the Mediterranean was in Arab hands. Yet pilgrims still poured into Jerusalem from all over Europe as well as the Near East. Convents, churches, monasteries, and other Christian establishments filled the city, which was overseen by a patriarch, and Christian princes vied with one another in the amelioration of the conditions under which Christians lived.

Those conditions were not as bad as might be thought. Muslims rarely interfered with pilgrims on their sometimes long and arduous journey, and Christians had not suffered particularly under Muslim rule. But of late, some unexpected violence had occurred. Just as Charlemagne's envoys were about to set out, disquieting news reached him that Arabs had pillaged a monastery, killing eighteen monks. Charlemagne asked his envoys to discuss the matter with the caliph and to urge him to curb misdeeds of this sort. He also exhorted them to secure the goodwill of all the Muslim princes they met and to find ways of distributing money to needy Christians throughout the Holy Land.

Harun received and lavishly entertained Charlemagne's mission and acceded to his requests. He had every reason to do so. If the protectorate Charlemagne asked for appeared to give him priority over Irene, it helped Harun to curb Byzantine influence in Palestine. It also made Charlemagne subordinate to himself. For Harun, this was a diplomatic coup. After the fashion of Persian monarchs, Harun regarded himself as the King of Kings. To him all other kings were vassals; from him they derived their royal estate. Harun had sought to establish this relationship by implication with the Byzantines by the tribute he exacted from them as the price of peace. That tribute implied that Byzantine authority stemmed from his own. He calibrated his relationship with Charlemagne with the same end in view. Not only did he agree to his proposal, but he sent him robes of honor such as vassals used to receive from Persian kings. Their acceptance by Charlemagne implied in Muslim eyes acknowledgment of his subordinate place. Moreover, Charlemagne could hardly pretend to a protectorate over Palestine without Harun's consent. Yet Charlemagne didn't care, for he had his own, transcendent end in view, which he had worked out in advance with Rome.

ALTHOUGH CHARLEMAGNE'S TWO ENVOYS DIED IN THE course of their return, Isaac survived and reached Aachen with the exotic gifts entrusted to his care. One of them was a white elephant named Abu al-Abbas, which had once belonged to an Indian raja (and would later be immortalized in stone in the cathedral porch of Bale). Charlemagne fell in love with this animal and it subsequently accompanied him on all his campaigns. Meanwhile, Harun had been intrigued enough by the mission of the Franks to respond with a mission of his own.

According to "Notker the Stammerer," a monk of St. Gall, the Baghdad envoys slipped through a Byzantine blockade and reached Aachen in the last week of Lent in 802. Charlemagne had urgent business at the time and did not receive them until Easter eve. He then donned himself in full royal attire—a brightly embroidered tunic fringed with silk and adorned with precious stones—which Notker naïvely assures us overawed the Arabs, for "he seemed to them so much more than any king or emperor they had ever seen."

Notker indeed recounts the whole embassy with a prejudiced eye. Charlemagne gave, for example, the envoys a tour of his palace complex, during which, we are told, "the Arabs were not able to refrain from laughing aloud because of the greatness of their joy." Compared to the imperial splendors of Harun's Golden Gate Palace, with its great green dome, Charlemagne's incomplete estate at Aachen was, of course, extremely modest, despite the marble columns and mosaics from Ravenna and Rome. (As for his country estate at Asnapium, which the Arab envoys may also have seen, it featured, according to one contemporary account, "a royal house built of stone in the very best manner, having three rooms." No matter what those rooms might have looked like, they were not likely to overawe.)

Following Easter service the next day, Charlemagne regaled the envoys at a banquet, but, according to Notker, they were so amazed at all they saw "that they rose from the table almost as hungry as when they sat down." (In fact, they found the food unappealing but were trying to be polite.) Afterward, Charlemagne, to demonstrate his own martial courage and prowess, took them into the forest to hunt wild oxen and bison. But "when [the Muslims] set eyes on these immense animals," we are told, "they were filled with mighty dread and turned and ran." Charlemagne, on the other hand, "knew no fear: sitting astride his spirited horse, he rode up to one of the beasts, drew his sword, and tried to cut off its head." Perhaps it was best for the king that the envoys had fled, for he botched the blow and "the huge beast ripped the Emperor's Gallic boot and leg-wrap," goring his leg with the point of its horn.

One evening during their stay, the envoys got soused on barley beer and indirectly betrayed what they thought of the king's might. Notker reports it this way:

> The envoys were more merry than usual, and jokingly said to him, who as always was calm and sober: "Emperor, your power is indeed great, yet it is much less than the report of it which is spread through-out the kingdoms of the East." "Why do you say that, my children?" he replied. "How has that idea come into your head?" "All the peoples of the East fear you," they replied, "much more than we do our own ruler, Harun. As for the Macedonians and the Greeks, what can we say of them? They dread your overwhelming greatness more than they fear the waves of the Ionian Sea. The inhabitants of all the islands through which we passed on our journey were as ready and keen to obey you as if they had been brought up in your palace and loaded by you with im-mense favors. On the other hand, or so it seems to us, the nobles of your own lands have little respect for you, except when they are actually in your presence. For when we entered your domains and began to look for Aachen, and explained to the nobles we met that we were trying to find you, they gave us no help at all but sent us away."

In other words, people a long way off may be impressed by rumors of your power, but up close it doesn't seem to amount to very much. Notker missed the point and thought Charlemagne was being praised for the awe he inspired in distant lands. Charlemagne, however, understood very well what was implied, at least with respect to those within his dominions. For "he deprived all the counts and abbots, through whose lands, the envoys had traveled, of every honor which they held, and he fined the bishops an enormous sum of money" to make sure the envoys were given clear direction out of his kingdom and shown every courtesy and care.

In the meantime, protocol was maintained and handsome gifts exchanged. The Arabs had brought him various spices and unguents, brass candelabra, bolts of silk fabric, ivory chessmen, a colossal tent with many-colored curtains, a pair of monkeys, and a water clock that marked the hours by dropping bronze balls into a bowl. "All who beheld it," acknowledged Notker, "were stupefied." As the balls dropped, mechanical knights or horsemen—one for each hour—emerged from behind little doors that shut neatly after them as they stepped forth. Included, too, was a beautiful astrolabe, along with a number of books on astrology, which Charlemagne at once commanded to be translated into Latin from Arabic. Thought Notker: "They seemed to have despoiled the East that they might offer all this to the West." Charlemagne reciprocated as best he could with some embroidered cloaks from Frisia, a few Spanish horses, and some hunting dogs "specially chosen for their ferocity and skill."

When the Arab envoys returned to Baghdad, Harun immediately put the dogs to the test. They were released to chase a wild lion, which they managed to corner, and this, Notker tells us, so impressed the caliph that he took their prowess as emblematic of Charlemagne's superior might. As evidence, Notker cited a letter in which Harun with ironic generosity affected to mourn the fact that the Holy Land was too far away for Charlemagne himself to defend, and so offered to defend it in his name.

THESE EXCHANGES COINCIDED WITH A REVOLUTION ON THE world's stage. Irene's atrocity against her son had paralyzed the Greeks and alienated the West. Her usurpation was regarded in both Rome and Aachen as an unlawful coup, and neither Charlemagne nor Pope Leo III at first recognized her crown. They therefore considered the Byzantine throne "vacant." The pope, spurned by the Byzantines and shamed by his own besotted past, seized opportunity by the forelock and developed a scheme to rehabilitate his image, enhance his power, and make Charlemagne the new universal, Roman emperor of the Christian world.

What followed was molded to that scheme.

Toward the end of 799, a monk sent by the patriarch of Jerusalem arrived at Aachen with a reliquary gift for Charlemagne from the Holy Sepulchre. Charlemagne sent the monk back a few weeks later in the company of Zacharius, a palace priest, with a rich donation of alms. Zacharius returned from Jerusalem with two more monks (notably, a Greek from the monastery of St. Sabas and a Latin from the Mount of Olives) bearing three sets of "keys"—to the Holy Sepulchre, to the city of Jerusalem itself, and to Mount Sion, together with a finely wrought gold casket containing a fragment of the True Cross. But they did not go to Aachen. They went to Rome, where Charlemagne had been "summoned" by the pope. Charlemagne made haste slowly, according to plan. Before setting out, he undertook a journey through the whole land of the Franks—to reaffirm the length and breadth of his dominions, pay homage to the relics his churches possessed, and pray at the tombs of the great saints. He entered Rome in state, and on December 23 met with Zacharius and his companions, who thanked him for the alms he had sent to Palestine and presented him with their precious gifts.

Two days later, on Christmas Day, the king attended Mass at St. Peter's, and as he rose from his knees before St. Peter's crypt, the pope anointed his head with oil and placed a crown on his head as the whole assembly in the packed church intoned, "Life and Victory to Charles the most pious Augustus, the Great and Peace-Giving Emperor, crowned by God." With that act a new Western empire was created that was independent of the Eastern or Byzantine. In a sense, of course, the coronation was nothing more than a formal recognition of an achieved state of things, for by his numerous conquests Charlemagne was an emperor in fact. Charlemagne also made it clear that "subordination to his will was now the price of the pope's security." Even in doctrinal matters, he maintained his independence, and with respect to image worship, refused to gloss over the fine distinctions in their views.

Charlemagne remained in Rome until Easter 801. After he left, he

LEFT: A sixteenth-century Persian miniature showing the Prophet Muhammad, veiled, ascending to heaven in a halo of fire on his human-faced horse, Burak, escorted by angels. (Courtesy of the British Museum, London)

BELOW: The Great Mosque at Damascus, built in the early eighth century.

The nave of the Great Mosque of Cordova (begun in 785 by Abd al-Rahman I) with its veritable forest of columns supporting double horseshoe arches of red brick and white stone.

Charles Martel halts the advance of the Moors at the Battle of Poitiers in 732 in an eighth-century manuscript illumination. (Courtesy of the Bibliothèque Nationale, Paris.)

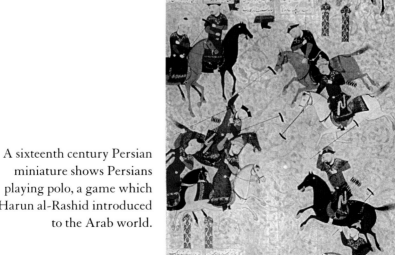

A sixteenth century Persian miniature shows Persians playing polo, a game which Harun al-Rashid introduced to the Arab world.

Abbasid horsemen in a twelfth-century engraving by al-Wasiti. (Courtesy of the New York Public Library.)

Persian miniature showing Harun al-Rashid as a young man.

Harun as a mature caliph.

A page from Hunayn ibn Ishaq's Arabic translation of the works of Galen. (Courtesy of the Princeton University Library.)

Constantinople during the time of Harun al-Rashid.

LEFT: The Byzantine Empress Irene on one of her gold Solidus coins. She is depicted here crowned, holding the scepter of empire. (Courtesy of the British Museum, London.)

CENTER AND RIGHT: Nicephorus I, who ruled the Byzantine Empire from 802–811, shown with his son, Staurakios, on a gold Solidus coin. (Courtesy of the Classical Numismatic Group, Inc.)

Icon mosaic of the Virgin and Child enthroned. This Byzantine icon is the oldest surviving mosaic in the Cathedral of Hagia Sophia, Istanbul. (Courtesy of Gryffinder Photos.)

The Emperor Charlemagne. Equestrian statue, made shortly after his death, Aachen.

Pope Leo III crowning Charlemagne, 800 A.D. Detail of fourteenth century fresco. (Courtesy of the Musée Goya, Castres, France.)

An arched entrance to the Alhambra, the fortress-citadel built by the Moors at Granada.

Crusader Fortress, Syria. Such castles were built throughout the Levant "from the snow-capped Taurus Mountains to the burning shores of Aqaba." Besieged twelve times, it fell at last in 1271.

never returned. Twelve years later, when he made his only surviving son, Louis, co-Emperor in 813, he conspicuously failed to invite the pope to preside, asserting Louis's divine right to rule without the pope's imprimatur.

Einhard, not incidentally, claimed that Charles had been taken by surprise by his coronation and would never have entered the church if he had known what would occur. But that can hardly be. The mosaic of attendant events reinforced its every theme. Directly after his coronation, Charlemagne gave the pope a heavy gold chalice, decorated with precious stones, and at his own country palace at Ingelheim he had new frescoes painted depicting himself alongside Constantine the Great.

The prestige of his new title prompted him to adjust his sights. Vast as his kingdom was, he knew, of course, that his universal empire was universal in name only, since unlike the Roman Empire of old, "it was a continental state without the Mediterranean Sea." Compared to the Caliphate, it was also a thinly populated area, not a flourishing, highly civilized land filled with commercial cities and towns. The town of Metz at the time had a population of about 6,000, Paris about 4,000—and this was considered grand. Charles, of course, recognized that his universal rule was a legal fiction. In order to lend it more substance, he seized opportunity by the forelock and opened negotiations with Constantinople, offering to marry Irene. The pope supported this move, with the object of reuniting the empire under a single dynastic rule. In the course of his negotiations, Charlemagne flattered the territorial greed of the Byzantines by holding out the hope that they might make common cause against the Abbasids. At one point, he told a Byzantine envoy: "Oh, would that that pool [the Mediterranean Sea] were not between us; for then we might divide between us the wealth of the east!"

Irene, who had already imagined such a union, was receptive to his overtures, for her regime was near collapse. Though a number of women in Byzantine history had acted as regents for their sons, Irene, as the first to rule in her own right, was handicapped by traditions that reduced her imperial role. One of the chief duties of the emperor, for example, was to command armies in war; but that, despite her forceful nature, she was not equipped to do. Charlemagne's coronation had also damaged her prestige;

moreover, her restoration of image worship in the end had gained her nothing with the pope. At the same time, her administration was marked by a heightened rivalry between the two most powerful eunuchs in her cabinet (in whom the machinery of government reposed), both of whom hoped to secure the empire for their own relatives after her death. Yet in a gesture of goodwill, Charlemagne declined for the moment to capitalize on her weakness and refrained from attacking Sicily, as his own envoys, accompanied by papal legates, made their way to her court.

PART TWO

The worldly hope men set their hearts upon
Turns ashes—or it prospers; and anon,
Like snow upon the desert's dusty face
Lighting a little hour or two—is gone.

And those who husbanded the golden grain,
And those who flung it to the wind like rain,
Alike to no such aureate earth is turned
As, buried once, men want dug up again.

—Edward Fitzgerald, *Rubaiyat of Omar Khayyam*

chapter ten

EVEN THE LOWLIEST
CAMEL DRIVER KNEW

In October 802, while Charlemagne's nuptial delegation was still in Constantinople, Harun and his two eldest sons were about to embark on a pilgrimage to Mecca that would decide the fate of the realm. The point of the journey was to confirm his transfer of power. But for Harun, nothing had gone as planned. Early on, he had tried to preempt dissension by erasing all doubt as to how the transfer would work. But even that laudable promptness went awry.

Indeed, Harun had not been caliph long before he had begun to think about who should succeed him. Though he ultimately had fourteen sons, few doubted that only the eldest two—Abdullah (Mamun) and Mohammad (Amin)—were viable contenders for the throne. The first, born on the Night of Destiny, was of course the son of the Persian slave Marajil, who had died in childbirth that same night. The second, born six months later to Zubaidah, was objectively revered because of Zubaidah's exalted position and Amin's doubly royal birth. The younger son therefore overshadowed not only Mamun but several sons born to Harun within the next few years. Among these were Ali, the son of Ghadir, and Kasim, the son of Kasif, a concubine.

In 791, just five years after he had mounted the throne himself as King of Kings, Harun had therefore announced that his five-year-old son, Muhammad, would be his heir. He gave him the honorific title of Amin (meaning, "the Truthful One") and the whole imperial court, according to custom, gathered to swear to uphold his sacred rights. Fadhl al-Barmak, who had fully endorsed Harun's move, was then serving as governor of Khurasan, and had the standing army there swear allegiance to the prince. Even so, the choice has been judged an innovation of sorts, since in the past the crown had often passed to the nearest of kin among adults (as from Saffah to Mansur), including collateral members of the line. Soon enough, Harun found himself wishing he had waited, for even before the two boys entered their teens, he began to doubt the wisdom of his choice.

In capacity, the two boys were certainly not the same. Harun saw that Mamun had manifold potential, which he was wont to cultivate, whereas Amin lacked aptitude. Once he came upon Mamun reading a book and wanted to know what it was about. "It is a book that stimulates the mind and improves one's social manners," the boy replied. "Praise be to Allah," said Harun, "who has blessed me with a son who sees with the mind's eye even more than he sees with his physical one." Harun's secret preference for Mamun may also have been influenced by the Night of Destiny itself. For by a kind of symmetry, it seemed to assign Mamun a fated role in the history of the Caliphate. Beyond that—given his own experience with his brother Hadi—Harun had begun to fret about the possibility of fratricidal strife.

When the two princes were still quite young, Harun had brought them out to meet the eminent scholar Ali ibn Fairuz, surnamed al-Kisai. They entered "like two stars illuminating the horizon," Kisai recalled. "Affable but dignified, they advanced, with eyes cast down, into the middle of the room. Al-Rashid then placed them, Muhammad (Amin) on his right and Abdullah (Mamun) on his left, and invited me to examine them on various aspects of their studies, including the Koran. They answered all my questions so well and with such grace that their father could not conceal his pride and joy. But after he had dismissed them with a tender embrace, I noticed tears running down his cheeks. He then confided to me his fears that they would one day become mortal rivals and fall victim to dissension and strife."

Around this time, Harun chose their tutors. One of those assigned to Amin was the grammarian Abu al-Ahmad. When ushered into the palace, he received some guidance from the caliph in a little speech: "The Prince of the Faithful is entrusting you with the being dearest to his heart. He gives you full authority over his son, and has told him that it is his duty to obey you. Try to be worthy of your task. Teach him to read the Koran, and instruct him in the traditions of the Prophet. Beautify his mind with poetry, and teach him how to behave. Show him how to weigh his words and speak to the point; regulate the amount of time he devotes to amusement; teach him to receive with respect the elders of the family of Hashim [Harun's bloodline] who come to see him, and to be considerate with the officials who attend his receptions. Let not an hour pass without turning it to some account for his edification. Do not be so severe as to kill the natural activity of his mind, or so indulgent that he becomes accustomed to idle ways."

The gentle affection and admirable good sense of this quiet exhortation could scarcely be surpassed.

Kisai was one of the tutors enlisted to help in the schooling of both boys, as was a scholar by the name of Yahya ibn al-Mubarak al-Yazidi, who guided their religious training and early study of the arts. At one point, a contest of sorts was witnessed by Harun and his vizier. Kisai was vanquished and Yazidi exulted in an unseemly manner before the caliph, by whom he was sharply rebuked. "By Allah, Kisai's mistake, joined to his good breeding, is better than your right answer joined to your umannerly act." Yazidi apologized. "The sweetness of my triumph," he said, "put me off my guard."

Kisai, a native of Kufa, might have been expected to be a good example for the boys, for he was one of the "seven readers," or leading reciters of the Koran. But he was not the best choice. He was a pedantic grammarian with many dry facts at his disposal but little imagination or literary sense. It was said of him that "of all those learned in grammar, no one knew less about poetry" than he. There was also something about him that repelled the opposite sex, and he once complained to Harun about his enforced celibate state. Harun sent him a beautiful slave girl, as well as a eunuch, but that was a poor way to find love. Amin seems to have learned almost nothing from him, except perhaps that sex could be leveraged by power. But that was not a good lesson to learn.

In the meantime, while Mamun devoted himself to advanced studies, Amin became a weight-lifting fanatic preoccupied with his physique. The difference between the two boys continued to widen and Harun's deep affection for them both did not blind him to the implications of that fact. As they entered adulthood, he was apt to remark that Mamun seemed "wise, statesmanlike, and reliable," blessed with "the piety of Mahdi and the resolution of Mansur." But he thought Amin "unstable, extravagant," and overly susceptible to the charms of women, concubines, and slaves.

One day the caliph sent for Yahya al-Barmak, now the elder statesman of the realm, to hash the matter out: Yahya found the caliph in a state of extreme mental distress, pacing about. Harun said, "The prophet of God, on whom be peace, died without a testament, when Islam was yet in the vigor of youth, and the faith was fresh. The Arabs were united. Then followed quarrels for the succession, with the melancholy results you know as well as I. As for me, I intend to regulate my succession, and let it pass into the hands of one whose character and conduct I approve of, and of whose political capacity I am assured. Such a one is Mamun. But my family incline to Amin to further their own Arab heritage and line, even though they know him to be capricious, extravagant, and a libertine. Now, if I show my preference for Mamun, I bring against me the hatred of my House; but if I make Amin my only heir, I fear it will bring disaster to the State."

At length, the two decided that the Hashemites (Harun's clan) had to be catered to, but that Mamun (meaning "the Dependable One") should be made next in line. The matter was officially settled first at Rakkah, then at Baghdad. Yahya's two sons took charge of the education of the princes in the art of governance, with Fadhl tutoring Amin; Jafar, Mamun. Sometime later, Harun hedged his bets further and named another son, Kasim, third in line.

Yet even with matters apparently settled, the Arab party (Mamun being the son of a Persian concubine) continued to lobby hard for Amin. After an eloquent exhortation by one partisan, Harun exclaimed, "Rejoice, for Amin shall surely have the throne!" "Prince of the Faithful," he replied, "I do rejoice, as a barren woman rejoices in a son, a sick man in new-found health, and plants in the rain. He is a peerless prince, who will defend his honor, and live up to the example his ancestors have set." "What," asked Harun, "do you think of his brother, Mamun?" "Good pasture," said the other, "but not like the saadan," i.e., rich, arable land. When the poet had departed, Harun exclaimed, "That man is an ignorant lout."

Zubaidah had also become concerned and redoubled her efforts to make sure her son's dynastic claims remained intact. After all, she had not forgotten that Harun's own father, Mahdi, had tried to change (almost at the last minute) the agreement he had with Hadi. But now another factor entered in. Amin and Mamun had come of age and were officially assigned parts of the empire to govern under the tutelage of their Barmak guides. Mamun was entrusted with the large but turbulent province of Khurasan and allotted a substantial military force with which to keep it stable and secure. Amin had been assigned the west, including Syria and Iraq. Kasim, under Amin, had been given authority over northern Mesopotamia and the provinces along the Byzantine frontier. Zubaidah saw danger to Amin's interests in this arrangement and questioned Harun about it. Foremost among her concerns was the existence of the large army under Mamun's control. She complained bitterly that Amin had been refused the military subsidies his brother had received.

Of late, it had become unusual for the royal couple to quarrel. But on this occasion, Harun rebuked her severely for meddling in state affairs: "Who are you to judge of my acts? Your son has a relatively easy, peaceful area to govern, whereas Mamun has one in a constant state of unrest. To govern effectively, he needs both the money and the troops." Then in candor, he added (for he knew her mind): "If there is any cause for either of them to be afraid of the other," he said, "it is Mamun who should be wary of your son, and not the other way around." Which was true, for Amin was said to have a strong vindictive streak.

In an effort to prevent a struggle between the two sons, Harun hammered out a formal compact between them, which both swore to uphold. Leaving Kasim behind, in December 802, Harun set out from Rakkah on his seventh pilgrimage to Mecca, accompanied by his chamberlain,

Fadhl ibn al-Rabi; Amin and Mamun; Yahya al-Barmak; and Yahya's two sons, Fadhl and Jafar. The whole population of the two holy cities, Mecca and Medina, turned out to greet them, for it was also Harun's purpose to publicly present the two princes to all the tribal elders and make his formal arrangements known.

According to the agreed-upon text, "Amin was to be caliph first, but Mamun was to succeed him even if Amin had grown-up sons of his own." Mamun was also to have almost complete autonomy within his allotted domain—roughly speaking, the empire's eastern half, based in Khurasan. Amin was to allow him access to all his estates and goods in any part of the empire, and not to interfere with any administrative appointments he made. Should Amin violate any part of these arrangements, the Caliphate would pass at once to Mamun. Amin signed the document, which seemed designed to protect Mamun from anticipated attempts on his brother's part to claim more than his share. The document signed by Mamun was less tendentious. By its terms, he promised to accept his brother as caliph, not to give aid to any of his enemies, and to send troops to help him if he were attacked.

After the texts were witnessed by judges, clerics, and army commanders to give them full force, Harun drafted letters for both Amin and Mamun to sign, exhorting them to abide by the agreement in the spirit of fraternal love. Both signed and publicly swore to be loyal to one another as they stood in the Kaaba itself. Amin's letter read in brief: "This is the document of the Prince of the Faithful, and was written by me, Muhammad [Amin], the son of Harun, Prince of the Faithful, in my right mind and of legal age, voluntarily, not under compulsion. The Prince of the Faithful has made me his heir, and this action has been accepted by the Muslims in good faith. He has left to my brother Khurasan and its frontiers, its defense and its troops, its taxes and its treasury. I am under obligation to grant these privileges to my brother Mamun. Moreover, after me, he will be Prince of the Faithful."

Sixteen years of age at the time, ruddy and robust, Amin rose before the great concourse assembled in the mosque at Mecca to read this document aloud. Amin acknowledged Mamun's autonomy and affirmed that anyone—including himself—who violated the terms of the arrangement would have to make the pilgrimage to Mecca fifty times, free all his slaves, and divorce all of his wives. Mamun made the same pledge. All the documents were inscribed on January 4, 803, and their content announced to the host of pilgrims who had assembled at Mecca from all over the Muslim world. Decrees confirming the agreement were also dispatched by courier to be read aloud in the manner of a proclamation in town squares throughout the realm. The heralded terms were given as God's will: "The command of God cannot be altered, His decree cannot be rejected or His judgment delayed." As one writer put it: "The authority of God, His caliph and the whole weight of Muslim public opinion had been marshalled in its support. All the grandeur of high-flown Arabic rhetoric had been employed to make it solemn and binding. No caliph had ever made such a public and comprehensive attempt to regulate the succession before."

But scarcely had the documents been affixed to the sanctuary wall than they fluttered to the ground. This was taken as a sign that the compact would not stand. Yet one needed no special gift of foresight to see what lay ahead. Even the lowliest camel driver, wrote one Muslim historian, could divine what was in store. Indeed, there was profound concern among Harun's advisors. On leaving the Kaaba, Jafar al-Barmak strode right up to Amin and demanded that he repeat three times, "May God desert me if I betray my brother!" But his very need to do this served only to inspire doubt. Factional strife joined to the division of the Caliphate presaged civil war.

chapter eleven

THE HARDER THEY FALL

The succession crisis had helped reveal the lethal tenor of Harun's court factions. As the fault lines widened, the Barmaks were unable to straddle the divide. In time they emerged as their own faction, which other factions opposed. This was perhaps inevitable, if only because of their unique domination, by family and patronage, of high imperial posts. Some courtiers chafed at being excluded from office or advancement; others looked with envy upon the vast wealth the Barmaks had amassed, which, it was said, "sometimes outshone the splendor of the court itself." The Muslim historian Ibn Khaldun wrote: "Envy and jealousy lifted their masks and the scorpions of calumny came to sting the Barmaks even on the couch that they had secured for themselves in the very shadow of the throne." Those who had real or imagined grievances against them "also watched their every move," wrote Tabari, "and reported their mistakes to the caliph, and these accumulated in his mind."

The fall of the Barmaks seemed sudden, and came in 803, right after the pilgrimage to Mecca, when the succession arrangements were confirmed. But the process tending to their destruction had perhaps begun as far back as the reign of Mansur when their paterfamilias, Khalid, minted coins in Khurasan with his own portrait on them in the image of a shah. Since then, a concealed river of resentment had gathered force against them like one of those snow-fed, hidden torrents in the Taurus Mountains that from time to time came crashing down into the Anatolian plain. Then, reminiscent of Ivan the Terrible's later sudden and somewhat mysterious liquidation of his Chosen Council of advisors, "Harun acted swiftly and secretly," as one scholar put it, "to destroy the power of the family that had done so much to ensure his accession to the caliphate and the success of the first seventeen years" of his rule.

No two historians seem to agree entirely on the reasons for his action or on why he acted when he did with such force. It may be, as Ibn Khallikan thought, that Harun had simply come to see that "the people's hopes were fixed on the Barmaks, not on himself," and so was moved by jealous rage: "In truth, they committed nothing to warrant al-Rashid's conduct towards them; but the day of their prosperity and power had been long, and that which continues long become irksome." He compared it to the discontent that had arisen against the Umayyad Caliph Omar, whose long reign had been characterized by unexampled prosperity and gains. Yet the people had been glad to see him go.

That may have been part of it. But a number of other factors contributed to their fall.

Within the religious culture of Islam, the Barmak family had always occupied an anomalous place. In part because of their Buddhist roots, the Barmaks were broad-minded and tolerant of divergent views; prudent in their politics; distrustful of fanatics; sympathetic to the Shiites (though not convinced Alids or disciples of Ali); and entertained relatively freethinking opinions on a variety of subjects not strictly governed by Islamic law. All this meant that the intellectual circles they favored repelled the orthodox.

In dealing with Alid or Shiite dissidents and rebels, they had always favored flexibility and conciliation where Harun leaned more readily toward ruthless means. Yahya had set the pattern by encouraging Harun, as much as possible, to leave Alids in peace. Fadhl and Jafar had followed suit, but in doing so exposed their own loyalties to attack. At the same time, since the Barmaks were both immensely popular and politically entrenched in Khurasan, where pro-Alid or Shiite feeling continued to thrive, the caliph began to suspect that the family might be scheming to appropriate part of Persia for themselves. Grown ever more jealous of his own prerogatives, his distrust turned to fear.

In the meantime, Harun found himself besieged by writs and petitions that disparaged the Barmaks and questioned the wisdom of his rule. One Sunni cleric gave Harun a screed that read: "Prince of Believers! what answer wilt thou give on the Resurrection Day, and how will you justify yourself before Almighty God, for having given to Yahya al-Barmak, his sons and relations, such unlimited control over the Muslims, and entrusted to them the government of the State, when you know that they are godless infidels?"

Harun had always been prone to suspect disloyalty even in those who had long since proved their devotion to his throne. And he could be impatient of results. In 792, for example, Yazid ibn Mazyad as-Shaibani (who had accompanied Harun in command of the troops on his victorious march to the Bosporus in 782) was sent into Armenia and Azerbaijan to put down a Kharijite or "separatist" revolt. The Kharijites were religious fanatics who sought a theocratic state. Shaibani had previously been governor of both provinces, and Harun used to call him "the Bedouin," with affection, because he was a rough-hewn, austere Arab from Jezira and, unlike most courtiers, averse to using talcum powder or perfume on his beard. But when no victory was forthcoming, Harun rebuked him sharply in a threatening note: "If I had sent a black slave in your place, he would have accomplished more than you. Show more aggression, or it will cost you your head."

Harun needn't have fretted. Shaibani knew precisely what he was about, and in girding his men for battle told them that the Kharijites, though formidable in the frantic zeal of their first charge, would be baffled if it failed and could then be easily routed in a counterstrike. Shaibani's men stood firm, struck back, and sent the rebels flying. According to Ibn Khallikan, Shaibani slew the rebel leader himself in single combat on the field.

Though Harun hated the Kharijites, he was not incapable of recognizing worth among those belonging to their sect. Once, when a rebel was brought before him, Harun asked him, "What do you expect me to do to you?" The man replied, "What you want God to do to you, when you stand before him in judgment." Harun remained pensive for a time, then said, "Let him go."

For Harun, it had been a difficult year. There had also been fighting in Damascus between two different Arab factions or tribal groups, which had spread south into Jordan as far as Amman. Many country villages were burned and plundered and the local governor replaced. Yahya al-Barmak's youngest son, Musa, was dispatched to restore order, and having done so, remained as governor in charge. Yet scarcely a year passed without some serious provincial unrest, with Umayyad factions still active in Syria and Mesopotamia and hostility to Arab rule in Khurasan. The oppression of various provincial governors ostensibly loyal to the crown added to Harun's woes. The very extent of the empire made it difficult to exercise a central authority strong enough to prevent such officials from asserting their own independence or making exactions upon the people for their own gain. Pretenders to the throne and impersonators of dead figures arose to stir the people up.

It may be remembered that after Husein ibn Ali had been killed by Hadi on the outskirts of Mecca in 786, his adherents had scattered. But wherever they settled and took root they returned to bite his brother's hand. One of Husein's cousins, Idris, had made his way to Egypt and from there to North Africa, where he proclaimed a rival caliphate among the Berbers centered at Fez. Harun arranged to have him poisoned by an assassin. But his son succeeded him, and the rival state survived. Meanwhile, another cousin, Yahya ibn Abdullah, had escaped to Rayy. Harun put a price on his head, but he continued his flight through Khurasan and Transoxania and finally reached Dailam, a coastal region of the Caspian Sea. There, in 792, supported by indigenous tribal chiefs and a broad segment of the population, he issued a call for revolt. Fadhl al-Barmak, then governor of Persia, was dispatched to deal with the rebellion and managed to induce Ibn Abdullah to capitulate with the proffer of a safe conduct from the caliph, countersigned by other notables at court.

Yet the writ was not upheld. In Baghdad, Ibn Abdullah was given a pension, but Harun soon trumped up charges against him of intriguing against his rule. Upon his arrest, he was placed in the custody of Jafar al-Barmak, who released him on his own authority, which allowed him to escape to Khurasan. Harun was irate and evidently swore he would one day kill Jafar for having trifled with his trust. "God slay me if I slay thee not!" he was heard to say under his breath.

The sporadic ability of Alids to raise a following against the state contributed to a gradual hardening of Harun's policy toward their schemes. And he faulted the Barmaks for having coddled some in their clan. It may be that the Barmaks had presumed too much on the familiarity that Harun allowed them. We have already seen how Jafar in particular dispensed favors in the caliph's name as if he were the caliph. At the same time, Harun had come to resent his own overreliance on the Barmaks as agents of his power.

Another possible reason for Harun's animus (particularly toward Jafar) was the generosity they had shown toward Abd al-Malik ibn Salih, a collateral member of Harun's own family whom the caliph suspected of conniving for his throne. Harun also learned that Jafar had drawn a large sum from the treasury on Abd al-Malik's behalf.

Malik and Harun had once been on familiar, if not friendly, terms. From time to time they had consulted about Syrian affairs, and Harun had trusted him enough to appoint him tutor to his son Kasim. Malik also had a pleasant disposition, and, being a Syrian magnate, occasionally joined the caliph on his Syrian tours. Once as they were out riding together, Harun said to him as they passed by Manbij, where Malik had his estate, "Is this your dwelling?" Malik replied, "It is yours, O Commander of the Faithful, and then mine through your favor!" Harun said, "What is the dwelling like?" He replied, "Not as fine as the edifice of my kinsfolk (i.e., your's), but superior to the rest of the dwellings of Manbij." Harun asked, "What are the nights like at Manbij?" Malik replied, "Like permanent dawn!"

The subsequent controversy surrounding his loyalty came to epitomize the rifts then fracturing the realm. When the Abbasids had come to power, Malik's father, Salih, had appropriated most of the former Umayyad lands in Syria, where he established a mighty base for his clan. Malik in turn had come to represent the "Syrian interest" at Harun's court. In the succession struggle under way, he therefore belonged to the "Arab party" and was allied with Amin. As Kasim's former tutor, he also supported Kasim's claims to share in Harun's division of the realm. There was nothing in any of this to arouse Harun's ire, except that the Arab and Persian factions had begun to devolve into shadow governments, each determined to preempt the other in its bid for power.

It so happened that just when Harun had become convinced that the Barmaks might have their own schemes for an independent Khurasan, Abd al-Malik had been denounced for concerting a plan with tribal leaders in Syria to overthrow Harun and/or claim the western part of the empire for themselves. To complicate matters, Malik was opposed by his own son, Abd al-Rahman, who belonged to the Persian party favoring Mamun—who in turn was tutored by Jafar. Yet it was Jafar who had recently subsidized Malik with government funds. As Harun tried to make sense of all these cross-connections, he endeavored to fend off the different factions while accommodating their legitimate if conflicting demands. Before long he could barely hear himself think above the crackle of confused slander. In that state, paranoia took hold of his mind. As one poet would write later of another monarch:

> Blood and revenge did hammer in my head,
> Unquiet thoughts did gallop in my brain:
> I had no rest till all my friends were dead,
> Whose help I used the kingdom to obtain.
>   My dearest friend I thought not safe to trust,
>   Nor scarce myself, but that perforce I must.

Abd al-Malik was denounced—by his private secretary as well as his son—and clapped in jail. But the evidence against him was hearsay at best. One day Harun sent for him and accused him of concocting treacherous designs. "No, Prince of the Faithful," answered Malik. "Had I done so, I should have been made to repent it. You are the vicegerent of God's Prophet over His people. It is our duty to obey you, and to give you good advice; and it is your duty to the people to rule them justly and pardon their faults."

"Ah," said Harun, "you are humble with your tongue and ambitious with your mind; here is your secretary, who testifies to your faithless deeds."

Replied Malik, "He has given you something which he had no competence to provide." When the secretary was summoned, Harun urged him to "speak out fearlessly without feeling overawed." But when the man had finished, Malik rebutted all his charges and said to Harun: "How should he not tell lies about me behind my back, when he slanders me directly to my face?"

"Well, there is your son Abd al-Rahman, too," said Harun. "He is prepared to corroborate all that your secretary said."

"My son," answered Malik, "is either acting under orders, or he is a rebellious child. If he is acting under orders, there is some excuse for him; but if he is rebellious, then he is an ungrateful scoundrel; God Himself warns us against such persons when He says, 'And amongst your very wives and children ye have enemies, so beware them.' "

At this Harun exclaimed, "Your case is as clear as day, but I will not act hastily. God shall judge between us!" "I am content," replied Malik, "to have God for my judge, and the Prince of the Faithful to execute His judgment, assured that he will not prefer his own wrath to the Lord's commands."

Some days later, the prisoner was brought before the caliph again. After the fashion of an Old Testament prophet, Harun began to fulminate: "It is as if I were looking at a heavy storm and a rain of blood, flashing clouds and an onslaught of vengeance and fingers without wrists and heads without necks falling like hail. For by God, it is through me that the rough ground has been made smooth for you and the turbid waters clear. Through me, you have been allowed to conduct your own affairs. So watch out, lest catastrophe befall you and retribution come upon you like a mighty stallion, striking the ground with its forefeet, and galloping with its hind feet raised in the air!"

Harun worked himself into a frenzy, but Malik stood his ground. "Fear God, O Commander of the Faithful," he said. "Do not set ingratitude in the place of thankfulness, or punishment in the face of reward! . . . How many nights, from dusk to dawn, have I endured

hardships on your behalf! In how many narrow places have I stood fast
in your defense!"

But Harun would have none of it. "By God," he declared, "if it were
not for sparing the blood of the Hashemites, I would cut off your head!"

Yet not long afterward, Abdullah al-Khuzai, who was then Harun's
captain of the guard, came to him and asked him why Abd al-Malik had
been imprisoned, since he understood Malik to be a faithful counselor
and an honorable man. Harun said, "I received some disquieting reports
about him. I'm not convinced that he's as loyal as he seemed. . . . I also
do not trust him not to stir up dissension between my sons, Amin and
Mamun." Khuzai replied that if that were the case, he must be confined,
but in a more dignified manner befitting his pedigree and rank. And this
was arranged.

Enter Fadhl ibn Rabi, the son of Rabi ibn Yunus, who had served as
chief minister for a time during the reigns of Mahdi and Hadi. Although
the Barmaks had guided the empire for three generations, the family of
Rabi ibn Yunus remained a potential rival to their clan. On the accession of Harun, Yahya al-Barmak and his sons had gained all the chief
posts—thanks in the main to the influence of Khaizuran, who had opposed any important post for Rabi's son. But upon Khaizuran's death in
790, Fadhl ibn Rabi had been restored to favor and the privy seal given to
his care. He aimed still higher and saw his opportunity in the Barmaks'
reckless rise. In 795, he increased his leverage and standing when Harun
dismissed Yahya's brother, Muhammad, as chamberlain, and put Rabi in
his place. That made him the gatekeeper to Harun's inner sanctum and
allowed "persons inimical to the Barmak faction to obtain access in future
to Harun."

Some historians regard this development as the first sign on the part of
the caliph that he no longer deemed it wise to allow the Barmaks to mo-
nopolize all the top posts. Meanwhile, Rabi "wrought against them underhand" and took advantage of anything questionable they did. Yahya
al-Barmak, now the elder statesman of the realm, was not unaware of
what such enmity might mean. Even before Rabi had become chamberlain, his potential for causing trouble aroused concern. One day, Yahya
was handling some petitions at court, with his son Jafar beside him,

when Rabi came in with ten petitions in his hand. Yahya refused his approval to each one. As Rabi gathered them up, he muttered, "Repelled and rejected. Fortune may yet alter her present course and produce some change." Yahya heard that, called him back, reconsidered the petitions, and approved them. But the enmity between them was not allayed.

As the influence of Rabi increased, Yahya felt the atmosphere around him chill.

This reversal of feeling is vividly delineated by an anecdote Jibril ibn Bakhtishou, Harun's personal physician, would tell. He recalled that early in Harun's reign he was once summoned by the caliph to the palace to treat some sickness besetting Zubaidah, when their attention was drawn to shouts of praise and thanksgiving that reached them from the audience hall. Harun was told that it was in honor of Yahya, who was just then addressing the public's petitions and appeals. "May Allah bless and reward him," said Harun, "for he has lightened my burden and shouldered the weight of my rule." Zubaidah, with equal enthusiasm, joined in his praise.

Years later Jibril found himself in the same chamber in conference with the caliph and his wife when similar shouts of gratitude to Yahya reached their ears. "May Allah do unto him," exclaimed Harun with bitterness, "according to his deeds, for he has taken hold of affairs to my exclusion and has conducted them according to his pleasure without reference to my will." And Zubaidah, too, joined in this tirade.

Although Zubaidah owed a very great deal to the Barmaks—not only had Yahya played a critical role in placing Harun on the throne, but Yahya's son, Fadhl, had helped to secure the nomination of her own son as heir—a single day of enmity can undo the debt of years. They had clashed over the management of her royal palace, and she took undying offense to what she viewed as hubris in his strict disposition of her affairs. Jafar's alliance with Mamun had also evidently soured her on the entire Barmak clan.

Harun did not long keep his resentment to himself. One day, for example, he scolded Yahya sharply for entering his presence without leave. Harun, who was talking to Jibril at the time, turned to the doctor and asked whether anyone ever did that to him. Jibril said, "No, and no one would presume to do that." The caliph then said, "What is wrong with me, then, that people come in without asking?" Yahya, abashed, pointed out that he had long been allowed to enter the private quarters of the caliph at all hours—even when Harun was undressing or preparing for bed. But in the future, he said, he would seek permission first. Harun then made light of his own rebuke, but Yahya's reduced stature thereafter was plain to all at court.

At about this time, Fadhl's portfolio was also reduced, and he was eventually relieved of most of his high functions, except for his post as tutor to the crown prince Amin. Jafar, too, became aware that the caliph's feelings had changed. But he could have scarcely guessed by how much.

Meanwhile, the Barmak family had grown rich in the service of the caliph, and their numerous holdings rivaled those of Harun himself. Khalid al-Barmak had adorned his own house with gold tiles; Jafar had built for himself a royal palace by the Tigris, with game parks, colonnades, sparkling fountains, audience chambers, and the like. From time to time, their enemies denounced them in anonymous letters to the caliph like this: "To God's trusty servant on earth, to him who has the power to loose and bind, Lo! the sons of Yahya are kings like you; there is no longer any difference between you; your behests are altered by them, but theirs are implicitly fulfilled. Jafar has built a palace, in the like of which no Persian or Indian ever dwelt. Its floor is set with pearls and rubies, and the ceiling is made of amber and aloes wood; we even fear he may inherit your kingdom when you are hidden in the grave. He is nothing but an arrogant slave to dare vie with you this way."

Harun took that in. A relative of the caliph, Ismail ibn Yahya, tells us that shortly before Jafar set out to take up his post as governor of Khurasan, he went to see him and said, "Jafar, you are taking up a lucrative post in a prosperous country. If I were you, I would make over one of my estates here in Baghdad to the caliph or to one of his sons as a gesture of thanks." "Ismail," he replied, "your cousin the caliph lives by my bounty, and it is only through us that his dynasty thrives. Is it not enough that I have left him nothing to trouble himself about, and have kept his treasury full, without my having to part with some of what I have acquired for my self, my family, and my son? Surely it cannot be that he envies what I have?"

"God forbid," said Ismail.

"Then why even suggest such a thing?"

Yet after Ismail departed, Jafar wished he had not spoken as he had, and grew wary. Nor was he wrong to feel unease. For one of Harun's spies repeated the conversation verbatim to Harun, which so upset him that he "shut himself up for three days, and would see nobody, but passed the time brooding over his schemes of revenge." Yet it is a measure of the interconnected power the Barmaks wielded that Harun, despite his own deep dissatisfaction, dared not act against them with overt force for some time, out of risk to himself.

At length, that time came.

In September 803, Harun, accompanied by Zubaidah, left Rakkah for Mecca on his eighth pilgrimage. He proceeded twelve miles a day, at a leisurely pace, pausing every three miles to rest beneath a tent that had been pitched for him beforehand with refreshments to give him ease. At the end of each day, he reviewed the day's dispatches that had arrived in the interim by carrier pigeon or pony express. Although Harun had vowed, in penitential fashion, to perform the whole pilgrimage on foot—without even wearing sandals or shoes—this was a practical impossibility, since the sand was strewn with gravel and sharp stones, which would have cut his feet. In passing across such areas, carpets were sometimes unrolled for him to tread on, then gathered up, carried forward, and unrolled again, as required. Overall, the pilgrimage covered about a thousand miles, and took him about three months to traverse. When he finally entered Mecca, great crowds of pilgrims came out to meet him "with cheers and shrill female trills, and cries of "Allahu Akbar," "God is Great."

After completing his devotions in and about the Kaaba, Harun started back. En route, he rested some days in a country house near Hira and then proceeded by boat up the Euphrates to near Anbar, where he disembarked and pitched his camp. There, Tabari tells us, the caliph summoned the Barmaks and, "after discussing affairs of state, gave them all robes of honor as if to dispel any rumor that they might be in disgrace." Harun remained in camp and feasted and relaxed as he often did whenever he luxuriated at a hunting lodge. On January 29, 803, however, events took a fateful turn. There are several versions as to what happened, but all come to the same end.

Early that day, Harun decided to hold court. As a number of officials came in, they saluted Harun and sat in their respective places at some distance from his raised, central seat. Then Jafar entered and Harun received him with unalloyed delight and they laughed and joked together as Jafar took his seat by the caliph's side. Jafar produced various recent petitions, and the caliph listened and decided upon their claims. At the conclusion of this audience, Jafar asked leave to go to Khurasan since Mamun was in need of his counsel and he had pressing matters to resolve.

The caliph sat perfectly still for a moment, then called for his astrologer, who was sitting nearby. He asked him what time it was. "Half-past nine o'clock," the man said, as he took the altitude of the sun. Harun then reckoned it up himself, and, it is said, looked in a bound volume of planetary tables and declared, "Today, my brother, is not a good day for you to go. Something serious might happen. Stay over for the Friday prayers, and go when the stars are better aligned." Jafar was surprised by the caliph's caution and asked the astrologer for his astrolabe so he could take his own reading of the hour. He saw that his own planet (by the time of his question) was in its detriment (opposite the house it ruled) and the moon (showing the trend of events) in its fall. "By Allah," he exclaimed, "you're right! I'd better wait for another time."

Somewhat later, Harun and Jafar went out hunting together and the caliph showed Jafar every sign of affection, even putting his arm around him, which he had never done before. The weather was balmy and almost springlike in its mild and cheerful brightness, "and the Euphrates was flowing smoothly between bordering palms whose fronds stirred in the breeze. . . . The game came out from under cover, the fields were feathery with yellow sprouts, flocks of white heron rose before their steeds." Some attendants noted that the splendor of Jafar's escort, horses, and equipment exceeded those of the caliph, but Harun appeared to ignore this, if he noticed it at all.

When the party returned at evening, weary from their exertions,

Harun excused himself to go frolic with his concubines, and urged Jafar to drink and make merry himself. Jafar insisted that he would rather keep the caliph company, but then they said good night and each went to his own abode.

After a while Harun sent someone to see how Jafar was faring, only to learn that he was subdued. So he commanded him once more to abandon himself to pleasure, swearing that he, the caliph, could not enjoy himself among his own slaves unless he knew Jafar was also having a good time. There was something too insistent about all this and Jafar turned to a blind musician named Abu Zakkar who was with him and confessed his unease. But the musician blithely reassured him of the caliph's goodwill. Soon another servant arrived from Harun with perfumes, sweetmeats, and dried fruits. Jafar could hardly refuse them, but he nibbled reluctantly at them with uncertain bites. Something was gravely wrong.

At length, around midnight, Harun emerged from his own harem and told Masrur—his "strong man" on such occasions—to "go at once to find Jafar and kill him and bring back his head." Masrur set off with a party of soldiers and found Jafar drinking with the caliph's physician and listening to the singing of Zakkar. The musician had just sung a song that ended with the lines: "No young man can escape it, come what may,/ Death comes at last by night or day."

When Jafar saw Masrur, he paled and began to shake. "The Prince of the Faithful is calling for you," said Masrur. Jafar knew what that meant. Frantic to find a way out, he stalled by asking if he could take the time to make his will. Yes, Masrur told him but he must be quick. "Jafar fell on his face and began to kiss my feet," Masrur recalled, "and begged me to allow him to go to his apartment to give final instructions to his family. I replied, 'You must stay here, but you can give what instructions you wish.' " The first thing Jafar did was free all his slaves. As he began to write out more instructions, he said to Masrur: "Take care, for [Harun] may have ordered you to do this simply because he was drunk. He may think better of it tomorrow. What then will he do with you?" And he urged him to go back to the caliph and confirm his intent.

In fact, Masrur thought this might be prudent. He left Jafar under

guard and returned to the caliph, whom he found sitting on a prayer carpet, sweating with rage. Harun had a cane in his hand, and was digging
it into the ground. When he saw Masrur, he demanded, "Where is Jafar's
head?" "Prince of the Faithful," replied the eunuch, "I can bring Jafar
himself." "That's not what I wanted. I want his head!" Masrur went back
to where he had left his captive and took off his head with a single stroke.
Then he "took it by the beard, carried it back to Harun, and threw it
before him all dripping with blood." The caliph sighed at the sight of it
and groaned and cursed. With tears in his eyes, he began to address the
severed head directly, and with each plaintive word he spoke he ground
his teeth and dug his stick into the ground.

A little while later, Harun called for Harthama ibn Ayain and sent
him into Baghdad with orders to arrest every member of the Barmak
family and surround their palaces and estates. He also sent the eunuch
Salam al-Abrash—a man often used for dread errands, like Masrur—
with a note in his own hand to Sindi ibn Shahik, one of his trusted aides.
"Sindi," it read, "if you are sitting down when you read this, get up! And
if you are standing, do not sit! but come to me!" Sindi went at once to
the caliph, who told him: "I have sent for you on a matter so secret that
if the button of my shirt knew it, I would throw it into the stream!" Then
he dispatched him to Baghdad to cooperate with Harthama in sweeping
the government free of all those who could be identified as Barmak loyalists or staff. That same night, Fadhl and the aging Yahya were arrested
and numerous members of the Barmak family slain.

The next morning, Jafar's remains were sent to the capital, where his
body was dismembered, divided into thirds, and hung on Baghdad's three
pontoon bridges for all to see.

Everyone was astonished by the swiftness of events. One official later
recalled that only a few days before he had stopped in at the treasury and
noticed a disbursement in one of the ledgers that read: "For a dress of
honor and decorations for Jafar, son of Yahya, 400,000 gold dinars." A
couple of days later, he found that same entry crossed out and in its place:
"Naphtha and shavings for burning the body of Jafar, son of Yahya, two
kirats [a twelfth of a dinar]." However, Jafar's decaying body would remain on public display for two years before it was finally cut down, and

only then was it soaked in two kirats' worth of naphtha and consumed on a bonfire of reeds.

Though there were reasons enough why the Barmaks met the fate they did, speculation abounded and novel explanations arose. These have echoed down the years. Tabari, for example, tells us that Jafar had illicit relations with Harun's sister, Abbasah, and that the two "would go off to copulate" after some of the caliph's soirees. Others say that Jafar behaved properly but Abbasah had her own desires. In the latter version, Abbasah was said to have flattered Jafar's mother with blandishments and gifts and persuaded her to find some means to get Jafar to share her bed. At length, Jafar's mother got her son drunk and in the darkness of her room offered him a beautiful young slave to enjoy. That rings oddly true. For Ibn Khallikan tells us that Jafar's mother used to make him "a present every Friday of a young virgin, with whom he passed the night, after drinking some wine."

In any case, so the story goes, in his stupor Jafar failed to recognize Abbasah until it was too late and he had satisfied his lust. When his mother expressed pride at her stratagem, he exclaimed, in despair: "You have thrown me away for nothing and brought me to the edge of the abyss."

As so often seems to happen (in history, at least) after one-night stands, Abbasah conceived but somehow disguised her condition and gave birth to a son. The child was sent to Medina in the care of servants, and came to Harun's attention only when Zubaidah got wind of the deceit and used it against the Barmaks, whom she had come to distrust in the developing struggle between Mamun and her son Amin. Annoyed at the extreme measures Yahya al-Barmak took to secure the women's quarters at night, she one day blurted out: "If he really looked after the harem, he would have prevented his own son from committing a crime!" "What are you talking about?" asked Harun. Zubaidah said, "As long as you are beguiled by the Barmaks, I can't talk to you frankly. But once you come to your senses, I will tell you something much harder for you to bear than what you have heard." When he demanded she make herself clear, she called for one of her slaves named Arzu, who knew about the secret affair. Arzu told Harun about it and about the child Abbasah had borne.

Harun was mortified. He was so beside himself, it is said, that he ordered Arzu beheaded simply for knowing what she knew.

Soon afterward he tracked down the child—potentially, of course, a dynastic rival—and killed him. In a further sinister embellishment, it is said that there were two offspring, not one; that he sent for them in Medina; and that when he beheld them he admired them, for they were as handsome, cultivated, and eloquent as other members of his house. He asked the elder, "What is your name?" The boy said, "Hasan." Then he asked the younger, "And what, dear child, is yours?" The child replied, "Husein." The caliph looked at them and wept. Masrur, it is said, later told a friend, "I thought he would relent and have pity on them. But he wiped his eyes" and had them killed.

As if all this weren't gruesome enough, it was even claimed that Harun, in revenge, "nailed his sister up in a chest with all her jewels, and then buried it in a trench under a mass of rubble and bricks." Abbasah's steward and ten servants "were massacred in turn." Their killers, hirelings of Masrur, were then supposedly "sewn into sacks and thrown into the Tigris River" to cover up all evidence and memory of the crime.

AFTER THE FALL OF THE BARMAKS, THEIR PROPERTIES ES-cheated to the state. Yahya and Fadhl languished in custody but were allowed comfortable quarters. Later they were imprisoned with great rigor, cross-examined harshly, and Fadhl was flogged. Meanwhile, when Yahya learned that Harun had killed Jafar, Yahya said, "So will his son be killed." And when told that the family palaces had been sacked, he said, "So, too, will his house be destroyed." This was reported to Harun, who paled. "I have never known him to foretell anything," he said, "that did not come to pass."

Not long afterward, Yahya's wife, who had been Harun's foster mother (having nursed him), obtained an audience with the caliph, and touchingly showed him a little keepsake box that she had kept for almost forty years. In it was Harun's own first baby tooth and a lock of his hair. By these sentimental tokens of her affection, she implored him to let her husband go. The caliph offered to buy them from her but showed no concern for Yahya's plight. At length, when she found she could make no headway with him, she threw the box at his feet.

One day Harun had Yahya brought out of his cell and demanded that he reveal all he knew about Abd al-Malik's seditious schemes. Harun even offered to restore him to power if he did. Yahya replied, "By heaven, I never noticed anything like treason in Abd al-Malik; but if I had, I should have stood between him and you, for your kingdom and authority were mine, and all my prosperity or adversity depended upon your own. How likely is it then that Abd al-Malik would have asked me to help him? I saw only that he was a fit and proper person, such as I was glad to find among your own family. Any of the appointments I approved for him were for merit and that alone."

Unable to force the answer he craved, Harun threatened to kill Yahya's son, Fadhl, if he did not tell the truth. Yahya replied, "You have us in your power; do as you please!" Father and son were incarcerated together and when Fadhl learned of the exchange, he assumed his life was done. The two parted in a touching scene. "Are you pleased with me, father?" "Yes; may God be the same!" Harun, however, was not done with them yet.

As the days passed, he decided to send Masrur to Fadhl and compel him to draw up a full and open inventory of all the property he owned. Masrur threatened to treat him as a common criminal if he did not comply. Fadhl replied, "By Allah, I have made no false statements. I would, if the choice were offered, prefer death to even one stroke of a whip, as the Prince of the Faithful well knows." Then he added: "You yourself know too that we have always maintained our reputation at the expense of our wealth; why then would we now shield our wealth at the expense of our selves?"

On November 25, 805, at the age of seventy, Yahya died. A note was found on his person that read: "The victim has gone on ahead to the tribunal, but the agent of his destruction will follow soon. The judge at their trial will be that just One who needs no witnesses and never errs." Fadhl, however, remained in close confinement for another three years. He was then released, but died soon afterward, a broken man.

On hearing of Fadhl's death, Harun is said to have remarked, "My

fate is close to his!" for astrologers had predicted that he would die soon
after his foster brother did.

Yahya's two surviving sons, Musa and Muhammad, remained in
prison until the next reign.

As might be expected, the few surviving Barmaks fell on hard times.
Officially, the Barmak name was anathema. Harun tried in vain to suppress any public expression of mourning, and was even prepared to kill
anyone known to express regret. Ibrahim ibn Uthman ibn Nahik, a
high treasury official, for example, allowed himself, in the privacy of his
own home, to show some sorrow, and now and then when drunk would
threaten to avenge Jafar. Eventually his own son betrayed him. Harun
asked him if anyone else could corroborate his charge. "Yes," he replied,
"his eunuch, Nawal." So Harun summoned the eunuch, who backed up
what the son had said. Still, Harun held back. "It would not be lawful
for me," he remarked, "to kill one of my own retainers on their word.
The two may have conspired together—the son because of his eagerness
to gain his father's property and rank, the slave out of some grievance
against his lord."

In time, Harun decided to ascertain the truth for himself. He sent for
Ibrahim ibn Nahik and in a show of friendship engaged him in conversation and offered him one cup after another of wine. The caliph drank,
too, began to lament Jafar's loss, and said that he had scarcely slept since
he had had him killed and would rather have lost his kingdom than his
friend. At this Ibrahim cried out that it was true, that they would never
see his like again. Harun rose up with a curse and Ibrahim rose, too, left
in horror and went straight to the home of his mother, and said: "I am
doomed." Not long afterward, he was killed by his son at the caliph's
command.

Yet Harun had it in him to relent—at least, there are stories to that
effect; and perhaps he suffered remorse. No one seems to know, or will
ever know. But the wound went deep. One day his sister Ulaiyah said to
him, "I have not seen you enjoy a day of perfect happiness since you put
Jafar to death. Why did you do it?" Harun replied, "What possible good
could it do you to know the reason? If I thought my shirt knew, I would

tear it in shreds." On another occasion, he told a friend, in answer to the same question, "If I thought my right hand knew the reason, I would cut it off." Yet he himself knew and thereafter, as one writer put it, he "lived but a luster, carrying to the grave a secret flaw which gnawed at his vitals even as the memory of his crime plagued his soul."

THE FALL OF THE BARMAKS WAS BURNED INTO THE MEMORY of the Caliphate and left an indelible stain on Harun's rule. The *Arabian Nights* would call it a stain of blood "which not even the four rivers could wash away." Jafar's dismal end in particular became a parable in Islamic history for the mutability of fate. However much the Barmaks had exalted their own standing, they had been generous as well as ostentatious, kind and gracious as well as proud. Religious toleration, as exemplified by their ecumenical embrace of nearly all creeds, soon began to fade with their passing. Indeed, their loss adversely affected the whole climate of the kingdom and created so much ill will in the capital that Harun thereafter seldom left Rakkah. Historians like Tabari would condemn him for it—"The memory of it will live on until the day of judgment," he wrote—while contemporary poets left a record of their dismay. One declared: "The hand of beneficence has shrivelled, the tide in the ocean of munificence has ebbed. This family provided our caravans with its guiding star." Another wrote: "Let us stop and rest our horses: there are no benefactors now, nor supplicants for their largesse. Tell Generosity: you died when Fadhl died; and call to Adversity: come, flaunt yourself each day." A third made Jafar into a martyr of the faith:

> By God, were it not for the denunciation of a slanderer
> And an eye of the caliph's which never sleeps,
> We would circumambulate the gibbet on which you are nailed and kiss it,
> Just as pilgrims circumambulate the Kaaba
> And kiss the Black Stone!

Even the poet Abu Nuwas, Harun's favorite, had to go into hiding after he daringly declared: "It was through them that the name and the glory of Harun al-Rashid clanged from the flats of Central Asia to the forests of the north, from the Maghreb and Andalusia to the farthest bounds of Tartary and China to the east."

The poets were not far wrong. The reign of the Barmaks, no less than that of Harun himself, would be remembered as unsurpassed.

chapter twelve

"RUM" AND KHURASAN

fter the fall of the Barmaks, Harun became preoccupied with new campaigns against the Byzantines and with threats to his regime sparked by his delegated rule of Khurasan. On both fronts, events had been moving fast. In Constantinople, Irene had been eager to conclude her marriage with Charlemagne, in part to forestall Muslim aggression, but leading court political and military officials objected on various grounds. They were unhappy with Irene's concessions to Harun, could discover no gain to the empire by her policy gambles, and had seen the throne itself disgraced. The Byzantines also resented Charlemagne's attempt to get his hands on their crown.

At dawn on October 31, 802, just as the marriage negotiations were reaching a critical point, Irene's finance minister, Nicephorus, took power. Irene was arrested, her top officials ousted, and Nicephorus crowned emperor in the Cathedral Church of Hagia Sophia by the patriarch. Subsequently, Irene was banished to the monastery she had founded on the island of Prinkipo, and afterward still further to the island of Lesbos, where she was forced to support herself under guard by working a spinning wheel until her death on August 9, 803.

In after years—despite her documented cruelties and crimes—the Eastern Orthodox Church would revere her as a martyred saint.

Nicephorus moved to restore Byzantine power and prestige. He challenged Charlemagne's title of Holy Roman Emperor (though it was not a title Charlemagne himself ever used), as well as his sovereignty over the Italian state of Venice; canceled some of Irene's social programs and tax breaks; put more men under arms; and notified Harun that Irene's humiliating agreement to pay tribute was null and void. Mindful of Harun's reputation as a chess master, he couched an insulting letter to him in the parlance of the game:

> Nicephorus, King of the Rum [East Romans], to Harun, King of the Arabs: The queen who reigned before me treated you as a rook while she assumed the posture of a pawn. She paid you tribute which, by right, you should have paid to her. This was but a woman's weakness. When you have read my letter, return the money you took and ransom yourself out of the trouble you are in. If you do not, the matter will be settled by the sword.

When Harun read this, he was so enraged that no one present dared meet his gaze. The caliph then called for a pen and ink, and taking up the letter, wrote on the back: "In the Name of God, the Compassionate, the Merciful. From Harun, the Prince of the Faithful, to Nicephorus, the Roman dog. I have read your letter, you son of a heathen mother. You will see my reply before you hear it. Farewell." Then he ordered his army into the field. Three columns advanced, made up of 135,000 men. They crossed the Taurus Mountains and halted before the gates of Heraclea on the Black Sea. Over the course of the next several days, the city was taken, plundered, and burned to the ground. Nicephorus had not expected such a swift, devastating response and was caught off guard. Having made no real defensive preparations of his own, he sued for peace and agreed to double the tribute he had so recently despised. Harun accepted that but also exacted a promise from the Byzantines that they not rebuild any fortress the Muslims dismantled or destroyed. As if to rub salt in the wound, Harun also imposed a humiliating poll tax on both Nicephorus and his son. This could scarcely be borne. As soon as winter descended and ice and snow blocked the mountain roads, Nicephorus repudiated the agree-

ment, expecting he would now have until the following summer to prepare for a Muslim attack.

But when news of the emperor's breach of faith reached Rakkah,
Harun gave orders for his army to march. His troops recrossed the frontier through ice and snow, overcame tremendous obstacles, and prepared
to lay waste and destroy the whole of Asia Minor if the Byzantines would
not submit. When Nicephorus balked, Harun crushed him at the Battle
of Krasos in Phrygia (in central Anatolia), put the region to the torch, and
annexed Tyana—at the foot of the Taurus Mountains, near the Cilician
Gates—where he also built a mosque.

Once more Nicephorus sued for peace, agreed to the former tribute, and even had to pay it in coins specially minted for the purpose and
stamped with the heads of Harun and three of his sons. Meanwhile, a
Muslim naval expedition had disembarked at Cyprus and ravaged the
island, withdrawing with abundant plunder as well as sixteen thousand
Christians to be sold as slaves.

All this could be borne even less—though the emperor was powerless
to redress such wrongs.

Yet in the bloody contest between the two powers, relations at the top
were not always bad. For his part, Harun had a general reverence for
sovereignty itself. As caliph, he one day ordered a hundred lashes for a
servant who casually belittled an ancient king. In explanation, Harun
remarked to a court official, "Power establishes a sort of union or family bond between sovereigns. I am punishing this man not only out of
respect for my own throne, but out of consideration for the shared respect that obtains among kings." In that spirit, past Arab and Byzantine
sovereigns had also exchanged gifts—diamond-encrusted gold belts, gar-
ments of rare silk, "men of gigantic size or strength," for example, and
slaves—usually to mark notable occasions like the signing of a treaty, an
exchange of prisoners, or the accession of an emperor or a caliph to their
respective thrones. The Umayyad caliph Muawiya had sent his Byzantine
counterpart fifty thoroughbred horses. The Empress Irene had sent thirty
thousand pounds of goats' hair cloth to Harun.

Relations between Nicephorus and Harun, at least on the personal plane, were also not beyond reach. In the wake of his humiliation, Nicephorus sought from the caliph a gesture of goodwill. One day two top Byzantine officials arrived in the caliph's camp with a letter from the emperor asking him to release a young girl, a patrician's daughter, engaged to be married to his son. Harun obliged and in addition sent the emperor medicinal drugs, including "tiryak" or opium, perfumes, raisins, treacle, khabis (a sort of pastry made from flour, milk, and honey), and dates. He also sent him one of his imperial tents. Nicephorus in return sent Harun several hundred embroidered silk robes, twelve hawks, four hounds, three thoroughbred horses, and fifty thousand dirhams loaded on a bay horse.

In the *Arabian Nights*, we find an occasional reference to such gifts. In one passage, for example, we read: "Now these are the presents which the lord of Constantinople sent to the caliph: fifty of the fairest virgins in all Greece, and fifty of the most glorious boys from Rome, dressed in gold-embroidered silken full-sleeved robes, with colored pictures in needlework upon them, and silver damascened gold belts holding up double skirts of brocaded velvet which fell in unequal lengths. They also had gold rings in their ears from which depended single round white pearls each worth a thousand pound weight in gold. The girls, too, were sumptuously decked. These were the two principal gifts, but the rest did not fall short of them in worth."

By such comity, Nicephorus may have hoped to save face. But he had more trouble than he could bear. On the other side of the Byzantine Empire lay the kingdom of the Bulgars, under their mighty khan. During his reign, the Bulgar kingdom had doubled in size and spread from the middle Danube to the Dnieper and beyond. In former times, the Byzantines and Bulgars had cooperated as allies against the Arabs, but of late their peoples had been almost constantly at war. In the end, it was not the Muslims but the Bulgars who swept Nicephorus from the stage. Constant skirmishing between the two escalated into major action when the Bulgars slaughtered the Byzantine garrison of Serdica (now Sofia) and Nicephorus sacked the Bulgar capital of Pliska in revenge. He scarcely had time to rejoice in his triumph before he was trapped in the mountain passes as he withdrew. For several days he sulked like Achilles in his tent. Then the Bulgars moved in and killed him along with his generals and the flower of his troops. The khan, exultant in his turn, claimed the emperor's head as a trophy and had the skull lined with silver to serve as a drinking cup.

EVEN AS A MEASURE OF STABILITY AND CALM SETTLED DOWN on the Byzantine front, Khurasan was roiled with discontent.

The great historian Edward Gibbon once remarked that a turbulent region within a kingdom is often more difficult to manage than an enemy without. For the realm as a whole can be mobilized against a foreign power; not so against a region on which the kingdom itself depends. Throughout their tenure as viziers, the Barmaks had cautioned the caliph about the need for a special administrative policy in Khurasan that would grant the province some autonomy. It was, after all, the headquarters of the Persian national party, as well as a hotbed of Shiite belief. Under Abu Muslim it had helped to overturn the Umayyads. Harun had reason enough to fear that if allowed to flourish in its own independent fashion it might overturn the Abbasids, too. Yet the wise and moderate advice of the Barmaks had served only to kindle the caliph's suspicions, prompting a heavy hand.

In 796, after Yahya al-Barmak had induced Yahya ibn Abdullah to turn himself in, Harun had made Ali ibn Isa, a member of the old Abbasid military guard, governor of Transoxiana and Khurasan. Yahya al-Barmak had opposed Ibn Isa's appointment, considering him unfit; but Harun had ignored his counsel—just as he had ignored Yahya's concerns the year before when he had replaced Yahya's brother, Muhammad, with Fadhl ibn al-Rabi as chamberlain. As governor, Ibn Isa proved a tyrant. Though he directed a steady stream of wealth from the province to the caliph's coffers, he was detested by the local population for his unjust and oppressive rule. Indeed, over time he created so much ill will by his extortions and exactions that the province teetered on revolt. Yahya one day pointedly remarked to the caliph that the stability of a province could not be measured reliably by the amount of money it brought in. But Harun failed to pay heed.

Ibn Isa seemed to have the Midas touch. When he first sent Harun a dazzling sample of his ill-gotten gains, the caliph was luxuriating in East

Baghdad in one of the Barmaks' palatial homes. Yahya al-Barmak was with him, and Harun said to him in a mocking tone: "This is the person you advised us not to appoint as governor over this frontier region, but we rejected your advice concerning him and a blessing has come out of our opposing your advice!" Yahya tactfully replied that he was always happy when Harun's judgment proved better than his own, and that there could be no doubting the richness of Ibn Isa's gifts—"if it were not that there lay behind it what the Commander of the Faithful would abhor." Harun said, "And what is that?" Yahya replied that the bounty the caliph had before him could not have been obtained without tyrannical means. He then offered to obtain for Harun twice as much by hard bargaining with various rich merchants for their costly merchandise. Those merchants might not be entirely happy with the deals they had to make, he said, under pressure from the crown, but "this would be a safer way to build the treasury up." According to Tabari, Harun was struck by Yahya's declaration but did nothing to alter the arrangements he had made.

That became more difficult as time went on. Complaints about Ibn Isa continued to pour in, and Harun was urged by leading figures in the province to appoint someone in his place. Harun asked Yahya whom he should name. Yahya proposed the famed general Mazyad al-Shaibani, but Harun declined to take his advice. At length, Harun decided to go to Khurasan to assess the situation for himself. In 805, on his return from another pilgrimage to Mecca, he bypassed Baghdad and on April 23 joined troops that had been concentrated at Nahrawan, twenty miles to the northeast. As Zubaidah traveled up the Euphrates from Baghdad to Rakkah, Harun, with two of his sons, Mamun and Kasim (leaving Amin in Baghdad with Fadhl ibn Rabi, now vizier), marched at the head of his columns to Rayy. Ibn Isa came over from Merv in Khurasan to meet him and brought many priceless gifts. These included twenty pieces of Chinese imperial porcelain "the likes of which had never before been seen," along with large sums of money, which he presented not only to Harun but all the officials in his train. By his bribes, self-confident demeanor, and fluent explanation of events, he managed to allay Harun's concerns.

Rayy was Harun's birthplace, of course, and he lingered there for several months. Perhaps there was sentiment in this, but policy was also on his mind. As the first caliph ever to visit the region, he took full advantage of the awe inspired by his royal presence to receive duty in person from the tribal chiefs of mountain districts, including Dailam and Tabaristan. Harun also gathered a number of provincial officials around him and asked them to reaffirm their oath of allegiance to Mamun. A kindred oath, one that acknowledged—yet again—Mamun's own succession rights, was also exacted at the caliph's command from Amin and his circle in Baghdad by Harthama ibn Ayain, Harun's commander of the guard.

Clearly, the matter of succession continued to roil Harun's thoughts.

After Harun returned to Rakkah, he expected to hear that Khurasan was calm. Instead he learned to his fury of new unrest. Directly and indirectly, Ibn Isa's misrule had brought to prominence an opportunistic noble by the name of Rafi ibn Laith. Rafi's family had been influential under the Umayyads and his grandfather was a popular governor of Samarkand. Harun told Ibn Isa to humble the man, but Rafi fled and placed himself at the head of the rebellious host. Ibn Isa attacked, but his forces were routed and it soon became apparent that he lacked the means to reestablish control. Meanwhile, the rebellion had spread.

Harun turned to Harthama ibn Ayain, now his general in chief, to straighten things out.

Harthama was to go to Khurasan, ostensibly with reinforcements (as Ibn Isa supposed it), but in fact to take him into custody as soon as he arrived. To make sure that no clerk or secretary saw his order, Harun wrote it out with his own hand. When Harthama was but a day's march from Merv, he asked Ibn Isa to send his chief aides to his camp. As they began to arrive that same evening, Harthama rode on ahead with an elite troop of cavalry to Merv. En route, he was met by Ibn Isa himself with great demonstrations of friendship, which Harthama returned. He had been told not to betray his true intentions by the least sign, and when the governor rode up he "bent his leg to dismount his horse" in a gesture of respect. Ibn Isa cried out, "By God, if you dismount, then I shall dismount." The two drew near and "embraced" and continued on side by side. Ibn Isa quizzed Harthama about Harun's health and disposition, until they came to the governor's palace, where dinner was served. When they were almost through eating, Harthama suddenly turned to his host and gave him an angry letter from Harun, which read: "In the name of God, the Merciful, the Compassionate. You son of a whore, I exalted your status and raised your fame, made Arab leaders follow you and made the descendants of Persian kings your slaves. In return, you have disobeyed me and cast my command behind my back. . . ." Before Ibn Isa could recover from his shock, he found himself in chains.

The next day Harthama went to the Great Mosque, and addressing a restive host, told them that the Prince of the Faithful had ordered Ibn Isa's arrest and that he himself would now assume the duties of interim governor and set things right. Ibn Isa was then dragged to the mosque and compelled to answer those whom he had defrauded and afterward taken to Baghdad on a camel "with no saddle-blanket beneath him, a chain round his neck, and heavy fetters on his legs." Meanwhile, all his friends and relations were arrested, and his treasure, including tons of gold and silver—found buried in the garden of his son—were carried to Baghdad by a caravan of fifteen hundred camels and appropriated by the state.

Yet the region would not be tamed. There were numerous separatist political and religious groups, some led by warlords who controlled their own wild mountain fiefdoms; renewed agitation by the Kharijites, who sought a theocratic state; and insurgents along the eastern borders linked to foreign religious groups. Since most of these movements had their headquarters in distant, even inaccessible, regions, they were impossible to contain. By the time the administration in Baghdad became aware of them, they had usually gathered force and spread. By 808, just such a commingled wave of discontent had grown anew. Added to the residual effects of Ibn Isa's misrule, a full-fledged revolt, whipped up by Rafi ibn Laith, who remained at large, and centered at Samarkand, had spread into eastern Persia and stretched from Ferghana to Azerbaijan. The revolt could not be quelled. Toward the end of 808, Harthama was recalled from the West, where in the summer of 807 he had been sent to mount another raid against the Byzantines, and Harun decided once more to go to Khurasan.

chapter thirteen

THE RED SOIL OF TUS

Legend is, after all, only the poetic sublimation of reality.

—Gabriel Audisio

Mamun's top aide at this time was Fadhl ibn Sahl, a Persian noble and former protégé of the Barmaks who had replaced Jafar al-Barmak as the prince's tutor and guide. When first introduced to Harun by Yahya al-Barmak not long before the family's fall, Ibn Sahl had been so overawed in the caliph's presence that he could scarcely utter a word. Harun turned to Yahya, "with the look of one who blamed his choice," but Ibn Sahl promptly recovered and said, "Commander of the Faithful! May it be deemed proof of your servant's merit that his heart is seized with such respect in the presence of his Master." Harun liked that and said, "If you kept silent that you might frame this answer, I must say that you have succeeded. But if it came to you extempore, it is better still." Harun then asked him questions on a host of subjects and Ibn Sahl acquitted himself so well that the caliph had no doubt as to his fitness for the post.

Harun was now weighed down by care. His days were joyless, his moods taciturn and black. Though scarcely forty years old and in his prime, he seemed to have aged prematurely, with stern, drawn features and graying hair. He had also (it is said) begun to drink heavily and was torn between rage and yearnings to forgive. In destroying the Barmaks he had arguably protected his throne and family from dynastic threat, but he had also hugely strengthened the Arab faction at court. That faction supported Amin, whom Harun did not trust, and therefore imperiled Mamun, whom he did. By his divided actions, which stemmed from a divided mind, he had become incapable of acting in concert with himself. He had also lost control of his regime.

In truth he had created this sorry situation for himself. He had neglected tried-and-true friendships, alienated kin, and ruled increasingly by fear. Few loyal figures remained in his entourage. Even his new vizier, Fadhl ibn al-Rabi, whose father had been vizier to Harun's father, Mahdi, had become the leader of the Arab faction at court. Those around him could see that Harun no longer commanded much authority. Moreover, he was enfeebled by some malady or disease.

In mid-February 809, leaving his son Kasim in charge of Rakkah, Harun embarked for Baghdad en route to Khurasan. He reached Baghdad on Friday, February 26, 808, and following his afternoon prayers, continued on, having entrusted the capital to Mamun. The caliph was in a morbid state. As he came to the outskirts of Nahrawan, twenty miles from the capital, he said to Sobah al-Tabari, a companion riding by his side, "Oh Sobah, I don't suppose that you will ever see me again. I don't think you know how ill I feel." "No, by God," said Sobah, "I did not know you were feeling unwell."

Harun pulled up, turned off the track, and dismounted in the shade of a group of trees fifty yards from the road. He took Sobah aside while the rest of his entourage remained at a distance and made him swear not to reveal to anyone what he was about to see. Then he opened the front of his clothing to reveal a silk sash wound tightly round his midriff, as if binding a grievous wound. At the time, Harun was suffering from intestinal ulcers. He told Sobah: "I have tried to conceal my condition, but everyone suspects I am sick. Each of my sons has a spy in my entourage. Masrur is now working for Mamun; Jibril ibn Bakhtishou, my own doctor, for Amin. These and others count every breath I draw. They all think I am living too long, and cannot wait for me to die. If you doubt it, call a horse for me now, and you will see that they will bring me a lean, stumbling old nag, to aggravate the discomfort I am in." Harun himself then called for a horse, and indeed a sorry steed was provided, just as he had said. The caliph gave Sobah a quick look, mounted, and rode on.

Harun had become a "homily indeed," as one writer put it, "of the useless emptiness of fame."

Meanwhile, scarcely had the caliph left Baghdad than Fadhl ibn Sahl remarked to Mamun, "You do not know what may happen to your father. But your brother Amin has taken precedence over you, and even though Khurasan is supposed to be yours, the best that you can hope for from him is that he will rob you of your rights, for he is the son of Zubaidah, and his relations are all of the Hashemi clan. You should therefore accompany your father, so if anything happens, and Amin proves faithless, you'll be at a safe distance from the capital and better able to assert your claims. You'll also be in Khurasan, where you have your power base." Mamun grasped at once the prudent wisdom of this advice and joined his father on the road.

After crossing the heights of Hulwan, Harun halted at Kermanshah and in a show of command harangued his troops. But the caliph's condition had worsened appreciably by the time he reached Jurjan, and he could only struggle on as far as Tus. There he had to be carried about by his attendants, which caused a great stir among the troops.

Harun had long since had a premonition that it would be at Tus that he would die. Yet he had not known this clearly. Some months before, while still at Rakkah, Ibn Bakhtishou, his physician, one day came to see him and found him paralyzed with fear. He had had a frightful vision, he said, of an arm and hand protruding from under his bed and holding a fistful of red earth. He recognized the arm and hand but couldn't recall to whom they belonged. Then he heard a voice say, "This is the soil of the land in which you will lie." Ibn Bakhtishou assured him it was just a bad dream, brought on by all his cares. But now at Tus, laid up in a house, he suddenly staggered to his feet and exclaimed, "My dream!" and told Masrur to bring him some earth from the garden. Masrur returned with red soil in his palm. Harun looked at his physician and said, "By God, this is the same arm I saw in my dream, and this the same earth in the same hand."

At about this time, Harun learned that Harthama, his general in chief, had finally begun to bring some order to Khurasan. He had taken Bukhara and was preparing to advance on Samarkand, where Rafi ibn Laith was then holed up. Harun was briefly heartened by this news and sent Mamun ahead to Merv with Ibn Sahl to take charge of the new administration and oversee the campaign. Yet nothing could cheer him for long. At times he gave himself up to bitter outbursts; at others he fell into a mournfully elegiac mood. It was now about mid-March. He called together some army commanders and told them: "All that lives must perish. All that is young must grow old: you see what destiny has made of me. I now urge upon you three things: keep religiously to your undertakings and be faithful to your imams; be united among yourselves; and watch over Amin and Mamun. Should one of them revolt against his brother, stifle his insurrection and condemn his perfidy." Then he added: "My wealth hath not profited me! My power hath perished from me"— words from the Koran.

One morning, he also recited aloud these lines: "Where are the kings, and all the others who lived before you? / They are gone where you will go when your time comes." Then he turned to one of his courtiers and asked: "Could it not be said that these words are especially appropriate for me?"

While Harun was in this hopeless state, Bashir, brother of the rebel leader Rafi ibn Laith, was brought in as a prisoner to his camp. Harun denounced him for helping to make the end of his own life so miserable and told him, "If I had no more time left than it would take me to move my lips, I would say 'He must die!' " Then he called for a butcher and had Bashir dismembered limb from limb. When his body lay in a pile, the caliph said, "Count it up." There were fourteen parts. For some reason, Harun found that number exciting and raised his hands toward heaven and cried, "O God, just as you have given me power to exact vengeance for you and power over your enemy, and I have now done it to your satisfaction, let me do the same to his brother, too."

This gruesome execution was his last public act.

As his own last hour approached, he supervised the digging of his grave in the garden and selected his winding sheet. Over the next few days, a number of readers intoned the whole of the Koran in his presence, each reciting different chapters in a confused medley, as the dying caliph went in and out of sleep. On the twenty-third of March 809, he suddenly opened his eyes and called for a thick blanket, that the attendant watching over him might wrap himself in it for warmth. Presently Harun called out, "Where are you?" The attendant answered, "Here. While the Prince of the Faithful suffers so much, my heart will not let me rest." At this, Harun unexpectedly laughed. "Remember the poet's lines: 'Those belonging to a great race / Must bravely bear the hardest fate.'" Then he died. He was buried in the garden at Tus from which Masrur had drawn the red earth, and where a magnificent domed mausoleum with two soaring minarets, known today as the Tomb of the Martyr, would be built nearby. But the martyr honored there is not Harun, who was no martyr, but a famed imam of the Shiites, whose adjacent tomb is a Shiite shrine.

Harun's legacy was both sorry and grand. "The preposterous position into which he had been born" automatically made him a kind of despot and "almost necessarily crushed all really human feelings in him," it is said, because of the largeness of the power he held. One may doubt it. For his wanton cruelties, at least, that seems a poor excuse. The derangement of his last years also nearly eclipsed what he achieved. Yet taking his reign as a whole, he was also an energetic ruler, "humbly performed the duties of his religion, and strove his utmost to increase, or at least preserve intact, the glorious inheritance that had been handed down to his care." Though he had failed to extend the empire of Islam in a physical sense—and here and there even lost some ground—he had held most of the immensity of what he had together, and had imparted a new ecumenical largeness to the culture of the faith by his embrace of the treasures of the past.

Yet whatever capacities Harun may have brought to the throne, there is also no doubt that his reign derived much of its luster from the eminent men around him who governed in his name.

What manner of man Harun really was remains obscure. Publicly devout, as we have seen, he performed a hundred prostrations with his daily prayers, made the pilgrimage to Mecca every two years, and was the only caliph to go the whole way on foot. Some anecdotes gently commend his impartial justice and sagacity; others—such as the story of a rich baker who was burned alive in his own oven for giving short weight—portray him as incredibly harsh. It was also in Harun's time that the great pontoon bridges across the Tigris were first used for public executions—where political offenders were crucified, and their heads stuck on poles as warnings to passersby. And who could forget the weird end of "Wasif the Eunuch," a prominent court favorite, whose body, partially embalmed in resin, was exposed on a bridge and recrowned with his severed head? In some respects, Harun was, as one writer put it wryly, "very unlike the merry monarch of the *Arabian Nights*."

At the same time, as the caliph of those tales, his memory is imperishably linked to their undying charm and romance. Despite a cruel and willful streak, he comes down to us as "Aaron the Just," the once and future king, whose fabled Baghdad is a timeless city where fishermen consort with genies and Aladdin forever rubs his magic lamp. As one of the great historians of Islam, Sir William Muir, once remarked, though "the witchery of Oriental romance has cast an adventitious glow around the life of Harun al Rashid; even when that has faded before the prosaic realities of history, enough remains to excite wonder and admiration at the splendor of this monarch's Caliphate."

chapter fourteen

THE SIEGE OF BAGHDAD

The news of Harun's death was rushed by courier to Amin in Baghdad in just a few days. At the time, Amin was living in the al-Khuld "Palace of Eternity" on the banks of the Tigris. Perhaps for security reasons, he moved at once into the Great Green Domed Palace within the Round City, and the following Friday led the prayers before a multitude of the faithful, many openly weeping and wailing in mourning, in the Great Mosque. He gave a short address promising to work for the good of the people and accepted oaths of allegiance from members of his own family and from high officials of the former regime.

By then a courier had brought the emblems of state for him to display as proof of his title—including the mantle of the Prophet, which he wore. The army, in restraint of its anarchic inclinations, had been given two years' bonus pay out of the overflowing coffers of the realm. In Merv, the capital of Khurasan, Mamun likewise "addressed the people from the pulpit, announced his father's death, and tore his clothes as a sign of grief."

Yet no one, perhaps, was sadder than Zubaidah, then at Rakkah. When word reached her of her husband's death, she assembled all the women of the royal household for a ceremony of public mourning and appealed to Ishaq al-Mausili to compose an elegy fit for Harun. But that peerless musician "could think of nothing original, and so adapted the words and melody of a dirge he had long ago heard sung in Medina" when the Umayyad Caliph Yazid II (720–24) had been mourned. Zubaidah then set out for Baghdad to be by her son. Amin and all the notables of the capital went out to meet her at Anbar, and there gave her a state reception, in accordance with the venerable stature she now enjoyed as imperial matriarch.

Meanwhile, the question had arisen as to what the army en route to Khurasan should do. Harun had told his vizier, Fadhl ibn Rabi, to transfer all the troops and money he had with him to Mamun, so he could deal effectively with Khurasan and manage his portion of the realm. Ibn Rabi not only had agreed to do this, but had reinforced his promise by a solemn oath. But no sooner was Harun buried than he went back on his word; for in the contest between the two brothers, he was in Amin's camp. He therefore publicly announced that all subjects were under an obligation to support "a reigning sovereign" (i.e., Amin) rather than one (Mamun) whose future reign might—or might not—come to pass. So the generals and their legions returned to the capital, abandoning their Khurasan campaign.

The two brothers, Amin and Mamun, both twenty-three years old, were now divided by over a thousand miles of rough terrain. But that seeming buffer was but a fragile screen. To test Amin's goodwill, Ibn Sahl, Mamun's top aide, asked him to allow Mamun's wife and two sons to travel unhindered to Khurasan. Amin replied that the journey was too dangerous and rough, but that he would be happy to act as the caretaker of Mamun's family, property, and goods.

That was a bad sign. Ibn Sahl warned Mamun to be careful and acquiesce to any reasonable request Amin might make. But he also told him to get ready to fight and rally the people of Persia to his side. Mamun grasped the practical wisdom of this advice, made peace with the rebels, and by means of tax breaks and other measures endeavored to ingratiate himself with the subjects of his domain. At the same time, instead of mounting any open challenge to Amin, he shrewdly chose to wait until Amin engaged in some aggression—as he was sure he would—so that his own response could be viewed as an act of self-defense.

Amin proved true to form. Urged on by his vizier, Ibn Rabi, he deprived his younger brother, Kasim, of the provinces allotted to him by Harun; demanded that Mamun remit to Baghdad any surplus revenue the province yielded up beyond that needed for administrative costs; and insisted that Mamun accept a new intelligence director for the province as a whole.

Mamun replied in a conciliatory note in which he asked Amin not to press him unjustly in view of his sincere loyalty to the crown. Letters hidden "inside hollow canes, sewn into clothing, or concealed in women's hair" were passed back and forth between secret agents in both camps. In the meantime, Amin disregarded his brother's protestations of loyalty and confiscated his personal property in the capital and placed his wife and family under house arrest.

Mamun expressed dismay at his brother's actions, but Amin would not relent. He next demanded that Mamun give up much of the territory under his jurisdiction. Mamun replied, "Son of my father, do not make me come into conflict with you when I would willingly obey, nor become estranged when I want to be on friendly terms." But Amin was determined to gather up all the reins of power into his hands. "I have received your letter," he replied, "in which you not only show your refusal to obey me but, worse, your ingratitude to God."

In the fall of 810, the die was cast. Amin annulled Mamun's succession rights in favor of his own infant son, Musa, and ordered Mamun's name omitted from the public Friday prayers. He also took the fateful step of seizing the signed succession documents displayed at Mecca, conveyed them to Baghdad, and publicly tore them up in scorn. In these rash, even sacrilegious, actions, he was encouraged by a number of suspect characters, including Ali ibn Isa, the ex-governor of Khurasan.

It is sometimes alleged that the two brothers might have managed to hammer out some détente between themselves had their two viziers, Fadhl ibn Rabi and Fadhl ibn Sahl, not kept their hostility alive. But Amin, as noted by his own father, had a degenerate and treacherous nature and needed little prompting to instigate a fight.

On Friday, February 21, 811, members of the royal family, court officials, and generals of note assembled for prayers in the Great Mosque in Baghdad, where Amin's vizier read out a long statement declaring Mamun in revolt. Tens of thousands of soldiers were massed in one of the large Baghdad parade grounds and readied to march.

Civil war began.

At the head of his army Amin placed Ali ibn Isa, whom he promised to reinstate as governor of Khurasan should be prevail. Since Ibn Isa was hated for his former unjust rule, this was an incredibly foolish move. In every way, it strengthened Mamun's hand and galvanized the Persian population to resist. It also enabled Mamun to appeal to all those united in their dissatisfaction with Baghdad and its ruling Arab elite.

Zubaidah was deeply distressed by these developments. Although Amin was her own son and she had been his advocate, she had also brought up both boys together and could not deny to herself how unstable Amin was. It must have been fairly obvious to all. Illustrations of his bizarre behavior abound in the chronicles. He dismissed key ministers in childish tantrums, arbitrarily burned official reports, and indulged his pleasures to the exclusion of state affairs. According to the historian Masudi, Zubaidah had always been deeply apprehensive about his fate. On the very night Amin was conceived—in a scene that Shakespeare might have imagined—she had dreamed that three women came into her room and sat down beside her, two on her right and a third on her left. "Each," she recalled, "in turn drew near and placed her hand on my womb. The first said: 'His yoke will be heavy.' The second: 'He will be a weak-willed king and by fortune betrayed.' The third: 'Wasteful of blood, surrounded by revolt.' " Then, on the night Amin was born, these three witches (like the doleful fates in *Macbeth*) reappeared, "sat down again, stared at me," and predicted a short and sorry reign. Somewhat later, when Amin was yet a toddler, they haunted her sleep for the third and last time. Their unanimous verdict was that he would prove "a tyrant, a wastrel, and a babbling fool. Dig his grave," they cried, "open his coffin, bring out his winding sheet!"

They were right. He proved a weak voluptuary, led at will by those about him, and surrounded by eunuchs and carefree women who encouraged his frivolity and vice. No sooner had he become caliph than he established for his own pleasure on the Tigris River five gondolas, in the shape of various beasts—a lion, an elephant, an eagle, a serpent, and a horse. On any given day or night, he could almost always be found on one of them engaged in private carousing or some Bacchanalian feast. In one typical extravaganza, a hundred naked singing girls were paraded before him and intoned his praises as they waved palm fronds in their hands.

Above all, Amin had a sexual passion for eunuchs, which his mother had tried to sublimate or divert. She did so by dressing up pretty slave girls as boys. Their "close-fitting, wide-sleeved robes with wide belts" were designed to "show off their waists and curves," writes one historian, and their hair, coaxed out "with fringes and lovelocks from beneath their turbans," was drawn "back at the nape of the neck like young men." But it did not work.

Even as she tried to humor and contain Amin, she did what she could to protect Mamun.

Before Ibn Isa left for the front, Zubaidah implored him to treat Mamun, if captured, like a prince, and bring him as a prisoner to Baghdad without subjecting him to any humiliation or harm. "Do not speak haughtily to him," she said, "for you are not his equal. . . . Should he abuse you, bear with him, and should he revile you, do not retaliate."

In mocking compliance with her request, Ibn Isa promised to bind him with a set of silver chains.

Ibn Isa set out from Baghdad on March 16, 811, at the head of an army of forty thousand men. Amin accompanied this host as far as Nahrawan, from which the army marched on to Hamadan, on the way to Rayy, sure of success. Facing him was the Persian general Tahir ibn al-Husain. The two were as opposite as the men they served. Ibn Isa was coarse, arrogant, and grasping. Tahir, the grandson of a governor of Herat, was a genteel, brave, and dedicated soldier who had lost an eye on the eastern front. He was also "an elegant scholar" of refined taste and fond enough of good poetry to have once pardoned a man for a capital offense when the man apologized in well-wrought lines.

When told that Tahir was at Rayy, Ibn Isa answered, "What of it? Can a fox stand up to a lion? There are only two courses open to him. Either he can shut himself up and be besieged, or he can retreat as soon as our cavalry approach his lines." On the face of it, that was likely enough.

Mamun had not had time to mobilize the army he needed and Tahir had with him a rather modest force—some say a tenth of what Ibn Isa had. But Tahir possessed superior skill and judgment and, the sources tell us, had the stars on his side. Ibn Sahl had promoted his appointment in part based on his horoscope and even determined the most propitious moment for him to set out. When that moment arrived, "he knotted Tahir's standard and placed it in his hand."

Tahir advanced and in early May came within sight of Ibn Isa's army in a plain between Rayy and Hamadan. Ibn Isa's troops seemed to fill it, the polished steel of their arms and armor flashing in the sun. There was little chance Tahir's own force could prevail in open combat. So he decided on a desperate ruse. He sent word that a flag of truce would be forthcoming, and Ibn Isa, in his conceit, assuming all was over, rode forward to dictate his terms. In so doing, he failed to protect himself. Suddenly, a solitary trooper emerged from Tahir's ranks, rode straight at him, and struck him with his sword. Ibn Isa fell from his horse, and a moment later his severed head was rolling on the ground.

In the ensuing engagement, Ibn Isa's leaderless army fared poorly. Part of it fell back to Hamadan. There it was trapped and surrendered after a short siege. By then Tahir's own forces had grown exponentially in strength and advanced toward Hulwan on the Baghdad road. At the same time, Harthama ibn Ayain, having restored order to Samarkand, arrived with his own legions and assumed overall charge of the campaign. Mamun proclaimed himself caliph; formally appointed Fadhl ibn Sahl his imperial vizier; and sent a fresh column of troops toward Ahwaz, as the road to Baghdad now lay open to their advance.

When the news of Ibn Isa's defeat reached the capital, Amin was fishing in the Tigris with a eunuch named Kauthar, with whom he was in love. "Don't bother me now," he exclaimed. "Kauthar has caught two fish, and I haven't yet caught one." His absurd distraction at a moment of national crisis boded ill for his prospects, especially since his open affair with the eunuch had estranged the court—just as the power-grabbing eunuchs in Constantinople had estranged the court of Irene. Yet the fate of empire was in their hands. "These two have splattered everyone, like a camel pissing," one official exclaimed, as he watched the hopes of the Arab party collapse.

Fadhl ibn Rabi sought to rouse Amin to a sense of the peril he was in, but the besotted monarch, immersed in pleasure, heeded only his sycophants. Meanwhile, Tahir took Hulwan, northeast of Baghdad, without much of a fight, turned west and occupied Wasit, while Harthama routed Amin's forces at Nahrawan in May 812. Before long Kufa, Basra, Mosul, Mecca, and Medina had all declared for Mamun. By the end of September, the capital was completely encircled, with Tahir to the west of Baghdad and Harthama entrenched to the east.

Once under siege, the city might have been expected to surrender promptly. Instead, it held out for a year. To the east, the caliph was protected by the wide and sinuous Tigris; to the west, by a man-made waterway that emptied into the river from the north. Its pontoon bridges, which "rose with flooding," were cut from their moorings, preventing a flanking attack. At the same time, the reticulated network of canals south of the Round City, Baghdad's heart, served both as a natural barrier and as arteries for goods and war materiel sent down the Euphrates from the west. Aside from these perimeter defenses, there were also, of course, the imposing outer and inner fortifications of the Round City itself, including its ringed complexes, checkpoints, great iron gates, massive protective walls, and a sixty-foot-wide moat. Each gate also had a right-angled entrance so that assailants could not strike through directly to the courtyard within. Baghdad, moreover, had its own arsenal of weapons, siege engines, and artillery for fighting back. The people, Arab nationalists for the most part, also armed themselves. Equipped with staves and slings, helmets of palm leaves, padded wool jackets, and shields of plaited rushes tied to their arms, they organized themselves into a civil defense force—though in the end, of course, they could not contend against Mamun's armored cavalry with its lances and swords.

Yet the city held out with unexpected resolve. Amin himself remained popular—in part because of all the money he lavished on the people to the exhaustion of his coffers; in part because the city was largely Arab and he was the only caliph the Arabs had.

Nevertheless, Baghdad was doomed. Catapults, planted around the walls, cast in shot; whole quarters were razed to the ground. Troops pressed into the suburbs, then into the city itself, advancing block by block and fighting from house to house. Amin was incapable of meeting the challenges he faced. At one point during the height of the siege, he became preoccupied with finding a goldfish that had escaped from a basin in his palace; in an effort to find it, he turned the place upside down. When Zubaidah, barricaded in the al-Khuld Palace, reproached her feckless son, he shouted, absurdly: "Silence! Crowns are not to be firmly secured through women's frets and fears. The caliphate demands statesmanship beyond the ability of women, whose function is to nurse children. Be gone!"

By then Amin had run out of money to distribute and communication between the east and west banks of the Tigris had been cut. The whole commercial quarter was occupied by enemy troops. Army discipline collapsed, the people began to surge about Baghdad in lawless mobs, and Amin's own military commander denounced him as a hermaphrodite. Eventually Amin saw that his cause was hopeless, took refuge in his mother's quarters, and judged that his only two options were surrender or escape. Some of his advisors urged him to try to break through the siege lines, make his way to Syria, and there concoct plans to recover his throne. Others urged him to seek mercy in defeat.

Amin decided to surrender to Harthama, who had known him as a boy, and who was more likely than Tahir to spare his life. Urgent messages were exchanged between them and arrangements for the surrender worked out. But Tahir objected and at length it was agreed that Amin would give himself up to Harthama, but the imperial regalia—the royal cloak, scepter, and ring—would go to Tahir.

On the night of September 25, 813, Amin said good-bye to his two little sons, "kissing and fondling them desperately, while the tears ran down his cheeks." Then, tearing himself away, he left the palace with a few companions and disappeared into the night. "Ahead of us," recalled an aide, "one candle lighted the way." They hastened down byways and slipped out of the city, down to the bank of the Tigris. Harthama was waiting there in a skiff moored under the embankment to carry him across. "But as we rode to board it," the aide wrote later, "the caliph's horse, in an ill-omen, suddenly came to a halt. It refused to move until the caliph struck it with his whip." It stepped on board, but as soon as Amin dismounted, it bolted ashore.

The caliph descended to a chamber on the lower deck, where Harthama and his staff were in council. As he entered, everyone stood up. Harthama received him with respect, and in the name of Mamun embraced him, kissed his hands and feet, and called him "My Lord." Amin gazed around the assembly, acknowledged its various members, and specifically thanked one of them for a past favor he had done.

The boat then shot out into the stream.

Yet the whole scheme had stuck in Tahir's craw. He was determined to thwart it, and suspected that Amin would not honor its terms. The boat came under attack by his men, who "began drilling holes into its hull and tried to overturn it." Amin panicked, thought himself betrayed, and plunged into the river. Within moments he was caught and dragged ashore to a nearby house. There he lay, "wrapped only in a cotton sheet, shivering with cold and fear."

"As we were in this situation," recalled a fellow captive, "someone entered in full armor. He stared hard at Amin and left. I knew then that he was a dead man. . . . Around midnight, I heard the noise of horses, there was a knock at the door and when it was opened, a group of Persians came in with their swords drawn. When Amin saw them, he said, 'We are God's and to Him we return!' " Then the soldiers killed him and cut off his head. Tahir exposed it briefly on the battlements before sending it with the imperial regalia to Mamun. In this dismal fashion, the sole son born to Harun and Zubaidah together, and the only caliph descended through both parents from the Prophet himself, met his end.

Mamun's vizier was not happy about this. "What has Tahir wrought?" he cried. "He shall unleash upon us renewed violence. We ordered him to send us Amin as a prisoner. Instead, he sent us his head." But Mamun replied: "What is past is past; let us find the means to exonerate Tahir." In fact, Tahir had done the caliph's will. During the siege, Tahir had asked Mamun what he should do with Amin if he caught him. Mamun said nothing in reply, but "sent him a shirt with no opening in it for the head.

By this, Tahir knew that he wished him put to death." It hardly seems likely, moreover, that Tahir would have killed Amin—or attacked Harthama's skiff—on his own account.

Even so, when Mamun saw the head of his brother, "he wept, and asked God to forgive him, and reminisced about some of the things that Amin had once done for him, and the good times they had had together in the time of Harun." Thereafter, Mamun could never look at Tahir without thinking of what he had done. In 822, a eunuch working for the caliph dispatched Tahir with a poisoned sauce.

chapter fifteen

INTERREGNUM

While Mamun and Amin had been fighting for control of the Caliphate, neither had concerned himself with the Byzantines or the Franks. There was not much to concern them, in fact, for the Byzantines were demoralized by their own calamities and Charlemagne was about to pass from the scene. In 809, at the age of sixty-four, he had divided his own dominions among his three sons—Pepin, Louis, and Charles—but Pepin and Charles soon died; and only Louis (known afterward as Louis the Pious) remained. If Amin had been too profligate, Louis proved too pious (or feckless) to manage what had been given to his care. Nevertheless, at a solemn ceremony, he had been raised from the rank of king to that of emperor, as Charlemagne intoned: "Blessed be Thou, O Lord God, Who hast granted me the grace to see with my own eyes my son seated on my throne!"

After a reign of forty-seven years, Charles died of pneumonia at the age of seventy-two on his palace estate. He was buried under the dome of the cathedral at Aachen, wrapped in a purple silk Byzantine shroud woven with the image of a charioteer.

It has been said that in spite of being a warrior-king, Charlemagne had "loved administration more than war" and fought only to forge a more peaceful Western Europe united by a common government and creed. If so, he failed. In the aftermath of his reign, the unity he had won by force of arms dissolved, and the continent of Europe once more broke apart in strife.

Like Harun, he had fearfully divined what lay ahead. Not long before he died, he had a prophetic dream. In it he was approached by a man who handed him a sword inscribed with four obscure Germanic words on the blade: "raht," "radoleiba," "nasg," and "enti." Charles recorded the dream that very night and attempted to interpret it the next day. The sword itself, in his view, signified the power of dominion. Then, on a declining scale, the first word meant "abundance"; the second "diminution"; the third "collapse"; the fourth, written near the sword's point, "end."

Other omens beset him. In the year he arranged for the succession, famine, epidemic disease, and calamitous storms struck the realm. A doleful message was sent to all the kingdom's bishops: "From these external events we can infer beyond all doubt that, inwardly, we are not finding favor with the Lord; . . . Therefore . . . every one of us should truly seek to do penance and humble his heart." The bishops were told to pass this message on to every community and parish church. In the fall of 807, an assembly of secular and ecclesiastical magnates called for a three-day fast. In subsequent seasons, soldiers failed to show up for duty; crime, poverty, and vagrancy increased; and the Danes stirred up rebellion among Slavic tribes on the frontier. Other portents also seemed to mark the approach of Charlemagne's passing. An earthquake-proof portico built to connect his palace and cathedral came crashing down; the church itself was struck by lightning; the great bridge he had labored for ten years to build across the Rhine near Mainz was consumed by fire; and the number of solar and lunar eclipses strangely increased. One morning just before sunrise, as he was setting out from camp on a campaign against the Danes, a meteor flashed across the clear sky in a blaze of light. As everyone stared at it in amazement, Charlemagne's horse reared and threw him to the ground. He landed with such violence that the buckle fastening his cloak broke and his sword was torn away. Then in June 810, Charlemagne's eldest daughter, Rotrud, and his beloved elephant, Abu al-Abbas, the gift of Harun, both died.

Although Charlemagne would one day be revered as a saint (if not officially canonized like the Empress Irene), he knew he had lived a worldly life; and in 811, when he made his last will and testament, he left most of his personal treasure to churches in the kingdom to subsidize continuous prayers for his soul.

THE BAGHDAD CALIPHATE MIGHT HAVE GONE THE WAY OF Charlemagne's Europe, but instead it rose phoenixlike from the ashes of civil war. The outcome had established Mamun as the rightful caliph—even though part of the court was still against him, and there was turmoil in Baghdad, where Arab sentiment was still entrenched. He therefore remained with his vizier in Merv, where they hoped to manage the empire from their Persian base. They also turned their attention to appeasing certain factions, especially the Shiites or Alids. In the spring of 817, Mamun named as his heir Ali al-Ridha, revered as an imam; changed the official black Abbasid flags to green (the traditional color of the Shiites); married Ali al-Ridha to his own daughter Umm Habib; minted coins with both their names; and gave another daughter, Umm al-Fadhl, to Ali al-Ridha's son. By this dynastic union, Abbasids were not cut out of the succession—but neither were the Alids.

In Baghdad, Sunni Arab nationalists—along with some Abbasids—went berserk. They coalesced as a faction in July 817; declared Mamun deposed; and put Harun's half brother, Ibrahim al-Mahdi (the poet, gourmet cook, and minstrel), on the throne. His title was affirmed to the public when prayers were said in his name in Baghdad's Great Mosque on July 24.

Ibrahim was not the right man. Though he had been close to Harun, he was not a statesman or leader of standing, but an artist and bon vivant. Known as "the Negro caliph" because of the black African color of his skin, he was little more than a figurehead for those in Baghdad who had cast about for a leader of royal blood. Though given the honorific name al-Mubarak, "the Blessed," to invest him with an imperial sheen, he felt himself cursed, and spent more time in his kitchen cooking than on affairs of state. He did not last long. He enacted no new policies of note and went into hiding as soon as it became clear that Mamun could oust him without a fight.

At the beginning of 818, as Mamun prepared to set out for Baghdad, he made concessions to the Arab party to smooth his return. He acquiesced to the assassination of his vizier, Fadhl ibn Sahl, who had become a divisive figure; disposed of Ali al-Ridha with a bowl of poisoned grapes; and brought his western army up from Rakkah to Baghdad, timing its arrival to coincide with his own, on August 10, 819.

Ali al-Ridha's fate might have been foreseen. That of Mamun's vizier, Ibn Sahl, had been foretold in his horoscope. After his death, the caliph reportedly found among his belongings "a coffer, locked, and sealed. On opening it, he found a little box, closed also with a seal, and within it a paper folded up, containing a piece of silk bearing the following inscription in his own hand: 'In the name of God, the Merciful, the Compassionate! This is the fate which al-Fadhl ibn Sahl has predicted for himself: he will live forty-eight years and be killed between water and fire.' " He lived to that age precisely and was murdered in his heated bath at Sarakhs (a Silk Road post in Central Asia) in February 818.

Meanwhile, Mamun was ready to make peace with his stepmother, Zubaidah, and his uncle and interim caliph Ibrahim. Ibrahim threw himself on Mamun's mercy; in a gracious speech, Zubaidah declared that though she had lost one son who was a caliph she had gained another son and caliph in Mamun. "My loss," she said, "is therefore my gain." He accepted her gesture and restored her wealth and rank. After this she seems to have lived a life of stately retirement until her death.

Mamun's reign thrived. As if to herald a new era of prosperity, glory, and renown, he celebrated in stupendous fashion his own marriage to Buran, the niece of his former vizier. Over the course of the festivities, huge ambergris candles, each weighing two thousand pounds, turned the night into day. Balls of musk the size of melons were scattered among the guests, each one containing a slip of paper bearing the name of an estate, a male or female slave, or some other coveted prize. A thousand pearls were also showered from a gold tray upon the royal couple, who sat on a golden mat. Zubaidah, in a further gesture of her acceptance and affection, gave the bride a royal jacket, with buttons made of diamonds and rubies, that had belonged to the wife of one of the Umayyad caliphs during that dynasty's halcyon days.

Along with the dispensation of such bounty, Mamun's reign ushered in a period of learning and scholarship that surpassed even that of Harun.

Mamun's court emulated the "freethinking" environment that had surrounded the Barmaks (in particular Jafar, who had been Mamun's chief
tutor as a young adult), and exalted the caliph's own faith in reason as the
test for veracity in religious texts.

In pursuit of his own hunger for classical learning, Mamun "established in 830 in Baghdad his famous House of Wisdom, which combined
a library, an academy, and a translation bureau into the most important
educational institute since the foundation of the Alexandrian Library in
the first half of the third century B.C." Learned Jews, Christians, Buddhists, and others flocked to the institute in great numbers; the monasteries of Syria, Asia Minor, and the Levant were combed for manuscripts.
Original research was advanced on every front—especially in geometry, astronomy, zoology, geography, chemistry, mineralogy, and optics.
Mamun also erected in Baghdad an observatory where scholars verified
the length of the solar year, the precession of the equinoxes, the obliquity
of the ecliptic, and other concepts expounded in Ptolemy's *Almagest*. Another observatory was built on the mount overlooking Damascus along
with several in Khurasan.

In rounding up men of knowledge and talent, Mamun reached out to
other monarchs, not always with success. He failed to persuade the Byzantine Emperor Theophilus, for example, to send him a scholar known
as Leo the Mathematician, whose specialized knowledge was deemed too
important to share. Leo's court status made him a sort of Byzantine Alcuin, and he later became head of Constantinople's own elite Academy
or school. Mamun offered Theophilus two thousand pounds of gold and
"eternal peace" for him, which must have been tempting. Ironically, Leo
was subsequently persecuted by the Byzantines as an iconoclast.

He might have fared better under Mamun. In Baghdad, prominent
scholars of all stripes often lived well. Foremost among them was Hunayn ibn Ishaq, a Nestorian Christian from Hira. Hunayn had worked
for an apothecary as a youth, studied Greek, entered the service of Jibril
ibn Bakhtishou, and was "subsequently appointed by Mamun superin-
tendent of his Academy or Institute. In that capacity, he had charge of all
the scientific translation work, in which he enjoyed the collaboration of
his son Ishaq and his nephew Hubaysh ibn al-Hasan, whom he trained."

Numerous works are ascribed to him, including Arabic renditions of Aristotle, Euclid, Galen, and Ptolemy. He is also credited with the earliest extant textbook on ophthalmology, and the translation of two Aristotelian treatises that introduced Muslims to the mathematical or scientific side of music as well as the physical and physiological aspects of the theory of sound.

Aside from the intellectual satisfactions Hunayn gained from his efforts, creature comforts were not lacking. He lived in a palatial home, and on any given evening, after a day's work, it was common for him to retire to one of the fancier public baths for a rubdown and manicure. After that, he would relax with friends and feast on fatted chickens, quinces, Syrian apples, and wine.

When the reigns of Harun and Mamun are taken together, the intellectual awakening that took place under their aegis—not nominally, but with their own active involvement—stands as one of the most significant in the whole history of culture and thought. Aside from its independent contributions, which were prodigious, their combined reign preserved and enlarged the heritage of Greco-Roman learning when that knowledge in the West was almost lost.

chapter sixteen

"OVAL, SQUARE, AND ROUND"

With less exalted results at first, the civil war within the Caliphate had been mirrored by fratricidal strife in Spain.

As the first strong ruler of Spanish Islam, Abd al-Rahman I had been too jealous of his own prerogatives to allow religious leaders to interfere with his conduct of affairs. But under the reign of his amiable and pliable son, Hisham, dubbed "the Just," their influence increased. Hisham was a model of virtue and a sincerely devout prince. He lived for salvation and at the time of his accession, he believed, based on his horoscope, that he had just eight years to live. He therefore "abjured all worldly pleasures," we are told, "and sought his own redemption by charitable works. Clad in the simplest garb, he would wander alone through the streets of [Cordova], mingle with the people, visit the sick, enter the hovels of the poor, and with tender solicitude interest himself in every detail of their needs and woes. Often at the dead of night, even in drenching rain, he would steal from his palace with food for some pious sufferer, and watch beside his lonely bed. Punctual in the performance of his religious duties, he encouraged his subjects to follow his example, and on stormy nights would distribute money to those attending evening service at the mosques." Yet, when required, he was also willing to resort to force to protect his kingdom, and from time to time he took the field to check some aggression by the Christians to the north.

When eight years had expired, Hisham died as predicted and bequeathed to his successor an undiminished realm. Yet "his very goodness
had but served to stir up a new factor of rebellion." These were the imams
or religious leaders he had allowed into his councils of state. Loathe to
give up their newfound power, they clashed almost at once with Hakam I,
the new emir. Hakam was a gay, sociable, and hedonistic man who found
their dour surveillance irksome. Their censure had no impact on his conduct, and after he expelled them from his councils he surrounded himself
with a formidable bodyguard of foreign (mostly European) troops. That
guard, popularly known as "the Mutes," offended both Arabs and Christian converts (also known as Renegades) since most of the Mutes could
not speak Arabic. In pulpit sermons, Hakam was excoriated as a "profligate" and denounced for his "foreign" and wayward ways.

The Mutes were not to be trifled with; nor was Hakam cowed. In
805, when riots erupted in Cordova, seventy-two of the ringleaders were
crucified. Uprisings in the Renegade suburb followed, culminating in a
full-scale revolt in 814. Out of fear for his life, Hakam barricaded himself
in his fortified compound as a mob of religious fanatics advanced toward
its gates. The Mutes, in converging columns, descended upon the march-
ers in a fury. The mob was dispersed, its leaders killed, and the suburb
burned to the ground. Thousands of families were expelled from Spain
and sought asylum in Fez, Alexandria, and Crete.

To preempt such a revolt in Toledo, also a hotbed of Renegade unrest, Hakam arranged for a banquet to which he invited those whose
loyalty he had reason to suspect. As each guest entered a courtyard, an
executioner stood ready with his sword. One by one they were all dispatched and thrown into a ditch. This massacre became famous in Spanish history; yet based on the versified memorandum Hakam addressed
to his son, he was convinced he had the right to act as he did: "Just as a
tailor plies his needle to sew together lengths of cloth, so have I used my
sword to keep my dominions united and intact. None of my frontiers
are under enemy jurisdiction and the skulls of rebellious subjects lie like
split gourds in the sun. . . . Peaceful then are the provinces which I hand
down to you, O my son! They are a couch on which you may repose

undisturbed: I have taken care that no rebellion should break in upon your sleep."

Hakam died in 822 after a reign of twenty-six years, and his son and successor, Abd al-Rahman II, had indeed a more tranquil reign. He luxuriated in his inherited bounty, adorned his court with literati, built up a large harem, and had twenty-four children by numerous wives. Somehow he also acquired the famous "dragon's necklace" that had belonged to Zubaidah, the wife of Harun al-Rashid. He built palaces, laid out gardens, beautified his capital with mosques, mansions, and bridges, patronized scholars, and fostered the arts. Thanks to the ingenuity of his hydraulic engineers, numerous gardens were supplied by water brought from the mountains by means of lead pipes and dispersed throughout the city to marble fountains, reservoirs, and tanks. To appease his appetite for learning—he was a dedicated bibliophile—his agents scoured the bookstalls of Cairo, Alexandria, Baghdad, and Damascus for rare and unusual works. Fittingly enough, he is generally commended for strengthening the connections between Spanish Islam and centers of Muslim culture in the East.

Under his rule, Cordova continued to thrive as a commercial metropolis, renowned for its silks, damascened leathers, and forged iron. The Mediterranean coast of Spain swarmed with fishermen and sailors; merchants and middlemen of all kinds provided his artisans with the raw materials they needed for their industries and crafts. Glassware, rugs, bound manuscript books, enamel, and sculptured ivory were all exported to the West. His court also attracted talent far and wide. One of its most celebrated members was an outstanding Persian musician named Ziryab, who had been driven out of Baghdad by Ishaq al-Mausili, the great musicologist and singer who had thrived under Harun and his son Mamun. Ishaq had been jealous of Ziryab's skill and striking innovations, which included the addition of a fifth string to the lute and the use of eagles' talons instead of wooden plectra for plucking the strings. Ziryab found refuge in Cordova (ever eager to be Baghdad's rival) and became a favorite of the emir. A "popular figure among the smart set," we are told, he became an arbiter of taste and fashion—much as Jafar Barmak had been in Baghdad in his time.

IN BAGHDAD, MAMUN REIGNED FOR TWENTY YEARS AND WAS forty-eight when he died near Tarsus in 833, on one of his Byzantine campaigns. Most caliphs met an "assisted fate" and that was probably the case with Mamun. It was a hot autumn day, and as he sat with his brother Mutasim on the bank of a mountain stream, he suddenly fell ill, then expired. He was promptly succeeded by Mutasim, the last of the three sons of Harun al-Rashid to reign.

Mamun's crown had been maintained with Persian support, and the result had been a vast increase of Persian influence at the Baghdad court. Mamun's successors failed to curb this trend. But already another element was stirring, for by almost the same process Persian power would be supplanted by that of the Turks. Muslim conquests in eastern Persia and Turkestan had brought a host of Turkic peoples into the Islamic fold, and in the course of their assimilation, caliphs began to rely on Turkish mercenaries to bolster their legions and strengthen their palace guard. This began to happen in the time of Mutasim. He reveled in the luxuries of court life, but in 836 popular hostility toward his Turkish escort forced him to leave Baghdad for Samarra, which became the seat of government for eight successive caliphs over the course of fifty years.

The story of one of the last, Mustain, reversed that of the first, when the Turkish bodyguard of his cousin and rival for the Caliphate, Mutazz, chased him down the Tigris to Baghdad, and there placed him under siege. How thoroughly the Abbasid Caliphate was undermined would be shown all at once in 861, when just twenty-eight years after Mamun's reign, the Caliph Mutawakkil was murdered by his own servants at the instigation of his son. Almost immediately imperial authority began to fail. Turkish troops raised and deposed succeeding rulers. In the great towns of the Tigris region there was popular tumult and revolt. One famous rising originated in the lake and marsh district around Basra, where large numbers of black slaves, mostly from the east coast of Africa, known then as "the land of the Zenj" (that is, Zanzibar), toiled in the mines.

Long before this crisis, parts of the Caliphate had been giving way to centrifugal strains. The independent kingdom of Spain continued to thrive under the hostile Umayyads; Morocco and Kairouan (Libya) had become separate states. At the end of the ninth century a Shiite sect known as the Karmathians took over Yemen and even carried off Mecca's Black Stone from the Kaaba; at the beginning of the tenth, the Fatimids, real or pretended descendants of Fatima, the daughter of the Prophet, made themselves masters of Syria, Egypt, and beyond. Some of these rulers recognized the caliph as their sovereign, stamped his name upon their coins, and gave him precedence in public prayer. But their deference was largely a formality. Even so, though other states fell away "like a bundle of unbound sticks," they remained Islamic, continued to diversify Muslim culture, and wielded their own might.

In short, while the Baghdad Caliphate contracted, the world of Islam grew. Its troops and agents made new inroads into Europe and Central Asia, and few courts could afford to be without their own Arab experts in the realms of diplomacy, commerce, and trade. Independent of Baghdad, the lesser North African emirates established their own spheres of influence across the Mediterranean Sea.

At the same time, Byzantine power had begun to wane. Developments within Armenia exemplified the trend. Armenia had long been divided between the Arabs and the Byzantines in a schism reflected in the country at large. For the Armenians, division was a familiar plight. Before Islam had come to dominate the region, Armenia had been caught between the Roman and Persian Empires. The country (not yet a nation) had been partitioned between them, until Greater Armenia had been consolidated as a single political entity by the Armenian king Trdat IV the Great. By then Christianity had spread from Syria into Cappodocia in Asia Minor, entering Greater Armenia from both the south and west. The official conversion of the country took place when Trdat the Great himself converted, declared Christianity the state religion, and established the Armenian Apostolic Church. As a monotheistic religion, Christianity provided the ideological foundations for a strong, centralized monarchy, which set the king, as the only deputy of a single God, at its head. Trdat the Great and his supporters saw this clearly and used the faith to their own ends. Pantheistic pagan traditions were uprooted and old temples destroyed. The Romans had supported these developments but the Persians did not sit idly by. Scarcely had Constantine the Great established his power base in Constantinople than the Persian king advanced his armies across the Syrian desert into Armenia and by 387 nearly 80 percent of Greater Armenia (including parts of Georgia) had been ceded to his troops. When Persia (and its imperial dominions) in turn fell to the Arabs, Armenia was formally annexed to the Caliphate in 701.

The Caliphate stationed Arab forces in key cities, imposed Islamic law, forced Armenian conscripts to serve in the caliph's legions, but allowed the Armenian Church to play an important role in Armenian life. Over the course of the next hundred years or so, pro-Arab and pro-Byzantine factions competed among the populace at large. Harun al-Rashid had tried to alter the country's demographics by promoting Arab settlements, and in western Armenia, Harun built and fortified a number of towns, including Haruniyah (named after himself), furnished with garrisons and mosques. In 806 he also rewarded an Armenian noble by the name of Ashot with the title of "Prince." Upon Ashot's death, Harun's son Mamun elevated Ashot's eldest son, Bagarat Bagratuni, to the post of "Prince of Princes," and appointed Bagarat's brother, Smbat, army chief of staff. But Armenia proved as unruly and recalcitrant a province to rule as Khurasan. The Caliphate could not maintain its control, and by 859 the independent kingdom of Armenia—under Ashot Msaker (the Meat Eater)—emerged. In the end, this was less of a loss for the Arabs than for the Byzantines, who failed to recover their former sway, while the Arabs had shifted their attention to more promising frontiers. Chief among these was southern Europe, where the conquest of Sicily was already under way.

The base for this new onslaught was the North African coast.

The heart of North Africa was known as the Maghreb (an area roughly equivalent to modern Tunisia) largely populated by Berbers— a non-Semitic, non-Arab tribal group. They were a "powerful, formidable, numerous, and brave people," as the Arab historian Ibn Khaldun described them, and at first they resented the intrusion of Islam into their lives. But like the Arabs, they were clansmen and had the same reverence for lineage and rank. In time a new imperial province called Ifriqiya (which encompassed all or part of Libya, Tunisia, Algeria, and

Morocco—essentially northwest Africa) was established with Kairouan (south of modern-day Tunis) at its heart.

Harun al-Rashid had appointed Ibrahim ibn al-Aghlab as its governor. Though serving at the caliph's pleasure, Aghlab and his successors, the Aghlabids, ruled independently as emirs until 909, presiding over a court that became a center for commerce, learning, and the arts. They built palaces, fortifications, and waterworks; a famed university attached to their great mosque, which attracted scholars from all over the Islamic world; and created their own large army, navy, and diplomatic corps. To protect their own interests—namely, the safety of their merchants and the coastline of their realm—the Aghlabids began to clash with the Byzantines in the eastern Mediterranean Sea.

Sicily soon emerged as the main contested prize. From its strategic location in the Mediterranean, the Byzantines had been able to control shipping and strike the coastal Muslim cities of North Africa and the Levant. They devoted considerable attention to the island's protection and had declared it a military province, or "theme." They installed a military governor at Messina, strengthened the coastal defenses, and fortified some inland towns. A kind of stalemate was reached, with each side maneuvering for advantage in the military and commercial spheres. Muslim fleets probed Byzantine coastal defenses; the Greeks stockpiled arms. Meanwhile, a series of trade agreements induced both sides from time to time to suspend hostilities, which allowed Byzantine merchants to operate in North Africa and Arabs to trade goods at Sicilian ports.

The fate of Sicily ultimately turned on the mercenary lust of a Byzantine admiral named Euphemius, who had ravished a nun. The Byzantine emperor demanded the admiral be punished, but the latter defied him and appealed for help to the North African emir. In effect, Euphemius offered Sicily to him as a tribute-paying province on condition that he be appointed its lord. The emir agreed, and on June 13, 827, an elite army of more than ten thousand men—Arabs, Berbers, Spanish Moors, and Sudanese blacks—embarked in a hundred ships, landed at Mazara del Vallo, Sicily, gained the southern shore of the island, and advanced on Syracuse. Syracuse repelled the assault (thanks in part to malaria, which thinned the besiegers' ranks) and for three years the conquest stalled.

Then Palermo fell in September 831, and thereafter the war for Sicily went on for fifty years.

District by district, the invaders made headway. Meanwhile, city-state rivalry among the Christian powers on the mainland facilitated wider gains. The Republic of Naples allied itself with the Arabs against the Lombards of Benevento, and, with Neapolitan help, the Arabs over-whelmed a Venetian fleet and occupied Brindisi in 838. From Brindisi they advanced along the Adriatic and Tyrrhenian coasts. Before long they had taken Taranto and Ancona, which they sacked and burned. In 846, some ten thousand Arabs in seventy-five ships appeared at the mouth of the Tiber and threatened Rome. Though Pope Gregory I had constructed a fortress at Ostia at the river's mouth, the Muslims pushed past it and sacked everything of value they could, including the Basilicas of St. Peter and St. Paul. The shrines of both saints were "profaned and plundered"; and the Franks—nominal protectors of the Holy See—failed "to lift a finger in its defense."

That was not surprising. For most in the Latin West, the new Arab aggression was seen as a problem mainly for the Byzantines. Even some Sicilians were reluctant to resist since they had grown weary of their Byz-antine yoke. What difference did it make whether they were obliged to pay tribute to the emperor of Constantinople or to an emir? Meanwhile, Sicily had become a bridgehead for the occupation of Sardinia as well as southern Italy. Rome would again be threatened, the pope obliged to pay a large annual tribute, and northern Italy subjected to Muslim raids. Calabria would be devastated, Capua destroyed. In 847, moreover, Bari became the capital of a small independent Islamic state. The only real setback suffered by the Muslims came in 849 when a Muslim fleet was destroyed by a Christian armada near Ostia, thanks largely to a storm that blew up when the engagement was under way. The armada returned to port safely, but the Muslim ships were scattered and wrecked.

On the island of Sicily itself, the Muslims began their final siege of Syracuse in the summer of 877. On the twenty-first of May 878, it fell. From a doleful cell into which he had been thrust with other church-men, a monk by the name of Theodosius recounted in a letter to his arch-deacon, Leo, the city's wrenching fate. The walls of the city, he wrote, had been undermined by tunnels and pounded day and night by a hail of stones hurled against them by catapults. The fighting on the sea had also been fierce, as one by one the ships of the Byzantines were sunk or set ablaze. Inexorably the Muslims had advanced to the very gates of the city in "tortoise-shell" formation with overlapping shields.

Meanwhile, the starving populace had been reduced to eating leather, animal skins, and bone dust (ground in a mill and mixed with water to form a gruel). On the black market, even a lump of dough was worth its weight in gold. Strange maladies, like lockjaw, arose from these conditions, and by the end of the siege many of the defenders were bloated like bladders, crippled, or paralyzed. The worst was yet to come. Once the city's main tower and rampart had been toppled, the Muslims poured in. As a general massacre began, Theodosius and two other monks quickly shed their clerical vestments and hid behind the cathedral altar, where they trusted to their bishop's prayers. No sooner had the latter begun to commend the church to its guardian angel than "behold the enemy was there. They wandered through the whole building, their drawn swords wet with blood. . . . then one of them moved round and came to the holy altar, and there he found us hiding between the altar and the bishop's chair. Yet he did nothing cruel, for in a miracle of mercy God had softened his heart." Soon afterward, the emir himself arrived, stripped the cathedral of every treasured thing, and pitched his tent in the nave. Theodosius himself was shut up for a month in a crypt aswarm with vermin, then taken to Palermo in chains.

After Syracuse was taken, only a few Christian enclaves remained. The Muslims scarcely gave them a thought. One of them, Taormina, held out until 902, seventy-five years after the invasion began. By then the Muslims had established some 320 fortresses throughout the island which they had divided into three administrative districts centered at Palermo, Messina, and Syracuse.

Under their aegis, "the land took on a new look." They encouraged the growth of small holdings, which increased the yield of farms; cleared the land; and to irrigate it fully, built canals and installed a system of siphons and waterwheels. They grew pistachios and almonds on hillsides and planted Persian melons, date palms, and vegetables along the island's rivers and streams. Aside from new fruits and vegetables, they brought in cotton, mulberry trees for silkworms, sumac for tanning and dyeing, and hemp for caulking ships. The development of agriculture generated a number of related industries, such as textiles, rope-making, matting, paper, and silk. Gold, silver, lead, mercury, vitriol, ammonium salt, antimony and alum were also mined (especially in the region of Mount Etna) and, to the dismay of the Byzantines, the Muslims now had access to some of the naphtha and sulfur deposits used for Greek fire. A timber industry also grew up around the forests in the broad valley above Cefalu. The scale of maritime traffic increased as new shipyards were built. Despite the official prohibition against drink, vineyards soon blossomed and Sicilian Arab poets saluted the wine distilled from native grapes. Enterprise in animal husbandry led to the raising of large herds of horses, cattle, sheep, and goats. Even the veteran fishermen of Sicily learned new techniques from the Muslims to improve their catch. When schools of tuna arrived each spring off Mazara, the Muslims corralled them by beating the water in a circle and rowing about in the teeming current in ever-tightening rings.

With advances in agriculture and commerce, towns and cities grew. Mazara, which lay at the wide mouth of a navigable river where many ships could be berthed, was transformed into an elegant port with courtyards, mosques, and public baths. In typical Muslim fashion, its intersecting alleyways and streets exfoliated like the limbs of a branching tree. Marsala (Mars-al-Allah, "port of Allah")—formerly known as Lilybaeum and a depressed town under the Byzantines—also became a major military base. Trapani, in turn, was developed by the Muslims as a commercial center, excelling in the working of coral and gold. At the same time, the demographics of Muslim settlement had a divergent impact on the island's economic life. Because most Muslims sailed for Sicily from the Tunisian headland, they settled in the island's western half. That favored the expansion of the port of Palermo over Messina and Syracuse. Palermo became the island capital, where the emir built his castle inland from the gulf. In its heyday, the city was famed throughout the Muslim world for its prosperity, beauty, mosques, and minarets and often compared to Cairo in Egypt and Cordova in Spain. It was also the preeminent place in Sicily where Arabs, Berbers, North African blacks, Greeks, Jews, Persians, and soldiers from as far away as Russia converged.

As a result of the conquest and occupation of North Africa and Sicily, trade with Europe greatly expanded, with Palermo, Mazara, Kairouan, and Fez serving as its hubs. An immense economic network stretched from Syria to Spain, and communication could be conveyed from one region to the next with near-telegraphic speed. It was said, in fact, that "a chain of watch-towers could flash news from Alexandria [in Egypt] to Ceuta [in Morocco] in a single day." Caravans from southern Morocco flowed in a steady stream to Tunisia and from there found their way to the markets of Sicilian ports. The Sicilian gold coin, the rubaya, or quarter dinar, was in demand from Syria to Palestine, while the bustling commerce at Kairouan alone reputedly brought into the public treasury annually "between seven hundred and eight hundred million dinars." In time, the wealth of Kairouan would be exceeded by that of Fez, which at its height boasted 785 mosques, eighty canals, forty-two "pools for ablutions," ninety-three public baths, 472 mills, 89,236 houses, a thousand shops, two silk markets, numerous textile factories, twelve copper foundries, four hundred paper manufactories, 188 pottery workshops, and assorted tanneries and other enterprises where items from soap to crystal were made.

One Syrian trader was so enthralled by all this bounty that he wrote a handbook for fellow merchants titled *The Beauties of Commerce*, in which he described the rules of his profession in detail. His financial sophistication would do credit to an analyst today. "There are three kinds of merchants," he explained: "he who travels, he who stocks, he who exports. Their trade is carried out in three ways: cash sale with a time limit for delivery, purchase on credit with payment by installments, and contracts whereby a merchant is entrusted with capital for investment in trade in return for a profit share. The investor bears all the risk on the capital, the merchant the labor cost."

None of the vagaries of the textile and spice trades escaped him. Any itinerant merchant, he pointed out, must also exercise great caution. He ought not to lull himself into the belief that his hopes will be fulfilled when he reaches his destination, because the journey may be delayed or interdicted or thwarted by some unforeseen event. He will then have to sell his wares, for better or worse, wherever he finds himself or disembarks. If he has not prepared himself in advance for such a contingency, he will suffer a great loss. . . . [With that in view], he should carry with him a price list, so he can determine the difference in the cost of his wares from place to place. He should also take into account the tariffs he may have to pay, and add these to the price he charges so he can accurately figure the profit to be made.

Finally, whatever item a merchant decides to stock up on, "he ought to buy in stages—not all at once but at four different times separated by intervals of fifteen days. . . . The reason being that the price of the purchased ware may rise, fall, or remain steady. If the price goes up, he can expect some profit. . . . On the other hand, if the price drops, he can congratulate himself in two respects—first, because he has protected himself against the drop; and, second, because he can now buy the item more cheaply. If the price remains unchanged, he can wait until it falls again to rebuild his stock."

Sicily's new prosperity reflected Islam's comparatively benign rule. Taxation overall, on Muslim and non-Muslim alike, was less onerous than under the Byzantines, and though some churches and synagogues were converted into mosques, most Christians and Jews were accorded the status of protected minorities (or "dhimmis"). That meant that in return for the payment of a poll tax, they were guaranteed the safety of their persons and property and largely free to live as communities according to their own laws. However, they were forbidden to proselytize or flaunt their beliefs—for example, by ringing church bells, drinking wine in public, or reading scripture aloud when (or where) it might reach a Muslim's ears. They were also prohibited from building houses higher than those of their Muslim neighbors, forced to yield the right of way to Muslims on the street, and forbidden to ride horses or bear arms.

Many conquered Sicilians converted to Islam—often, no doubt, to reduce their tax burden—even as the makeup of the population changed.

When the Muslims first arrived, Sicily had a population of about 1.5 million. Muslim immigration increased it by a third, to about 2 million; by the end of the period of Muslim rule, about half the population "had their roots in the Islamic world." Arabs dominated in the north; Berbers around Agrigento in the south. Palermo had 300,000 inhabitants, more than all the cities of Germany combined. One Christian who came to Sicily in 883 described it as "so full of citizens and strangers that there seems to be collected there all the Saracen folk from East to West and from North to South. . . . Blended with the Sicilians, Greeks, Lombards, and Jews, are Arabs, Berbers, Persians, Tartars, and blacks—some wrapped in long robes and turbans, some clad in skins. The faces you see are oval, square, and round, of every profile and complexion, with beards and hair of every variety of color or cut."

Even though Sicily belonged to the periphery of the Islamic world, several factors helped the arts and learning to thrive. Weekly and sometimes daily public lectures on a variety of topics were open to all, and those who taught in schools linked to mosques were exempt from fighting in wars. Dissident, independent scholars fleeing persecution in North Africa, Spain, and the Caliphate also found a refuge in its cities and towns. Conversely, Muslim scholars based in Sicily traveled during periods of turmoil to North Africa or Egypt, or ventured farther east. Their comings and goings kept Sicily in the mainstream of Islamic innovation and scholarship.

chapter seventeen

"CITY OF THE FLOWER"

et Sicily could not compare to Spain. Despite near-constant turmoil and strife, Spain's emirs had maintained themselves at Cordova in a manner that rivaled Baghdad in its Golden Age.

As the emirate evolved, however, such grandeur might have seemed in doubt. Though Abd al-Rahman II had sustained the semblance of a prosperous and coherent kingdom, all the permanent causes of discord— race, religion, tribal jealousy, personal ambition—remained and limited his capacity to rule. When Abd al-Rahman III ascended the throne in 912, at the age of twenty-one, he found the land torn by racial division, religious hate, lawless violence, and a potentially disastrous attempt on the part of both Toledo and Seville to establish themselves as independent city-states. He also had to contend with a powerful rebel in Andalusia named Omar ibn Hafsun, the Muslim descendant of a Gothic count. Operating out of an ancient castle on Mount Bobastro, Omar had challenged the hegemony of three emirs over the course of thirty-seven years. After many vicissitudes of fortune he succeeded in isolating Cordova and tried to make himself ruler of Spain. To attract the help of Christian powers, he renounced Islam, embraced Christ, and adopted Samuel as his baptismal name.

The new emir might have been daunted, for all the boasted achievements of his forebears seemed undone. Not so; and he would prove the greatest of the line. He was energetic, resolute, and daring; quelled the rebellious cities; subdued Arab lords who wished to enjoy a feudal sovereignty on their estates; and maintained his authority on the Mediterranean by powerful fleets. He also "invited to his councils men of diverse faiths, adjusted his alliances to maintain a balance of power among his neighbors, and administered the government with industry and attention to detail." Omar ibn Hafsun was ultimately humbled, and after he died, Muslims cried for vengeance and his "impure bones" were exhumed and impaled on stakes.

Meanwhile, the emir had been engaged in a holy war against the Christians of the north. Here the land of the Basques occupied the center, bridging the Pyrenees. To the east lay the still embryonic kingdoms of Navarre and Aragon; to the west, those areas that developed into the kingdoms of Castile and Leon. In 914, the king of Leon had captured a Muslim general and "nailed his head to the wall of a frontier fort." In 920 the emir took the field himself, demolished a number of Christian strongholds, and at Val de Junqueras ("vale of reeds") met and defeated the forces of Navarre. After overrunning part of the region, he recovered Saragossa and reestablished his undisputed sway.

Under Abd al-Rahman III, Spanish Islam achieved its golden age. In 929, at the height of his fortune and prestige, he also assumed the title of caliph, and so declared himself the rival and equal of the Abbasids of Baghdad and the Fatimids of Cairo and Fez. To lend further significance to his gesture, he adopted a religious surname: "al-Nasser li-Din Allah," "he who fights for Allah." By then, Baghdad's own power had pitifully dwindled, but the Fatimids, on the rise, had begun to compete with the Spanish Umayyads for hegemony of the western Mediterranean and the Maghreb. Not to be preempted, Abd al-Rahman swept along the North African coast and claimed it for his own.

Meanwhile, a few miles from Cordova he had begun to erect a palace that soon became a city unto itself: Medinat al-Zahra, "City of the Flower." Named after al-Zahra, "the Fairest," one of his wives, Medinat would occupy twenty-five years of his reign and much of that of his son. Ten thousand workmen labored daily at its building, installed some four thousand columns of marble and onyx, and fifteen hundred doors coated with polished brass. Its soaring Hall of the Caliphs featured sixteen ebony doors and numerous ivory arches resting on crystal pillars as transparent as glass. In the center of the room stood a basin of quicksilver "whose undulating surface reflected the dancing rays of the sun."

The caliph preferred Medinat al-Zahra to any other abode and placed his court there to escape Cordova's bustling crowds. "On cool evenings," we are told, he "would converse with friends in Latin or enjoy the sallies of his blind jester while sipping a cup of mint-flavored tea. Sometimes young dancing girls, their legs swathed in transparent chiffon pantaloons, would whirl about, waving scarves to the rhythm of tambourines and flutes." Despite this whiff of decadence, he proved a man of self-restraint, and from the range of his interests and learning would be remembered as "the Harun al-Rashid of the West." The epithet was more than just. For in every sphere of research and study Spanish Islam had come to rival, and perhaps excel, Baghdad at its height.

It was at al-Zahra that Abd al-Rahman III also granted audiences to envoys from foreign powers. He did not hesitate to flaunt his power. One day,

when he wanted to impress some Christian plenipotentiaries, he had matting spread from the gates of Cordova to the portals of the grounds. A double row of soldiers lined the way on either side, the tips of their unsheathed swords forming a canopy of steel over the heads of the ambassadors, who walked beneath this shining arch. When they came to the entrance hall they saw a long brocaded rug and, seated on both sides, richly gowned lords. The Christians bowed low to each of the noblemen, thinking him the emir. Finally they arrived at a courtyard where the ground was strewn with sand; in the center, his head bowed, sat Abd al-Rahman III. A Koran, a sword, and a burning fire were before him. As the ambassadors knelt, the monarch raised his head and said: "Allah has commanded us to request that you yield to Him," and he pointed to the Koran. "Should you refuse, we will use force," and he pointed to the sword. "If we kill you, you will go there," and he pointed to the fire. Overcome with fear, the envoys acquiesced. . . . and left without another word.

Much like his great forebear Abd al-Rahman I, however, Abd al-Rahman III seems to have lived in a hell of his own. When he died, he left behind, in his own handwriting, a note in which he stated that in the course of his whole life, with all its apparent earthly blessings, he had enjoyed only fourteen days of "pure and genuine happiness and content."

In 961, he was succeeded by Hakam II, his son, who sought to emulate his father, kept the Christian kingdoms of the north in check, but unwisely became enmeshed in an African war with the Idrisites of Morocco, an instance of the Sunni-Shiite feud. Hakam was succeeded by his own son Hisham II (976–1008), whose long reign was wholly dominated by Muhammad Ibn Abi Amir, his famed vizier. The latter was master of the realm. He courted all factions; had his name inscribed on the coinage and mentioned in the Friday prayer; wore royal robes; and after 992 replaced the caliph's name with his own on all official documents and scripts.

Twice each year he also led fierce campaigns against the kingdoms of the north. These culminated in 997 with the devastation of the magnificent church of Santiago de Compostela, a sacred Christian shrine. In honor of his achievements, he assumed the surname of al-Mansur (in Spanish "Almanzor," "the Victorious through God"), and when he died in 1002, he was buried with his head on a pillow filled with the dust that had clung to his armor on campaign. The following epitaph was engraved on his tomb:

His story in his relics you may trace,
As though he stood before you face to face.
Never will Time bring forth his peer again,
Nor one to guard, like him, the gaps of Spain.

That was true. After his death, no one so able and Argus-eyed arose to take his place. The abdication in 1008 of the fainthearted Hisham II ushered in a period of bloody internecine struggles in which five or six caliphs followed each other in rapid succession on the throne. This self-rending began when Almanzor's own son was poisoned by his brother, who in turn was overthrown. With a quaintness characteristic of royal spite, one subsequent caliph had the severed heads of his opponents converted into flowerpots to adorn the banks of the Guadalquivir. Another, to escape assassination, hid himself in a bathroom heater, only to be discovered and dragged to his death. Two years later, the caliph who had killed him tried to evade a similar fate by disguising himself in flight as a veiled singing girl. He, in turn, was poisoned by one of his own aides. In the attendant turmoil, even Cordova was pillaged by rival powers. By then Islamic Spain had been dismembered into a number of small provincial states, each the seat of more or less ephemeral Arab and Berber ruling families, known as the Reyes de Taifas (or "provincial kings"). That opened the door to militant Muslim brotherhoods from North Africa who crossed into Spain to help beat back Christian inroads led in part by the warrior El Cid.

ISLAM'S DAY IN SICILY, TOO, WOULD PASS. THE ARAB AND Berber populations never fused, and the Muslim army was rent by garrison rivalries, conflicting ambitions, and tribal quarrels. The Sunni-Shiite schism that bedeviled Islam also found its way to Sicily and undermined Muslim strength. Since most Sunnis were Arabs and most Berbers Shiites, the two problems overlapped. At first the Sunnis held power, but over time Shiite standing, fostered by the Fatimid caliphs of Cairo, grew. By 909, they had toppled the former regimes and gained Sicily and Tunisia for their own.

In the latter part of the eleventh century, Sicily would fall to the Normans, whose conquest was swift and fierce. A century of civil war preceded their advent, and in the course of that war the once-united island had dissolved (as did Spain) into a number of principalities or petty states. Beginning with the conquest of Messina in 1061, the Normans displaced several emirs, with the fractious Muslims unable to coalesce against their advance. Yet in indirect ways the Muslims prevailed. Many of the Normans who settled in Sicily embraced Muslim culture, which was accorded a privileged position at the Norman court; and most Norman rulers proved generous patrons of Greek and Islamic learning and the arts. Accepting the multiethnic society they acquired, they wisely held that

"Latins, Greeks, Jews, and Saracens shall be judged by their own judges each according to their laws."

There was sound policy in all this, of course. The Normans were outnumbered by their Muslim subjects and sought to tame the religious fervor that might have seethed through their ranks. Even so, a genuine Arab-Norman culture developed, which mobilized Arab architects and artisans to build monuments and adorn churches, enlisted Muslims to serve in the army and Arab military engineers to build siege engines and forts. Sicily also became a clearinghouse where Eastern and Western scholars could meet, and since the Norman kings and their successors held not only the island but southern Italy, they provided a bridge for the transmission into Europe of Islam's vibrant cultural life.

Arab rather than Byzantine influence, moreover, was predominant in the organization and protocol of the Norman court. Three of the Norman kings of Sicily assumed Arabic royal names, which appeared on their coinage; and the personal stamp of one of them, Roger II, bore an Arabic motto in praise of God based on a verse in the Koran. On various documents he also called himself, in Arabic, "the great and holy (or venerable) king." Though the crown he wore was Byzantine, his coronation mantle was adorned with an Arabic inscription and dated, in true Muslim style, from the year of Muhammad's flight. Like some other Norman kings, he also spoke perfect Arabic. With his harem, eunuchs, and so on, moreover, he lived much like a Muslim prince. His physicians were also Arabs, as was the admiral commanding his fleet; his chief minister was a veritable Grand Vizier with the title of "Emir of Emirs."

It was at the court of Roger II that the greatest of Arab geographers, Idrisi, wrote his monumental compendium of geography known as "Kitab Rujjar" ("the book of Roger") and drew his famed map of the world. A Moroccan Arab, Abu Abdallah Muhammad al-Sharif al-Idrisi composed this work based on his own extensive travels and a collation of numerous navigators' accounts. Completed in 1154, it took him fifteen years to write and was the most elaborate description of the world in medieval times. In it he described the earth as a globe with a circumference of 22,900 miles and pictured it as "stable in space like the yolk of an egg." He distinguished hemispheres, climates, oceans, seas, rivers, gulfs, mountains, deserts, and even major caravan routes and roads; correctly depicted the relative position and number of the lakes that form the tributaries of the Nile (not "discovered" by Western explorers for another seven hundred years); and included some account of the customs, religion, dress, trade, and other characteristics of many countries in the world. In his description of the British Isles, for example, he wrote: "The island of l'Angleterre [England] is a great island, shaped like the head of an ostrich; in it are populous cities, high mountains, flowing streams, and level ground. It has great fertility and its people are hardy, resolute, and vigorous. The winter is permanent. The nearest land to it is . . . the land of France, and between [England] and the continent there is a strait twelve miles wide. . . ." He singled out various English localities as worthy of remark, including London, Durham, Lincoln, Dover, Southampton, and "the narrow part of the island called Cornwall which is like a bird's beak." Scotland, he wrote, "adjoins the island of England and is a long peninsula to the north." Idrisi's crowning achievement, however, was a large, composite map transported onto a huge silver planisphere six feet in diameter and weighing four hundred pounds. One side of it featured the zodiac and its constellations; the other depicted lands, regions, countries, and seas.

Yet too idyllic a picture of Sicilian Muslims should not be drawn. The Norman conquest had rendered the Muslim populace dependent; Muslim rebels were deported; and in their foreign policy, the Norman kings championed the Cross.

epilogue

TURBAN AND COWL

Over time, the Byzantines and Muslims had found little new reason to contend. Byzantine concerns had long since turned to other fronts. In 944 and 971, the empire had hammered out a far-reaching commercial treaty with the Russians, kept up its battle with the Bulgars to the northwest; forged trade relations with Italian city-states; and involved the Venetians in its successful attempt to prevent the Normans from wresting the Balkans from its hands. In return, the Venetians exacted the unique privilege for its merchants of trading in nearly all Byzantine ports free of customs dues. In 1155, a similar pact was forged with Genoa to further contain Norman power. But the fate of the empire would ultimately be decided by the rise in western Asia of the Seljuk Turks.

Indeed, even as Islamic conquests began to falter in the West, far to the east they made notable gains. There Turkish dynasties carved out new kingdoms for themselves north of the Hindu Kush. Before long, hungry Muslim eyes beyond the mountain passes looked down upon the rich Ganges plain. Muslim invaders were led by the Ghaznavids, Central Asian converts to Islam of Turkic stock who had advanced from slaves and mercenaries of the Caliphate to masters of an expanding Afghan domain. Chief among them was Abdul Kasim Mahmud, known as "Mahmud of Ghazna." For his ruthlessness and might, Mahmud would one day rank with Tamerlane and Genghiz Khan.

Zeal for Islam was his theme, and as a staunch Muslim he considered the treasure acquired in his warring no more than his pious reward. His mixed forces—Afghan, Uighur, Arab, Turk—were ferocious in war and plunder, and his steppeland cavalry habitually outflanked "the ponderous phalanx of elephants that was still the pride of Hindu battlefields." Massacre and destruction marked his path, as slaves of both sexes were carried off by the hundred thousand, and temples and treasuries looted and stripped. He pierced to the heart of Hindustan, to Kanauj on the Ganges, through the desert to Kathiawar and the fabulously rich temple of Somnath on the coast, where fifty thousand Hindus were killed in a three-day battle and the famous shrine despoiled.

At Ghazna, his capital, in the Afghan hills, the plunder was put on display in his palace, where his subjects came to gape at diamonds the size of pomegranates, unbored pearls and rubies, emeralds as green as "sprigs of young myrtle," and jewels that "glistened like iced wine."

Meanwhile, to the west, he had also established himself at Bukhara and Samarkand—that is, across the whole region that Rafi ibn Laith, the rebel against Harun, had tried in vain to seize in the caliph's last days. Mahmud's field of action extended from Iraq to the Ganges.

Nothing like it had been seen since Alexander the Great.

Ultimately, the Ghaznavids, as Mahmud's dynastic line was called, fell victim to one of the unruly Afghan tribes within their own sphere. These were the highlanders known as the Suri, who occupied the rugged hills of Ghor. Their chieftain, Muhammad Ghori, led a series of campaigns deep into India and unlike Mahmud's conquests, Ghori's would last. Muslim rule was extended southward, and for hundreds of years Muhammadan kings—known as Moghuls—occupied the Delhi throne.

Much of today's turmoil throughout the entire region may be traced directly to this time, when so many dragon's teeth were sown.

THE RAMIFICATIONS OF SOME THINGS NEVER END. BEGINning at the end of the eleventh century, Latin Christianity and Islam clashed in a series of confrontations known as the Crusades. Their aim was the redemption of the Holy Land but led immediately to an attempt to establish a Christian state (the "Latin Kingdom of Jerusalem") in the

Muslim east. That turned the Mediterranean basin into a battleground between Christian and Muhammadan power.

The First Crusade began in 1096. At that illusory moment, the circle of history seemed to be completing its sacred course. Five hundred years after the first Muslim conquests began, the True Cross was once more planted in Jerusalem and Jerusalem itself returned to Christian hands. Christian knights, however, proved unable to consolidate their gains. They failed to occupy strategic sites, such as Aleppo and Damascus, and no sooner had they expanded across the Jordan River, dividing Syria from Egypt, than they were exposed to attack from Iraq. Meanwhile, the capture of Jerusalem had been sullied by the wholesale slaughter of Jews and Muslims, and the fragile unity of Christian might divided when the Crusaders broke with their Byzantine allies. Saladin, a Kurd, made himself master of the Nile Valley in 1171, emerged as sultan, and a decade later completely enveloped the Crusader kingdom except for Aqaba, its Red Sea port. When Christian troops rashly attempted to seize Mecca and Medina, Saladin declared a jihad, and on July 4, 1187, at the Horns of Hattin, above Lake Tiberias in Galilee—where Christ had delivered the Sermon on the Mount—annihilated the Christian army. In October the Kingdom of Jerusalem fell. After Saladin's victories, the dream of the Crusades began to fade. Within a few years, nothing remained in Christian hands but Antioch, Tripoli, and Tyre. The last of these surrendered in 1291. Other Crusades failed to recoup Christian losses and wandered far afield—to Constantinople, Egypt, and Tunis—with no impact on Palestine.

History gives us many cautionary tales. The Crusades are one. They began with the Muslims encamped on the edge of Asia and ended with their armies on the Danube in the heart of Europe itself. As for the "Great Cross" of the Crusaders, thought by some to be the True Cross of Christ, it was seized by Saladin as a trophy and buried beneath the threshold of one of Baghdad's city gates. A part of it was allowed to protrude from the ground, where it was trampled underfoot.

Yet the impact of the Muslim conquests lay far beyond the fields of war.

The inheritance of Islam is woven into the culture of the West as intricately as the knotted strands of a Persian rug. Is there any aspect of life it has not touched? The number of Arabic and Persian words common to Western usage reflect this at a glance. Terms of trade (caravan, bazaar, dinar, traffic, and tariff); seafaring (arsenal and admiral); domestic life (jar, syrup, alcove, carafe, sofa, mattress); the occult (amulet, talisman, julep); chemistry or alchemy (alkaline, antimony, elixir, alembic); the names of fruits (orange, lemon, and apricot); vegetables (spinach, artichokes, and shallots); spices and scents (sesame, carob, and saffron; indigo and sandalwood; alum, aloe, and clove); precious stones (lapis lazuli); medicines— "bezoar" (Persian: "pad-zahr," that is, "protecting against poison") and camphor; colors (azure, carmine, and lilac); fabrics (gauze, cotton, and satin); dyes (aniline); and a host of other familiar words and terms like *risk, caliber,* and *magazine* (the last from the Arabic "makhazin," meaning stores). In short, by trade, diplomacy, war, and other forms of engagement the abstract learning and practical achievements of Islam had a tremendous impact on the West.

Arabic learning, moreover, had a huge ethnic range and included contributions from every population under Muslim rule. It was not simply (or even primarily) Arab, but Persian, Hindu, Hebrew, Spanish, Syrian, Armenian, Roman, Coptic, and Greek. "Arab," like "Roman," became an imperial term. In all occupied areas, the Arabs found native craftsmen and builders who combined their know-how with native Arab skills. But the result was all "Arab" in the sense that Arabic (like Latin in the West) was the language of learning, diplomacy, and trade.

In time, under the Arabs, the complete medical and philosophical works of Galen, the *Physics* of Aristotle, the Old Testament (from the Septuagint Greek), Plato, Hippocrates, Ptolemy, Dorotheus, Archimedes, Euclid, and others were all translated, as the liberal arts flourished along with scientific research. Advances were made in spherical astronomy, geometry, algebra, trigonometric functions, chemistry, and integral calculus, to name just a handful of fields. Arabs also excelled in alchemy and botany, both closely allied to medicine. Alchemy (from the Arabic "al-kimiya") was an Arab "science" founded by a Kufan, Jabir ibn Hayyan, who was also the first to describe the two principal operations of chemistry—calcination and reduction. From Jabir and his colleagues we get such terms as *alembic, alkali*, and *antinomy*. Moreover, the Arabs discovered algebraic equations, invented the zero, introduced Arabic (really Hindu) numerals, created the decimal system, perfected the lunar calendar, and from Spain to Samarkand built new observatories that enabled them to double the level of celestial observations that the Greeks had attained. The great Muslim astrologer Abu Mashar, also known as Albumasar, of Khurasan, explained that the laws governing the tides were related to the rising and setting of the moon and helped determine the latitude and longitude of numerous places on earth. Enshrining the contribution many astrologers made to astronomical research, a host of prominent stars (like Altair and Deneb, Betelgeuse, and Rigel) have Arabic names, while terms such as azimuth, nadir, and zenith are of Arabic origin, too.

When the West eventually reaped the harvest of what the Arabs had achieved, even bigoted Christians were astonished and amazed. From Islam came the windmill, wheel irrigation, articles of dress and fashion, powders, glass mirrors, inlaid metalwork, colored glazes, and so on— even the Catholic rosary, perhaps, came from the Buddhist prayer beads of India by way of the Syrian trade. Syria produced colored glass vessels covered with patterns in artistic designs, often inlaid with gold and set with precious stones—a style of luxury glasswork later cultivated under Syrian direction by Venetians and known as Venetian glass. The best sword blades in the Near East were made of damascene steel (literally, fashioned in Damascus) and excelled the blades of the Franks.

In the realm of textiles and fabrics, the contributions were no less diverse: shawls came from Persia; damasks from Damascus; grenadines from Grenada; fustian from Fustat, Egypt; and muslins from Mosul, Iraq. *Mohair* comes from the Arabic word "mukhayyir" ("choice," "select"), and *taffeta* comes from "taftan," the Persian verb "to spin." "Attabi" silk, known as taby in England, was first produced in Baghdad and gave its name to the tabby cat.

Western heraldry was also influenced by Muslim crests and shields, while out of the ferment of Arab military culture came the crossbow; chain mail for knights; quilted cotton pads for underarmor; innovations in sapping, mining, and other siege tactics; mangonels and battering rams; "concentric" castles (derived from modifications made by the Arabs to Byzantine forts); even the carrier pigeon for the military dispatch. The now-universal custom of celebrating a military victory with fireworks and other illuminations was originally Arab, too.

Modern methods of book production also gained from medieval Muslim enterprise and skill. Paper, though a Chinese invention, came to Europe by way of Islam, and the first Western paper factories were established by the Muslims in Sicily and Spain. Early European books displayed features common to Muslim bindings, including marbled end-papers and boards with leather or vellum folded over the edges to keep them from being frayed. When European binders began to impress de-vices upon their leather covers with metal dies, Muslim artisans in Venice and Cordova enriched the stamped designs with gold leaf.

The accumulated architectural debt of the West to Islam is likewise large. In domestic architecture, the houses of Western nobles often fol-lowed the Arabic pattern of a courtyard with marble fountains; to Islam we also owe the cusped, ogee, and pointed arch; the use of engaged shafts at the angles of piers in Gothic vaulting; and Renaissance campanili or freestanding bell-towers. The lattice-wood screen, common to Arab homes and mosques, was copied in the English metal grille.

From Arab law we get such legal entities as the limited partnership; from Arab music, a number of instruments, including the lute, rebec, and guitar. The troubadour, "the quintessential musician of medieval Euro-pean chivalry," in one description, "was someone who knew 'taraba,' an Arabic word meaning to 'entertain with music.' The troubadour played a lute, whose name is a contraction of the Arabic name 'al-oud.'" The use of measured frets with the places of the notes fixed on the fingerboards was originally Arab, while the Arab habit of embellishing a melody by simultaneously striking a note together with its fourth, fifth, or octave gave European music its first prompting toward harmony. In theater, the Spanish word "mascara," like the English "masker" ("play actor"), is from the Arabic "maskhara" ("buffoon") and refers to the makeup used in early minstrel shows. The idea of a chaste, romantic love with no hope of consummation was semi-Arab (as well as Greek Platonic) and carried by the Arabs to Spain, where it helped inspire the chivalric ideals of courtly love. Even the sumptuous medieval European pageant with its "fields of Cloth-of-Gold" was inspired by the Baghdad caliph's lavish parades.

The example of Arabic poets helped inspire European vernacular verse. Arab meters are found in early Italian canticles and carnival songs, and the court poetry of Andalusia inspired the poetry of Provence. Some of the plots of Boccaccio's *Decameron* were Arab-inspired; and Chaucer's "Squire's Tale" (with its famous legend of the House of Brass) is an "Arabian Nights" tale. *Tristan and Isolde* was closely modeled on a Persian story, and Indian fables such as the romance of the *Seven Sages* (or Sindbad the Sailor) entered Western literature by way of Arabic. *The Dictes and Sayings of the Philosophers*, the very first book printed in English (by William Caxton), was a translation of sayings compiled in Egypt in the eleventh century by Mubashshir ibn Fatik. Picaresque adventure novels, which later took Europe by storm, were originally inspired by the "Maquamat," an Arabic literary form.

The first complete work in universal history (published in fifteen volumes) was undertaken by a Persian from Tabaristan, Muhammad ibn Jarir al-Tabari (838–923), who arranged his material chronologically by year. For his monumental work he drew from extant sources, oral tradition, and his own travels in Persia, Syria, Egypt, and Iraq. The first Arab historian to use the topical or thematic method was Abu al-Hasan al-Masudi of Baghdad (died 956), "the Herodotus of the Arabs," whose thirty-volume work, *The Meadows of Gold* (surviving only in an abridged version or epitome), was an encyclopedic compilation full of striking historical, ethnographic, and scientific notes. The Tunisian-born Aby Zayd ibn Khaldun, educated in Granada, was the first to introduce the idea of recurrent cycles in economic and political history. His understanding of market economics also anticipated Adam Smith.

The first European universities were also patterned to some extent on Muslim institutes. At the famed academy of Gundeshapur in southwest Persia, Greek scholars had consorted with their Syrian, Persian, and Hindu colleagues, and books, as we have seen, were translated from Sanskrit into Pahlavi (Middle Persian), and into Persian or Syriac from Greek. The famed Nizami Institute of Baghdad, founded in 1098 (around the time of the Norman Conquest of England), had branch buildings for research; Baghdad's great Mustansiriyah or College of Law contained four separate law schools, a large library, bathhouse, hospital, cafeteria, and other such modernish facilities as well as a great clepsydra, or water clock. Other notable universities were established at Nishapur, Jerusalem, Cairo, Alexandria, and Damascus long before they appeared at Bologna, Paris, Montpellier, and Oxford in the West.

While the study of medicine languished in the West under the name of "physics" (hence "physician") in monastic schools, the Arabs built upon their knowledge of Hippocrates and Galen. Al-Razi (Rhazes, 865–925), a physician of the Baghdad school, was the first to make a clinical distinction between measles and smallpox; Al-Majusi (died 994), known to the West as Haly Abbas, provided a rudimentary description of the capillary system and proof that, in delivery, an infant is expelled from the womb by muscular contraction; Ibn Sina (Avicenna, 980–1037), recognized the contagious nature of tuberculosis; and Al-Zahrawi (Abulcasis, died circa 1013), court physician to the Umayyad caliph in Cordova, introduced the cauterization of wounds and the crushing of bladder stones.

The Arabs were also the first to illustrate medical writings; developed the chemistry of prescriptions; introduced pharmaceutical preparations such as syrups, alcohol, and tragacanth; improved the art of dispensing by using scented waters for bottled preparations; explored the possibilities of anesthesia by inhalation (the precedent for ether); invented (to relieve the pain of surgery) the "soporific sponge," steeped in opiates and applied to the nose and mouth; used urinalysis to diagnose pregnancy; and introduced the idea of qualifying examinations for medical degrees. The first accredited medical school would not appear in the West until the twelfth century, when it was founded in 1140 by Roger II of Sicily, the Norman king and devoted Arabist. Even then, Arabs led the way. For example, Ibn Rushd (also known as Averroes, 1126–98) of Cordova and Seville, recognized in his medical work the principle of immunity in cases of smallpox and correctly explained the function of the retina of the eye.

If, as one scholar remarks, we are tempted to find among the great figures of the Middle Ages those only who "look down upon us from the vizor of the knight and the cowl of the monk," the Arab tradition brings to mind yet another great figure, that of the Arab physician-philosopher "with his gold and silver brocaded turban, his halo of intellectual curiosity, and his broad tolerance" for experimental learning in every field.

The contrast could hardly be more striking. While turbulent conditions in Europe led to intolerance, ignorance, and a general hostility toward intellectual pursuits, a succession of caliphs and emirs in Baghdad, Cordova, Toledo, Seville, Sicily (a seat of Arabic culture from 878 to 1091), and elsewhere fostered education among their subjects and afforded protection and encouragement to scholars of all faiths. In the tenth century, when London and Paris were still shabby towns, Cordova—"the mother of philosophers," the "light of Andalusia"—was the most civilized city in the West. At the height of its glory, it contained 300 mosques, 200,000 houses, 50 hospitals, 70 libraries (including a main library with at least 225,000 volumes); excellent public baths; miles of paved streets illuminated at night; and a trained and talented population of surgeons, dressmakers, singing-masters, architects, and so on, who served Muslim communities from Barcelona to Navarre. In Cordova, it was said, "every boy and girl of twelve was able to read and write—at a time when the barons and ladies of Christendom were scarcely able to scrawl their names."

The Christian reconquest of Spain brought the two civilizations into a general engagement that opened Western eyes. Toledo fell to Christian arms in 1085, Cordova in 1236, Seville in 1248, and finally Granada in 1492. Sicily, which had been under Muslim control for more than 200 years, fell to the Normans in 1091. In Toledo, a society of translators was formed to claim Islamic culture for the West. The result was reminiscent of the translation period in Baghdad three centuries before. Just as the Caliph Mamun had established his great "House of Wisdom," so the new translation school became a clearinghouse for knowledge of all kinds. Under royal patronage and supervision, encyclopedic compilations on everything from the virtues of precious stones to board games like backgammon and chess were made from Arabic sources, with the help of Jewish scribes. Scholars arrived from all over Europe—among them Robertus Anglicus (Robert "the Englishman"), the first translator of the Koran into Latin; Adelard of Bath; Michael Scot; Burgundio of Pisa; Johannes Hispalensis; and Gerard of Cremona, among the brightest lights. Adelard translated Euclid; Scot, the biological and zoological works of Aristotle; Burgundio, Galen; Hispalensis, al-Farabi; and Gerard (the most prominent and prolific) nearly eighty works—including portions of Hippocrates, Galen, Aristotle, Avicenna, Serapion, Isaac Judaeus, and works by Rhazes, Al-Kindi, Albucasis, and Ptolemy's *Almagest*. In a sense, Gerard did for the Latins, it has been said, what Hunayn ibn Ishaq (the foremost scholar-linguist under Mamun) had done for the Arabs in the scope of his enterprise. Another remarkable figure was the converted Jew "Avendeath" (that is, Ibn Dawud, son of David), who translated a number of mathematical and astronomical works.

There was much to keep their industry at a fever pitch. Before long, their influence reached to the very summit of thirteenth-century Christian thought. Two hundred years later the Renaissance of the fifteenth century would bloom in part because the Arabs had preserved ancient knowledge and kept the spirit of research alive.

BAGHDAD HAD BEEN FOUNDED AT A TIME DEEMED PROPI-tious by Mansur's court astrologer, who cast for the appropriate day and hour. The chart augured well for Baghdad's early glory but also implied it would one day be undone by war. Fate played itself out. In 1258 the city was sacked by the Mongols under Hulagu Khan, the grandson of Genghiz Khan, and its great library burned to the ground. Scholars, civic leaders, and a large proportion of its inhabitants were slaughtered and a mountain made of their skulls. The Caliph Mustasim—the last of the Abbasids—deluded himself into surrendering upon the promise that his life would be spared, but once in Mongol custody was "beaten to death in a sack." In 1401, the city was plundered again and ravaged by the Mongol Tamerlane. These devastating onslaughts were naturally followed by social disintegration and political disarray. Thereafter, in subsequent centuries Baghdad was repeatedly riven by factional violence, and fought over by the Persians and Ottoman Turks. The Turks seized it in 1638, but by then it was not much of a prize. It had lost its commercial importance, and in time tribal-based pastoral nomads drifted in to occupy its ruined remains.

Yet there is little more startling or compelling than the epic story of Islam during its formative and triumphant years. The landscape it occupies is immense, and some of the monumental figures of history—the Prophet Muhammad; the caliphs Omar, Mansur, Harun al-Rashid, and Mamun; the invincible Muslim general Khalid ibn al-Walid (known to Islam as "the Sword of God"); Charles Martel, Charlemagne, Almanzor, El Cid, Saladin, Mahmud of Ghazna; and Ibn Khaldun and Avicenna among them—enrich the saga with their own storied lives. Here, too, are some of the most consequential military movements and battles ever fought—in Spain, Asia Minor, North Africa, India, and the Near and Middle East: the Battles of Yamanah, Kadisiya, Yarmuk, Guadelete, Poitiers, Manzikert, Somnath, Hattin, and Tarain; the first historic siege of Baghdad; and the imperishable art of Muslim poets, craftsmen and builders, from the cathedral mosques of Cairo, Baghdad, and Damascus, to the epic verse of Firdawsi and *The Thousand and One Nights*.

If the preeminence of Islamic culture eventually waned, Islam itself maintained its importance on the world's stage. In the long view, its triumphs—and atrocities—are not less than those of the Christian West.

Most Americans, even among the educated, know almost nothing about Islam except that Muslims profess it and that Christians and Muslims clashed at the time of the Crusades. Most of those who have heard of the Crusades think the Christians won. Islam, in fact, has seldom lost ground. Even when its temporal power has waned, its faith has spread. It continues to have a home in Europe (in Kosovo, Albania, and the Balkans) and today extends not only throughout the Near and Middle East, but much of Africa (not just the north), Central Asia, the Indian subcontinent, and the Pacific isles. The only two lands ever "conquered by Islam and heavily Islamized," as one survey notes, that have ever "reverted to Christian rule" are Sicily and Spain.

We ought to know its history better than we do.

The world is wrapped round in one brocaded robe or shroud. In an epitome of this, one of the silk robes that Charlemagne may have received as a gift from Harun later served as a shroud for the body of St. Cuthbert at Durham Cathedral in 1104. Though Cuthbert was a Christian saint, his shroud bore a Kufic Arabic inscription: "There is no God save the One."

ACKNOWLEDGMENTS

Much to my surprise, I am getting on in years and this may be the last history I write. Other work beckons (poems, essays, a little memoir, perhaps); but after fourteen books of history in thirty-three years, with scarcely an intermission, I hope I have earned a rest. During that time, my agent, Russell Galen, and my editor, Bob Bender, have given indispensable support to the scope of my enterprise. Writing can be an arduous task, whatever pleasure it may afford: but I could scarcely have afforded that pleasure in any sense had they not sustained me in my work. Their loyalty has been priceless, and I am delighted to dedicate this book to them as a gesture of my thanks.

The history of early Islam is a daunting subject. Despite the illuminating contributions of a number of fine scholars, it remains (for many) a darkened plain. I have not sought to traverse the whole of it so much as bring part of its story alive. That itself would have been impossible without the work of those who have also traced its narrative lines. Even so, this book went through many dramatic changes before assuming its final form. In the end, Bob Bender did much to sharpen my focus, and with his usual editorial wisdom helped shape the text. For her able (and ever personable) handling of myriad details, I am also indebted to his steadfast assistant, Johanna Li. Gypsy da Silva once more supervised the copyediting process with care and diligence; Tom Pitoniak's sharp pencil saved me from a number of inelegant expressions and mistakes. The team at Dix Digital Prepress somehow managed to incorporate my numerous emendations and corrections—no mean task. To make the look and feel of the book all one, Joy O'Meara and Christopher Lin, respectively, devised the lovely and captivating book and jacket designs.

As ever, I am grateful to the staff of Butler Library of Columbia University (my alma mater), where the steep ladder of my research always starts; and (an overdue notice of sorts) to those at Brooks Memorial Library in my hometown of Brattleboro, Vermont, for the alacrity with which they seem able to obtain almost any book through interlibrary loan.

Finally, without the cheerful patience of my wife, the encouragement of family and friends, and the spirited company of our pets—who daily exemplify that irrepressible zest for life we all long for—this book would surely have faltered along the way. That it didn't is a tribute to their united and converging love.

—March 15, 2012

APPENDIX

THE UMAYYAD CALIPHS OF DAMASCUS

Muawiyah I, 661–680

Yazid I, 680–683

Muawiyah II, 683–684

Marwan I, 684–685

Abd al-Malik, 685–705

Al-Walid I, 705–715

Suleiman, 715–717

Omar ibn Abd al-Aziz, 717–720

Yazid II, 720–724

Hisham ibn Abd al-Malik, 724–743

Al-Walid II, 743–744

Yazid III, 744

Ibrahim, 744

Marwan II, 744–750

THE ABBASID CALIPHS OF BAGHDAD (TO 842)

Al-Abbas, 747–754

Al-Mansur, 754–775

Al-Mahdi, 775–785

Al-Hadi, 785–786

Harun al-Rashid, 786–809

Al-Amin, 809–813

Al-Mamun, 813–833

Al-Mutasim, 833–842

NOTES

Many quotations given in early medieval Muslim sources have a dated or archaic character. Modern secondary sources also sometimes cite them in that form. No two translations agree. I have not hesitated to render quotations into idiomatic English, in order to get the sense of them both readable and right.

CHAPTER ONE: MINARET AND TOWER

PAGE

1 *"An indescribable joy"*: Kaegi, *Heraclius: Emperor of Byzantium*, p. 206.

1 *"a triumphant"*: Nöldeke, *Sketches from Eastern History*, p. 60. Nöldeke, however, confuses the commemorative date in the Church Calendar with the date of the event itself. See Kaegi, *Heraclius*, p. 206. For further discussion of the dates, see Baynes, "The Restoration of the Cross at Jerusalem," *EHR*, pp. 287–99.

1 *"a deep, silent disdain"*: Arnold and Guillaume, eds., *The Legacy of Islam*, p. 40.

4 *"furnished the community"*: Hitti, *The Near East in History*, p. 261.

6 *"a land of wealth and luxury"*: Lane-Poole, *Medieval India Under Mohammedan Rule*, pp. 4–5.

7 *"all he could require"*: Keay, *India: A History*, p. 183.

7 *"their intrepidity and vigor"*: Bosworth, *The Ghaznavids*, p. 205.

8 *"desert power"* and *"a sea of sand"*: Verhoeven, *Islam: Its Origin and Spread*, p. 30.

8 *"naphtha-firemen"*: Hell, *The Arab Civilization*, p. 78.

8 *"passion for sex"*: Muir, *The Caliphate: Its Rise, Decline, and Fall*, p. 72.

11 *"vengeance for Husain"*: Nöldeke, *Sketches from Eastern History*, p. 82.

11 *"almost as holy"*: Ibid.

11 *"ungodly usurpers"*: Hitti, *The Near East in History*, p. 239.

13 *"Put not off"*: Abbott, *Two Queens of Baghdad*, p. 5; Nöldeke, *Sketches from Eastern History*, p. 133.

13 *"He who has no money"*: Clot, *Harun al-Rashid*, p. 16.

14 *"Founded by God"*: Le Strange, *Baghdad During the Abbasid Caliphate*, p. 11.

16 *"it was equally"*: Lassner, *The Shaping of 'Abbasid Rule*, p. 197.

16 *"as if by an enchanter's wand"*: Le Strange, p. 13.

16 *"In the name of the Lord!"*: Muir, *The Caliphate: Its Rise, Decline, and Fall*, p. 454.

CHAPTER TWO: THE NIGHT OF DESTINY

PAGE

19 *"How sweet would the world be"*: De Slane, trans., *Ibn Khallikan's Biographical Dictionary*, vol. 1, p. 522.

20 *"had a dark complexion"*: Clot, *Harun al-Rashid*, p. 22.

20 *"slender and graceful"*: Ibid., p. 23.

20 *"Take her to my son"*: Ibid.

20 *"to ride out"*: Kennedy, *When Baghdad Ruled the Muslim World*, p. 183; Glubb, *Haroon Al Rasheed*, p. 125.

20 *"as if she had been a great prince"*: Glubb, *Haroon Al Rasheed*, p. 125.

21 *"Restless Butterfly"*: Kennedy, *When Baghdad Ruled the Muslim World*, p. 106.

21 *"He who has two wives"*: Audisio, *Harun al-Rashid*, p. 15.

22 *"A man who behaves ill"*: Lane, *Arab Society in the Time of the Thousand and One Nights*, p. 255.

22 *"freedman"*: Glubb, *Haroon Al Rasheed*, p. 215.

22 *"women," it seems, "had been"*: Ibid., p. 120.

22 *"the Speckled One"*: Kennedy, *When Baghdad Ruled the Muslim World*, p. 30.

23 *"began his court career"*: Ibid., p. 35.

23 *"O Ali, do not follow"*: Glubb, *Haroon Al Rasheed*, p. 245.

23 *"saw a girl who was like an oryx"*: Ibid.

23 *"as a willow's twig"*: Lane, *Arab Society*, p. 215.

23 *"When you have recovered"*: Abbott, *Two Queens of Baghdad*, p. 42.

24 *"because of the direction she would give"*: Ibid., p. 53.

25 *"with goatskins full of muddy water"*: Glubb, *Haroon Al Rasheed*, p. 135.

26 *"You wouldn't have some wine"*: Ibid., p. 145.

27 *"That looks good"*: Ibid., p. 143.

28 *"By no single act"*: Philby, *Harun al-Rashid*, p. 31.

28 *"a big, ill-tempered boy"*: Audisio, *Harun al-Rashid*, p. 35.

28 *"hard and coarse"*: Clot, *Harun al-Rashid*, p. 27.

28 *"oxen trampling round"*: Bosworth, trans., *The History of Al-Tabari*, vol. 30, p. 11.

29 *After a while, he returned*: Ibid., p. 45.

30 *"I realized," Rabi told his family*: Ibid., p. 85.

30 *"Who is better, you or I?"*: Ibid.

30 *"You must do this for me"*: Glubb, *Haroon Al Rasheed*, p. 148; Audisio, *Harun al-Rashid*, p. 39.

30 *"Thereafter," according to Tabari, "she spoke"*: Bosworth, trans., *The History*, vol. 30, p. 43.

31 *"O Harun, it seems to me"*: Ibid., p. 53.

31 *"I will bring that to pass"*: Abbott, *Two Queens of Baghdad*, p. 93.
31 *"O Prince of the Faithful"*: Glubb, *Haroon Al Rasheed*, p. 149; Bosworth, trans., *The History*, vol. 30, p. 49.
31 *"anointed himself"*: Bosworth, trans., *The History,* vol. 30, p. 50.
31 *"O Yahya, what is the relationship"*: Ibid.
32 *"Keep far away"*: Ibid., p. 51.
32 *"What difference does it make to me?"*: Ibid., p. 60.
33 *"night of destiny"*: Abbott, *Two Queens of Baghdad*, p. 110; Glubb, *Haroon Al Rasheed*, p. 241.
33 *"O good Muslims!"*: Glubb, *Haroon Al Rasheed*, p. 157.

CHAPTER THREE: KING OF KINGS

PAGE
35 *"swarmed about"*: Audisio, *Harun al-Rashid*, pp. 44–45.
36 *"stood out like splashes of kohl"*: Ibid., p. 47.
36 *"My father! I owe my position"*: Glubb, *Haroon Al Rasheed*, p. 158.
36 *"Did you not see how the pale"*: Bosworth, trans., *The History of Al-Tabari*, vol. 30, p. 98.
37 *"Make way for the heir-apparent!"*: Ibid., p. 95.
37 *"To hear is to obey"*: Ibid.
37 *"with vast audience and reception"*: Clot, *Harun al-Rashid*, p. 40.
37 *"reviews and parades"*: Ibid.
38 *"with ponds and waterfalls"*: Ibid.
38 *"a small garden planted"*: Ibid.
38 *"lines of living color"*: Burton, *The Book of the Thousand Nights and a Night*, 152nd Night, p. 200.
38 *"pious advice"*: Audisio, *Harun al-Rashid*, p. 14.
39 *"a complete master"*: De Slane, trans., *Ibn Khallikan's Biographical Dictionary*, vol. 2, p. 123.
39 *"he never professed"*: Ibid., p. 124.
40 *"come to power on the crest"*: Lewis, *The Arabs in History*, p. 90.
41 *"The Persians ruled"*: O'Donnell, "Twenty-Five Centuries of Persia," p. 53.
42 *"When we consider the distances"*: Palmer, *The Caliph Haroun Alraschid*, p. 30.
42 *"Harun leans on God"*: Audisio, *Harun al-Rashid*, p. 99.
42 *"a pilgrimage is one"*: Ibid.
42 *"she ordered a shelter"*: Clot, *Harun al-Rashid*, p. 37.
43 *"walked barefoot through the mud"*: Kennedy, *When Baghdad Ruled the Muslim World*, p. 186.
43 *"recited the famous"*: Clot, *Harun al-Rashid*, p. 39.
44 *"north and west"*: Kennedy, *When Baghdad Ruled the Muslim World*, p. 45.
44 *"you would have thought"*: http://en.wikipedia.org/wiki/Sassanid_empire.

44 *"the main Muslim siege weapon":* Kennedy, *The Armies of the Caliphs*, p. 184.

45 *"[The vizier] is our representative":* Hitti, *History of the Arabs*, p. 319.

46 *"Rain where you like":* Glubb, *Haroon Al Rasheed*, p. 232.

48 *"an uninhabited ruin":* Kennedy, *When Baghdad Ruled the Muslim World*, p. 39.

49 *"in many ways the public face":* Ibid., p. 43.

49 *"No one," we are told, "was refused admission":* Ibid.

50 *"With Caliphs," he once said, "to argue":* Clot, *Harun al-Rashid*, p. 36.

50 *"Little Vizier":* Philby, *Harun al-Rashid*, p. 85.

50 *"By the pardon":* De Slane, trans., *Ibn Khallikan's Biographical Dictionary*, vol. 1, p. 302.

51 *"The Prince of the Faithful—may God exalt":* Palmer, *The Caliph Haroun Alraschid*, p. 41.

51 *"upwards of a thousand":* De Slane, trans., *Ibn Khallikan's Biographical Dictionary*, vol. 1, p. 302.

52 *"as rich as Jafar":* Clot, *Harun al-Rashid*, p. 55.

52 *"Is there not one man":* Palmer, *The Caliph Haroun Alraschid*, p. 47.

52 *"I want you to dispel":* Ibid., p. 171.

53 *"little Butterpat":* Glubb, *Haroon Al Rasheed*, p. 244.

53 *"with marvelous outpointing":* Abbott, *Two Queens of Baghdad*, p. 215.

53 *"inexpressibly sweet face":* Glubb, *Haroon Al Rasheed*, p. 193.

54 *"cool mountain pools":* Ibid.

54 *"undulating form":* Palmer, *The Caliph Haroun Alraschid*, p. 177.

54 *"Petronian feasts":* Audisio, *Harun al-Rashid*, p. 90.

54 *"drawn back at the waist":* Ibid., p. 88.

54 *"they were cajoled":* Ibid.

55 *"My love for her":* Masudi, *The Meadows of Gold*, p. 200.

55 *"was not," as often imagined, "a glorified brothel":* Kennedy, *When Baghdad Ruled the Muslim World*, p. 145.

55 *"seven slave girls":* Ibid.

55 *"She laid her lute in her lap":* Irwin, *The Arabian Nights: A Companion*, p. 173.

56 *"Let a man who receives":* Glubb, *Haroon Al Rasheed*, p. 169.

57 *"I never saw two claimants":* Palmer, *The Caliph Haroun Alraschid*, p. 219.

57 *"Sell her to me":* Ibid., pp. 157–59.

58 *"like a hornet's nest":* Palmer, *The Caliph Haroun Alraschid*, p. 136.

59 *"Spring of Zubaidah":* Philby, *Harun al-Rashid*, p. 53.

59 *"as a forward base against the Byzantines":* Kennedy, *When Baghdad Ruled the Muslim World*, p. 47.

60 *"They only want you to drink":* Palmer, *The Caliph Haroun Alraschid*, p. 161.

61 *"Is there anything you want?":* Glubb, *Haroon Al Rasheed*, p. 167.

61 *"You have grown old":* Palmer, *The Caliph Haroun Alraschid*, p. 170.

62 *"a sincere and benevolent":* Glubb, *Haroon Al Rasheed*, p. 331.

62 *"he suffered greatly"*: Audisio, *Harun al-Rashid*, p. 72.

62 *"strolled in and out"*: Ibid.

62 *"What would you like to tell me?"*: Glubb, *Haroon Al Rasheed*, p. 185; El-Hibri, *Reinterpreting Islamic Historiography*, p. 24.

62 *"quickly in tears"*: Glubb, *Haroon Al Rasheed*, p. 186.

62 *"Tell me, by your kinship"*: El-Hibri, *Reinterpreting Islamic Historiography*, p. 26.

CHAPTER FOUR: BAGHDAD

PAGE

65 *"lamb cooked over a spit"* and *"smeared with fat"*: Berlinski, *The Secrets of the Vaulted Sky*, p. 82.

66 *"marble steps"*: Bloom and Blair, *Islamic Arts,* p. 80.

66 *"Thousands of gondolas"*: Ibid.

66 *"Due to the scarcity"*: Ibid., p. 43.

67 *"I leave it to the bather"*: Aaland, "The Islamic Hammam Is Born," www.cyber bohemia.com/Pages/sweat.htm.

67 *"Whenever a woman enters"*: Ibid.

68 *"The unification of the Muslim"*: Clot, *Harun al-Rashid*, p. 128.

69 *"disgracing him"*: Palmer, *The Caliph Haroun Alraschid*, p. 190.

69 *"weights and measures"*: Irwin, *The Arabian Nights*, p. 157.

70 *"criminal brotherhoods"*: Ibid., p. 174.

70 *"in red leather"*: Ibid.

70 *"children would make"*: Clot, *Harun al-Rashid*, p. 176.

70 *"with the palaces"*: Ibid.

71 *"crowds would gather"*: Ibid., p. 177.

71 *"bootleggers of Baghdad"*: Hitti, *History of the Arabs*, p. 338.

71 *"On a rainy day"*: Clot, *Harun al-Rashid*, p. 177.

72 *"Permission Please!"*: Lane, *Arab Society in the Time of the Thousand and One Nights*, p. 37.

72 *"In the name of God"*: Irwin, *The Arabian Nights: A Companion*, p. 205.

73 *"Good dreams are from God"*: Lane, *Arab Society*, p. 88.

73 *"Know that what Allah"*: Irwin, *The Arabian Nights*, p. 198.

73 *"There is no god but God"*: Glubb, *Haroon Al Rasheed*, p. 205.

73 *"I bathed and perfumed myself"*: Burton, *The Book of the Thousand Nights and a Night*, 17th Night, p. 88.

75 *They travel from west to east*: Lewis, *The Arabs in History*, p. 97.

75 *"a fictional reworking"*: Irwin, *The Arabian Nights*, p. 182.

76 *"The trustworthy merchant"*: Lewis, *The Arabs in History*, p. 99.

77 *"to draw a check"*: Ibid., p. 100.

78 *"The ink of a scholar"*: Hitti, *The Near East in History*, p. 269.

CHAPTER FIVE: THE CULTURE OF PROSPERITY

PAGE

82 *"told that his astronomers did not know enough"*: Clot, *Harun al-Rashid*, p. 210.

83 *"ode of nostalgic longing"*: Blair and Bloom, *Islam: A Thousand Years of Faith and Power*, p. 142.

83 *"the roughness"*: Audisio, *Harun al-Rashid*, p. 143.

84 *"even famous men of letters"*: Glubb, *Haroon Al Rasheed*, p. 193.

84 *"interrupt them to suggest"*: Ibid.

84 *"O Commander of the Faithful!"*: Palmer, *The Caliph Haroun Alraschid*, p. 196.

84 *"an Arab of the desert"*: Ibid., pp. 165–67.

86 *"Now improvise"*: Glubb, *Haroon Al Rasheed*, p. 195.

86 They are the tent ropes: Ibid.

86 *"Abu Obeidah"*: Palmer, *The Caliph Haroun Alraschid*, p. 213.

86 *"It so happened"*: Ibid.

87 *"May you live long"*: Lane, *Arabian Society in the Time of the Thousand and One Nights*, p. 115.

87 *"The Prince of the Faithful"*: Ibid.

88 *"of wine, its taste"*: Clot, *Harun al-Rashid*, p. 218.

88 My body is racked: Kennedy, *Abu Nuwas: A Genius of Poetry*, p. 56.

88 *"the poems of Atahiyah"*: De Slane, trans., *Ibn Khallikan's Biographical Dictionary*, vol. 2, p. 43.

88 Stunned by my sin: Clot, *Harun al-Rashid*, p. 217.

89 *"He who bears the weight"*: De Slane, trans., *Ibn Khallikan's Biographical Dictionary*, vol. 1, p. 392.

89 *"Multiply your sins"*: Ibid., p. 393.

89 *"One or two"*: Ibid., p. 205.

89 *"For you must know"*: Clot, *Harun al-Rashid*, p. 216.

89 *"You're really going to kill me"*: Palmer, *The Caliph Haroun Alraschid*, p. 150.

90 *"Where are you going?"*: Ibid., p. 205.

90 *"we searched his whole house"*: De Slane, trans., *Ibn Khallikan's Biographical Dictionary*, vol. 1, p. 393.

90 *"discovered several new musical modes"*: Ibid., p. 21.

90 *"to beat the rhythm with a wand"*: Hitti, *History of the Arabs*, p. 425.

91 *"al-Nadim al-Mausili"*: De Slane, trans., *Ibn Khallikan's Biographical Dictionary*, vol. 1, p. 183.

91 *"a constant companion of the caliphs"*: Ibid.

91 *"thoroughly schooled"*: Ibid.

91 *"like a nightingale"*: Hitti, *The Near East in History*, p. 268.

91 *"prompted by Jinn"*: Ibid.

92 *"A table without vegetables"*: Clot, *Harun al-Rashid*, p. 173.

92 *"Whoso eateth a mouthful"*: Lane, *Arabian Society*, p. 160.

93 *"Harun took the pan"*: Clot, *Harun al-Rashid*, p. 172.

93 *"This is even better than eating"*: Glubb, *Haroon Al Rasheed*, p. 205.
94 *"The Arabs found themselves"*: Ibn Khaldun, quoted in Ibid., p. 201.

CHAPTER SIX: AL-ANDALUS

PAGE
95 *"My land has fresh water"*: Sedgwick, *Spain: A Short History*, p. 15.
96 *"when the wind blew"*: Descola, *A History of Spain*, p. 95.
97 *"screaming Berber horsemen"*: Ibid., p. 96.
97 *HIC REQUIESCIT*: Ibid.
97 *"This is Solomon's Table"*: Ibid., p. 105.
98 *"SUCH MEN SHALL CONQUER"*: Sedgwick, *Spain*, p. 24.
99 *"stood shoulder to shoulder"*: Hitti, *History of the Arabs*, p. 500.
99 *"The Arab-Berber wave"*: Ibid., p. 501.
100 *kind-hearted, disposed to mercy*: Lane-Poole, *The Story of the Moors in Spain*, p. 68.
101 *"the Kabbah of Western Islam"*: Ibid., p. 134.
102 *"My fellow-Christians"*: Dozy, *Spanish Islam*, p. 268.
103 *"whose devotion to their paymaster"*: Lane-Poole, *The Story of the Moors in Spain*, p. 67.

CHAPTER SEVEN: GREEK FIRE

PAGE
106 *"set back from the street"*: Rautman, *Daily Life in the Byzantine Empire*, p. 92.
107 *"drained into"* and *"waste was collected"*: Ibid., p. 76.
107 *"to stimulate affection"*: Ibid., p. 51.
108 *"Let us throw off"*: Ibid.
108 *"the solitary temperament"*: Ibid., p. 239.
108 *"spiritual athletes"*: Nöldeke, *Sketches from Eastern History*, p. 214.
108 *"despised all worldly"*: Ibid.
109 *"pelting each other"*: Harris, *Constantinople, Capital of Byzantium*, p. 30.
110 *"the envy of"*: Ibid., p. 15.
110 *"the Mandylion of Edessa"*: Ibid., p. 64.
110 *"God-guarded city"*: Ibid., p. 44; Vasiliev, *Byzantine Empire*, vol. 1, p. 236.
110 *"did have an extraordinary"*: Ibid.
110 *"of all the great"*: Ibid., p. 43.
111 *"chain of hilltop"*: Ibid., p. 65.
112 *reproduce the perfect*: Ibid.
112 *"so that he could gaze"*: Ibid., p. 67.
113 *"images are an abomination and the work"*: Koran, verse (sura) 92.
113 *"Christianize the spirit of Roman Law"*: Vasiliev, *History of the Byzantine Empire*, vol. 1, p. 246.

114 *"I am emperor and priest"*: Ibid., vol. 1, p. 259.

114 *"enshrined the principles"*: Herrin, *Women in Purple*, p. 45.

114 *"cursed out of the Christian Church"*: Vasiliev, *History of the Byzantine Empire*, vol. 1, p. 260.

115 *"idolaters and lovers of darkness"*: Ibid., p. 262.

CHAPTER EIGHT:
LOMBARDS, SAXONS, AND A POISONED CROWN

PAGE

118 *"contempt for Christianity"*: Ogg, *A Source Book of Medieval History*, p. 119.

118 *"holy work"*: Riche, *Daily Life in the World of Charlemagne*, p. 80.

118 *"military almoners"*: Ibid., p. 81.

118 *"three masses"*: Ibid.

118 *"ordered his army to fast"*: Ibid.

118 *"the Maccabees"*: Ibid.

120 *"bride-show"*: Garland, *Byzantine Empresses: Women and Power in Byzantium*, p. 73.

122 *"the pious began once more"*: Ibid., p. 78.

122 *"ashamed to have governed"*: Herrin, *Women in Purple*, p. 83.

123 *"Nika!" or "Victory!"*: Ibid., p. 79.

123 *"the Council could claim"*: Ibid., p. 89.

124 *"co-ruler," "Irene Augusta," "as a beardless youth"*: Garland, *Byzantine Empresses*, p. 83.

CHAPTER NINE: "IRON CHARLES"

PAGE

127 *"always stately and dignified"*: Thorpe, *Two Lives of Charlemagne: Einhard and Notker the Stammerer*, p. 76.

128 *"his dress differed"*: Ibid., p. 78.

128 *"the stories and deeds"*: Ibid., p. 78.

128 *"as well as his native"*: Ibid., p. 79.

128 *"used to keep tablets"*: Ibid.

129 *"well-skilled"*: Ibid., p. 80.

129 *"it had been impossible to lift"*: Fichtenau, *The Carolingian Empire: The Age of Charlemagne*, p. 34.

129 *"very active in aiding"*: Thorpe, *Two Lives of Charlemagne*, p. 80.

129 *"get help and relief"*: Ibid.

129 *"to reestablish the ancient"*: Ibid., p. 81.

129 *"There is no evidence"*: Fichtenau, *The Carolingian Empire*, p. 29.

129 *"even insisted"*: Ibid.

130 *"every man to seek"*: Durant, *The Story of Civilization*, vol. 4, p. 464.

130 *"whoring"* and *"drunkenness"*: Ibid., p. 467.

130 *"what they meant by"*: Ibid.

130 *"rode about in silk"*: Fichtenau, *The Carolingian Empire*, p. 121.

130 *"That fellow sang well!"*: Thorpe, *Two Lives of Charlemagne*, p. 114.

130 *"Country bumpkins"*: Ibid.

131 *"with the fingers"*: Fichtenau, *The Carolingian Empire*, p. 94.

131 *"Many crimes are enumerated"*: Riche, *Daily Life in the World of Charlemagne*, p. 53.

131 *"Today we see"*: Ibid., p. 74.

132 *"constant companion"*: Ibid., p. 75.

132 *"solidity and bite"*: Ibid., p. 147.

132 *"Kill my mother"*: Ibid., p. 75.

132 *"well-muscled loins"*: http://en.wikipedia.org/wiki/Destrier.

132 *"coil and spring"*: Ibid.

132 *"preferred for hard battle"*: Riche, *Daily Life in the World of Charlemagne*, p. 146.

132 *"rested on this organized"*: Durant, *The Story of Civilization*, vol. 4, p. 463.

133 *"flooded over"*: Riche, *Daily Life in the World of Charlemagne*, p. 79.

133 *"ferreted out"*: Ibid.

133 *"bristled with ears"*: Thorpe, *Two Lives of Charlemagne*, pp. 163–64.

133 *"Iron Charles"*: Fichtenau, *The Carolingian Empire*, p. 32.

133 *"literally forced"*: Ibid., p. 33.

134 *"There are only free men"*: Barbero, *Charlemagne: Father of a Continent*, p. 330.

134 *"the Franks arrived"*: Bloom and Blair, *Islam: A Thousand Years of History*, p. 95.

134 *"was to be counted among the Just"*: Fichtenau, *The Carolingian Empire*, p. 36.

134 *"saluting the men"*: Durant, *The Story of Civilization*, vol. 4, p. 463.

135 *"The King wished to know"*: Ibid.

135 *"sworn groups"*: Ibid.

136 *"to cultivate learning"*: Price, *Medieval Thought*, p. 66.

136 *"to come and sit"*: Durant, *The Story of Civilization*, vol. 4, p. 466.

136 *"proved accomplished"*: Thorpe, *Two Lives of Charlemagne*, p. 96.

136 *"there was not one"*: Ibid., p. 103.

138 *"as if he had lost a brother"*: McBrien, *Lives of the Popes*, p. 125.

141 *"he seemed to them"*: Thorpe, *Two Lives of Charlemagne*, p. 144.

141 *"the Arabs were not able"*: Ibid.

141 *"a royal house built of stone"*: Ogg, *A Source Book of Medieval History*, p. 127.

142 *"that they rose from the table"*: Thorpe, *Two Lives of Charlemagne*, p. 144.

142 *"when [the Muslims] set eyes"*: Ibid., p. 145.

142 *"knew no fear"*: Ibid.

142 *"the huge beast"*: Ibid.

142 *The envoys were more merry*: Ibid., p. 146.

143 *"he deprived all the counts"*: Ibid.

143 *"All who beheld it"*: Clot, *Harun al-Rashid*, p. 103.

143 *"They seemed to have despoiled"*: Thorpe, *Two Lives of Charlemagne*, p. 147.

143 *"specially chosen"*: Ibid.

144 *"Life and Victory"*: Vasiliev, *History of the Byzantine Empire*, vol. 1, p. 267.

144 *"subordination to his will"*: Cheetham, *A History of the Popes*, p. 66.

145 *"it was a continental state"*: Fichtenau, *The Carolingian Empire*, p. 31.

145 *"Oh, would that that pool"*: Ibid.

CHAPTER TEN:
EVEN THE LOWLIEST CAMEL DRIVER KNEW

PAGE

152 *"It is a book that stimulates"*: Abbott, *Two Queens of Baghdad*, p. 178.

152 *"Praise be to Allah"*: Ibid.

152 *"like two stars"*: Palmer, *The Caliph Haroun Alraschid*, p. 117.

153 *"The Prince of the Faithful"*: Glubb, *Haroon Al Rasheed*, p. 162.

153 *"By Allah, Kisai's mistake"*: Abbott, *Two Queens of Baghdad*, p. 176.

153 *"of all those learned"*: De Slane, trans., *Ibn Khallikan's Biographical Dictionary*, vol. 2, p. 237.

154 *"wise, statesmanlike"*: Glubb, *Haroon Al Rasheed*, p. 255.

154 *"The prophet of God"*: Palmer, *The Caliph Haroun Alraschid*, p. 119.

154 *"Rejoice, for Amin"*: Ibid., p. 118.

155 *"Who are you to judge"*: Clot, *Harun al-Rashid*, p. 82.

155 *"If there is any cause"*: Ibid.

156 *"Amin was to be caliph"*: Kennedy, *When Baghdad Ruled the Muslim World*, p. 70.

156 *"This is the document"*: Glubb, *Haroon Al Rasheed*, p. 258.

157 *"The command of God"*: Kennedy, *When Baghdad Ruled the Muslim World*, p. 71.

157 *"The authority of God"*: Ibid.

157 *"May God desert me"*: Clot, *Harun al-Rashid*, p. 83.

CHAPTER ELEVEN: THE HARDER THEY FALL

PAGE

159 *"sometimes outshone"*: Glubb, *Haroon Al Rasheed*, p. 270.

159 *"Envy and jealousy lifted"*: Audisio, *Harun al-Rashid*, p. 156.

160 *"Harun acted swiftly"*: Kennedy, *When Baghdad Ruled the Muslim World*, p. 73.

160 *"the people's hopes were fixed"*: De Slane, trans., *Ibn Khallikan's Biographical Dictionary*, vol. 1, p. 309.

161 *"Prince of Believers!"*: Palmer, *The Caliph Haroun Alraschid*, p. 83.

163 *"God slay me"*: De Slane, trans., *Ibn Khallikan's Biographical Dictionary*, vol. 1, p. 309.

163 *"Is this your dwelling?"*: Bosworth, trans., *The History of Al-Tabari*, vol. 30, p. 238.

163 *"Syrian interest"*: Ibid., p. 230.

164 Blood and revenge: Berry, ed., *The English Works of Giles Fletcher the Elder*, vol. 1, p. 100.

164 *"No, Prince of the Faithful"*: Palmer, *The Caliph Haroun Alraschid*, p. 132.

165 *"He has given you something"*: Bosworth, trans., *The History of Al-Tabari*, vol. 30, p. 232.

165 *"My son," answered Malik, "is either"*: Palmer, *The Caliph Haroun Alraschid*, p. 132.

165 *"It is as if I were looking"*: Bosworth, trans., *The History of Al-Tabari*, vol. 30, p. 233.

165 *"Fear God, O Commander"*: Ibid., p. 234.

166 *"By God"*: Ibid.

166 *"I received some disquieting"*: Ibid., p. 235.

166 *"persons inimical"*: Glubb, *Haroon Al Rasheed*, p. 270.

166 *"wrought against them underhand"*: De Slane, trans., *Ibn Khallikan's Biographical Dictionary*, vol. 2, p. 469.

167 *"Repelled and rejected"*: Ibid.

167 *"May Allah do unto him"*: Abbott, *Two Queens of Baghdad*, p. 194.

167 *"No, and no one would presume"*: Bosworth, trans., *The History of Al-Tabari*, vol. 30, p. 202.

168 *"To God's trusty servant"*: Palmer, *The Caliph Haroun Alraschid*, p. 83.

168 *"Jafar, you are taking"*: Ibid., p. 88.

169 *"shut himself up"*: Ibid., p. 89.

169 *"with cheers and shrill"*: Glubb, *Haroon Al Rasheed*, p. 284.

169 *"Allahu Akbar," "God is Great"*: Ibid.

169 *"after discussing affairs of state"*: Clot, *Harun al-Rashid*, p. 85.

170 *"Half-past nine o'clock"*: Palmer, *The Caliph Haroun Alraschid*, p. 94.

170 *"and the Euphrates was flowing"*: Audisio, *Harun al-Rashid*, p. 183.

171 *"go at once to find Jafar"*: Clot, *Harun al-Rashid*, p. 86.

171 *"No young man can escape it"*: Bosworth, trans., *The History of Al-Tabari*, vol. 30, p. 217.

171 *"The Prince of the Faithful is calling"*: Glubb, *Haroon Al Rasheed*, p. 278.

171 *"Take care, for [Harun] may"*: Clot, *Harun al-Rashid*, p. 86.

172 *"Where is Jafar's head?"*: Palmer, *The Caliph Haroun Alraschid*, p. 97.

172 *"Sindi," it read, "if you are sitting"*: Kennedy, *When Baghdad Ruled the Muslim World*, p. 73.

172 *"For a dress of honor"*: Palmer, *The Caliph Haroun Alraschid*, p. 99.

172 *"Naphtha and shavings"*: Ibid.

173 *"would go off to copulate"*: Bosworth, trans., *The History of Al-Tabari*, vol. 30, p. 230.

173 *"a present every Friday"*: De Slane, trans., *Ibn Khallikan's Biographical Dictionary*, vol. 1, p. 306.

173 *"You have thrown me away"*: Clot, *Harun al-Rashid*, p. 91.

173 *"If he really looked after"*: Palmer, *The Caliph Haroun Alraschid*, p. 91.

174 *"What is your name?"*: Ibid.

174 *"nailed his sister up"*: Clot, *Harun al-Rashid*, p. 91.

174 *"sewn into sacks"*: Ibid.

174 *"So will his son be killed"*: Glubb, *Haroon Al Rasheed*, p. 279.

175 *"By heaven, I never noticed"*: Palmer, *The Caliph Haroun Alraschid*, p. 135.

175 *"You have us in your power"*: Ibid., p. 133.

175 *"By Allah, I have made"*: Ibid.

175 *"My fate is close to his!"*: Ibid., p. 100.

176 *"Yes," he replied, "his eunuch, Nawal"*: Bosworth, trans., *The History of Al-Tabari*, vol. 30, p. 245.

176 *"I am doomed"*: Ibid.

176 *"I have not seen you enjoy"*: De Slane, trans., *Ibn Khallikan's Biographical Dictionary*, vol. 1, p. 310.

177 *"If I thought my right hand knew"*: Abbott, *Two Queens of Baghdad*, p. 200.

177 *"lived but a luster"*: Philby, *Harun al-Rashid*, p. 103.

177 *"which not even the four rivers"*: Clot, *Harun al-Rashid*, p. 84.

177 *"The hand of beneficence"*: Ibid., p. 88.

177 *"Let us stop and rest our horses"*: Ibid., p. 87.

177 By God, were it not: Bosworth, trans., *The History of Al-Tabari*, vol. 30, p. 228.

177 *"It was through them"*: Clot, *Harun al-Rashid*, p. 89.

CHAPTER TWELVE: "RUM" AND KHURASAN

PAGE

180 *Nicephorus, King of the Rum*: Muir, *The Caliphate: Its Rise, Decline, and Fall*, p. 475.

180 *"In the Name of God, the Compassionate"*: Ibid.

181 *"Power establishes"*: Audisio, *Harun al-Rashid*, p. 18.

181 *"men of gigantic size"*: Glubb, *Haroon Al Rasheed*, p. 313.

182 *"Now these are the presents"*: Clot, *Harun al-Rashid*, p. 114.

184 *"This is the person you advised"*: Bosworth, trans., *The History of Al-Tabari*, vol. 30, p. 251.

184 *"if it were not that there lay"*: Ibid.

184 *"this would be a safer way"*: Ibid., p. 252.

184 *"the likes of which"*: Glubb, *Haroon Al Rasheed*, p. 308.

185 *"bent his leg"*: Bosworth, trans., *The History of Al-Tabari*, vol. 30, p. 277.

185 *"By God, if you dismount"*: Ibid.

186 *"In the name of God, the Merciful"*: Ibid., p. 273.

186 *"with no saddle-blanket"*: Ibid., p. 281.

CHAPTER THIRTEEN: THE RED SOIL OF TUS

PAGE

187 Legend is, after all: Audisio, *Harun al-Rashid*, p. 70.

187 *"with the look of one who blamed"*: De Slane, trans., *Ibn Khallikan's Biographical Dictionary*, vol. 2, p. 472.

188 *"Oh Sobah, I don't suppose"*: Glubb, *Haroon Al Rasheed*, p. 321.

188 *"I have tried to conceal my condition"*: Palmer, *The Caliph Haroun Alraschid*, p. 114.

189 *"homily indeed"*: Glubb, *Haroon Al Rasheed*, p. 324.

189 *"You do not know what may happen"*: Ibid.

189 *"This is the soil of the land"*: Palmer, *The Caliph Haroun Alraschid*, p. 123.

189 *"By God, this is the same arm"*: Bosworth, trans., *The History of Al-Tabari*, vol. 30, p. 301.

190 *"All that lives must perish"*: Glubb, *Haroon Al Rasheed*, p. 327.

190 *"Where are the kings"*: Clot, *Harun al-Rashid*, p. 138.

190 *"Could it not be said"*: Ibid.

190 *"If I had no more time left"*: Bosworth, trans., *The History of Al-Tabari*, vol. 30, p. 298.

190 *"O God, just as you have given"*: Ibid.

191 *"Remember the poet's lines"*: Palmer, *The Caliph Haroun Alraschid*, p. 125.

191 *"The preposterous position"*: Ibid., p. 222.

192 *"Wasif the Eunuch"*: Le Strange, *Baghdad During the Abbasid Caliphate*, p. 181.

192 *"the witchery of Oriental romance"*: Muir, *The Caliphate: Its Rise, Decline, and Fall*, p. 483.

CHAPTER FOURTEEN: THE SIEGE OF BAGHDAD

PAGE

193 *"addressed the people"*: Kennedy, *When Baghdad Ruled the Muslim World*, p. 86.

193 *"could think of nothing original"*: Abbott, *Two Queens of Baghdad*, p. 205.

194 *"a reigning sovereign"*: Ibid.

195 *"inside hollow canes"*: Glubb, *Haroon Al Rasheed*, p. 344.

195 *"Son of my father"*: Kennedy, *When Baghdad Ruled the Muslim World*, p. 89.

195 *"I have received your letter"*: Ibid.

196 *"Each," she recalled, "in turn drew near"*: El-Hibri, *Reinterpreting Islamic Historiography: Harun al-Rashid and the Narrative of the "Abbasid Caliphate,"* p. 62.

197 *"close-fitting, wide-sleeved"*: Kennedy, *When Baghdad Ruled the Muslim World*, p. 188.

197 *"Do not speak haughtily to him"*: Abbott, *Two Queens of Baghdad*, p. 215; Glubb, *Haroon Al Rasheed*, p. 345.

197 *"an elegant scholar"*: De Slane, trans., *Ibn Khallikan's Biographical Dictionary*, vol. 1, p. 651.

197 *"What of it?"*: Glubb, *Haroon Al Rasheed*, p. 346.

198 *"he knotted Tahir's standard"*: De Slane, trans., *Ibn Khallikan's Biographical Dictionary*, vol. 2, p. 473.

198 *"Don't bother me now"*: Palmer, *The Caliph Haroun Alraschid*, p. 205.

199 *"rose with flooding"*: Lassner, *The Shaping of 'Abbasid Rule*, p. 184.

200 *"Silence! Crowns are not"*: Abbott, *Two Queens of Baghdad*, p. 218.

200 *"kissing and fondling"*: El-Hibri, *Reinterpreting Islamic Historiography*, p. 78.

200 *"Ahead of us"*: Ibid.

201 *"My Lord"*: Ibid., p. 79.

201 *"began drilling"*: Glubb, *Haroon Al Rasheed*, p. 357.

201 *"wrapped only"*: Ibid.

201 *"As we were in this"*: El-Hibri, *Reinterpreting Islamic Historiography*, p. 80.

201 *"What has Tahir wrought?"*: Ibid., p. 67.

201 *"What is past is past"*: Ibid.

201 *"sent him a shirt"*: De Slane, trans., *Ibn Khallikan's Biographical Dictionary*, vol. 1, p. 650.

202 *"he wept"*: El-Hibri, *Reinterpreting Islamic Historiography*, p. 67.

CHAPTER FIFTEEN: INTERREGNUM

PAGE

203 *"Blessed be Thou"*: Durant, *The Story of Civilization*, vol. 4, p. 471.

203 *"loved administration more"*: Ibid., p. 462.

204 *"raht"*: Fichtenau, *The Carolingian Empire: The World of Charlemagne*, p. 177.

204 *"From these external events"*: Ibid., p. 182.

206 *"a coffer, locked, and sealed"*: De Slane, trans., *Ibn Khallikan's Biographical Dictionary*, vol. 2, p. 243.

206 *"My loss"*: Abbott, *Two Queens of Baghdad*, p. 229.

207 *"established in 830"*: Hitti, *History of the Arabs*, p. 310.

207 *"eternal peace"*: Vasiliev, *History of the Byzantine Empire*, vol. 1, p. 298.

207 *"subsequently appointed"*: Hitti, *History of the Arabs*, p. 312.

CHAPTER SIXTEEN: "OVAL, SQUARE, AND ROUND"

PAGE

209 *"abjured all worldly"*: Dozy, *Spanish Islam*, p. 242.

210 *"his very goodness"*: Lane-Poole, *The Story of the Moors in Spain*, p. 72.

210 *"the Mutes"*: Ibid., p. 75.

210 *"profligate"*: Dozy, *Spanish Islam*, p. 245.

210 *"Just as a tailor plies"*: Ibid., p. 259.

211 *"dragon's necklace"*: Descola, *A History of Spain*, p. 115.

211 A *"popular figure"*: Hitti, *History of the Arabs*, p. 515.

212 *"the land of the Zenj"*: Nöldeke, *Sketches from Eastern History*, p. 149.

214 *"powerful, formidable"*: Lane-Poole, *The Story of the Moors in Spain*, p. 53.

216 *"profaned and plundered"*: Cheetham, *A History of the Popes*, p. 68.

216 *"to lift a finger in its defense"*: Ibid.

217 *"tortoise-shell"*: Crawford, *The Rulers of the South*, vol. 1, p. 82.

217 *"behold the enemy"*: Ibid., p. 92.

217 *"the land took on a new look"*: Ahmad, *A History of Islamic Sicily*, p. 37.

219 *"a chain of watch-towers"*: Smith, *A History of Sicily*, p. 7.

219 *"between seven hundred"*: Lopez and Raymond, *Medieval Trade in the Mediterranean World*, p. 53.

219 *"pools for ablutions"*: Ibid., p. 75.

219 *"There are three kinds of merchants"*: Ibid., pp. 24–27.

221 *"had their roots in the Islamic world"*: Benjamin, *Sicily*, p. 139.

221 *"so full of citizens"*: Zaimeche, *Sicily*, p. 43.

CHAPTER SEVENTEEN: "CITY OF THE FLOWER"

PAGE

224 *"invited to his councils"*: Durant, *The Story of Civilization*, vol. 4, p. 88.

224 *"impure bones"*: Hitti, *History of the Arabs*, p. 521.

224 *"nailed his head"*: Ibid., p. 523.

224 *"vale of reeds"*: Ibid.

225 *"whose undulating surface"*: Durant, *The Story of Civilization*, vol. 4, p. 90.

225 *"On cool evenings"*: Descola, *A History of Spain*, p. 117.

225 *"the Harun al-Rashid of the West"*: Gabrieli, *The Arabs*, p. 143.

225 *when he wanted to impress*: Descola, *A History of Spain*, p. 119.

226 *"pure and genuine"*: Durant, *The Story of Civilization*, vol. 4, p. 88.

226 His story in his relics: Hitti, *History of the Arabs*, p. 533.

228 *"Latins, Greeks, Jews"*: Smith, *A History of Sicily*, p. 17.

228 *"the great and holy"*: Ahmad, *A History of Islamic Sicily*, p. 63.

228 *"Emir of Emirs"*: Smith, *A History of Sicily*, p. 25.

228 *"stable in space"*: Lewis, *The Muslim Discovery of Europe*, p. 147.

EPILOGUE: TURBAN AND COWL

PAGE

232 *"the ponderous phalanx"*: Prasad, *History of Medieval India*, p. 79.

232 *"sprigs of young myrtle"*: Lane-Poole, *Medieval India Under Mohammedan Rule*, p. 21.

232 *"glistened like"*: Ibid.
236 *"the quintessential musician"*: Bloom and Blair, *Islam: A Thousand Years of Faith and Power*, pp. 101–2.
237 *"fields of Cloth-of-Gold"*: Glubb, *Haroon Al Rasheed*, p. 203.
237 *"the Herodotus of the Arabs"*: Hitti, *The Near East in History*, p. 254.
238 *"look down upon us"*: Campbell, *Arabian Medicine and Its Influence on the Middle Ages*, p. xvi.
239 *"with his gold and silver"*: Ibid.
239 *"the mother of philosophers"*: Arnold and Guillaume, *The Legacy of Islam*, p. 9.
239 *"every boy and girl"*: Campbell, *Arabian Medicine*, p. xv.
240 *"beaten to death in a sack"*: Huxley, *From An Antique Land*, p. 188.
241 *"conquered by Islam"*: Bloom and Blair, *Islam*, p. 101.
242 *"There is no God save the One"*: Buckler, *Harun al-Rashid and Charles the Great*, p. 53.

BIBLIOGRAPHY

Aaland, Mikkel. "The Islamic Hammam Is Born." www.cyberbohemia.com/Pages/sweat.htm.

Abbott, Nabia. *Two Queens of Baghdad*. London: Saqi Books, 1986.

Ahmad, Aziz. *A History of Islamic Sicily*. Edinburgh: Edinburgh University Press, 1975.

Ahmad, Qeyamuddin, ed. *Alberuni's India*. With introduction and notes. New Delhi: National Book Trust, 1983.

Al-Hassan, Ahmad Y., and Donald R. Hill. *Islamic Technology: An Illustrated History*. New York: Cambridge University Press, 1986.

Allan, J., Sir T. Haig, and H. H. Dodwell. *The Cambridge Shorter History of India*. New York: Macmillan, 1934.

Arnold, Thomas, and Alfred Guillaume, eds. *The Legacy of Islam*. London: Oxford University Press, 1968.

Audisio, Gabriel. *Harun al-Rashid, Caliph of Baghdad*. New York: Robert M. McBride, 1931.

Baas, J. H. *Outlines of the History of Medicine*. Translated by H. E. Handerson. New York, 1889.

Baker, Derek, ed. *Medieval Women*. Oxford: Basil Blackwell, 1978.

Baker, Patricia L. *Islamic Textiles*. London: British Museum Press, 1995.

Barbero, Alessandro. *Charlemagne: Father of a Continent*. Berkeley: University of California Press, 2004.

Baynes, Norman H. "The Restoration of the Cross at Jerusalem," *The English Historical Review*, vol. 27, pp. 287–99 (New York: Longman's, Green and Co., 1912).

Bendiner, Elmer. *The Rise and Fall of Paradise: When Arabs and Jews Built a Kingdom in Spain*. New York: G. P. Putnam's Sons, 1983.

Benjamin, Sandra. *Sicily: Three Thousand Years of Human History*. Hanover, NH: Steerforth Press, 2006.

Berlinski, David. *The Secrets of the Vaulted Sky*. Orlando, FL: Harcourt, 2003.

Berry, L. E., ed. *The English Works of Giles Fletcher the Elder*. Vol. 1. Madison: University of Wisconsin Press, 1964.

Bloom, Jonathan, and Sheila Blair. *Islam: A Thousand Years of Faith and Power*. New Haven, CT: Yale University Press, 2002.

————. *Islamic Arts*. London: Phaidon, 1997.

Bobrick, Benson. *The Fated Sky: Astrology in History*. New York: Simon & Schuster, 2005.

Bosworth, Clifford Edmund. *The Ghaznavids: Their Empire in Afghanistan and Eastern Iran*. Edinburgh: Edinburgh University Press, 1963.

————, trans. *The History of Al-Tabari: The Abbasid Caliphate in Equilibrium*. Vol. 30. Albany: State University of New York Press, 1989.

Breckenridge, J. D. "The Two Sicilies." In *Islam and the Medieval West*, edited by Stanley Ferber. Binghamton: State University of New York at Binghamton, 1975.

Brenan, Gerald. "When Islam Ruled Iberia," *Horizon* 5, no. 1 (Sept. 1962), pp. 73–93.

Broadhurst, R. J. C. *Travels of Ibn Jubair*. London: Jonathan Cape, 1952.

Browne, E. G. *Arabian Medicine*. Cambridge: Cambridge University Press, 1921.

Buckler, F. W. *Harun al-Rashid and Charles the Great*. Cambridge, MA: Medieval Academy of America, 1931.

Burton, Richard F. *The Book of the Thousand Nights and a Night: A Plain and Literal Translation of the Arabian Nights Entertainments*. 6 vols. New York: Heritage Press, 1934.

Bury, John Bagnell. *A History of the Later Roman Empire from Arcadius to Irene (395 A.D.–800 A.D.)*. New York: Adamant Media, 2005.

Butt, John J. *Daily Life in the Age of Charlemagne*. Westport, CT: Greenwood Press, 2002.

Cable, Mary. "The Grand Seraglio," *Horizon* 1, no. 5 (May 1959), p. 60.

Campbell, Donald. *Arabian Medicine and Its Influence on the Middle Ages*. 2 vols. London: Kegan Paul, Trench, Trubner, 1926.

Cheetham, Nicolas. *A History of the Popes*. New York: Barnes & Noble Books, 1982.

Clot, André. *Harun al-Rashid and the World of the Thousand and One Nights*. London: Saqi Books, 2005.

Crawford, F. Marion. *The Rulers of the South*. 2 vols. London, 1901. ("The Epistle of the monk Theodosius to the Archdeacon Leo concerning the capture of Syracuse," vol. 1, pp. 80–98.)

Crosby, Alfred W. *Throwing Fire: Projectile Technology Through History*. New York: Cambridge University Press, 2002.

Croutier, Alev Lytle. *Harem: The World Beyond the Veil*. New York: Abbeville, 1998.

Dawood, N. J., trans. *The Koran*. New York: Penguin Classics, 1995.

De Gramont, Sanche. "Mohammed: The Prophet Armed." *Horizon* 13, no. 3 (Summer 1971), pp. 18–23.

Descola, Jean. *A History of Spain*. New York: Knopf, 1963.

De Slane, MacGuckin, trans. *Ibn Khallikan's Biographical Dictionary*. 2 vols. Beirut: Librairie du Liban, 1970.

Dozy, Reinhart. *Spanish Islam: A History of the Muslims in Spain*. New Delhi: Goodword Books, 2001.

Dunn, John. *The Spread of Islam*. San Diego: Lucent Books, 1966.

Durant, Will. *The Story of Civilization*. Vol. 4, *The Age of Faith*. New York: Simon & Schuster, 1968.

El-Hibri, Tayeb. *Reinterpreting Islamic Historiography: Harun al-Rashid and the Narrative of the "Abbasid Caliphate."* Cambridge: Cambridge University Press, 1999.

Elliot, H. M., and J. Dowson. *The History of India as Told by Its Own Historians: The Mohammedan Period*. 8 vols. London, 1866–77.

Ellis Davidson, Hilda R. "The Secret Weapon of Byzantium." *Byzantinische Zeitschrift* 66 (1973), pp. 61–74.

Embree, Ainslie T., ed. *Alberuni's India*. With introduction and notes. New York: Norton, 1971.

Ferishta, Mohammed Kasim. *History of the Rise of Mohammedan Power in India*. Translated by John Briggs. Calcutta: Editions India, 1966.

Fichtenau, Heinrich. *The Carolingian Empire: The Age of Charlemagne*. New York: Harper Torchbooks, 1957.

Finley, M. I. *Ancient Sicily*. Totowa, NJ: Rowman & Littlefield, 1979.

Fraser-Tytler, W. K. *Afghanistan: A Study of Political Developments in Central Asia*. London: Oxford University Press, 1950.

Gabrieli, Francesco. *The Arabs*. New York: Hawthorne Books, 1963.

Garland, Lynda. *Byzantine Empresses: Women and Power in Byzantium, A.D. 527–1204*. London: Routledge, 1999.

Glubb, John Bagot. *Haroon Al Rasheed and the Great Abbasids*. London: Hodder & Stoughton, 1976.

Goddard, John Calvin. *A Leave of Absence*. Boston: The Pilgrim Press, 1902.

Grabar, Oleg. "Ceremonial and Art at the Umayyad Court." PhD diss., Princeton University, 1955, chapter 1. www.fordham.edu/halsall/med/grabar1.html.

———. *The Formation of Islamic Art*. New Haven, CT: Yale University Press, 1987.

Harris, Jonathan. *Constantinople, Capital of Byzantium*. London: Continuum, 2007.

Haskins, Charles Homer. *The Renaissance of the 12th Century*. New York: Meridian Books, 1960.

Hell, Joseph. *The Arab Civilization*. Translated by S. Khuda Bakhsh. Lahore: Ashraf Press, 1943.

Herrin, Judith. *Women in Purple: Rulers of Medieval Byzantium*. Princeton, NJ: Princeton University Press, 2001.

Hinks, Roger. *Carolingian Art*. Ann Arbor: University of Michigan Press, 1962.

Hitti, Philip K. *The Near East in History*. New York: Van Nostrand, 1961.

———. *History of the Arabs from the Earliest Times to the Present*. New York: St. Martin's Press, 1970.

Holt, P. M., Ann K. S. Lambton, and Bernard Lewis, eds. *The Cambridge History of Islam*. Vol. 2. Cambridge: Cambridge University Press, 1970.

Huxley, Julian. *From an Antique Land*. London: Max Parrish, 1954.

Ikram, S. M. *Muslim Civilization in India*. New York: Columbia University Press, 1964.

Inserra, Beniamino. "Emperor Frederick II." *Best of Sicily Magazine*, 2002, www.best ofsicily.com/mag/art57.htm.

Irving, Washington. *Chronicle of the Conquest of Granada*. Philadelphia: David McKay, 1850.

Irwin, Robert. *The Arabian Nights: A Companion*. New York: Penguin, 1994.

Jeffreys, Elizabeth. *Byzantine Style, Religion and Civilization: In Honor of Sir Steven Runciman*. New York: Cambridge University Press, 2006.

Julien, Charles-Andre. *History of North Africa*. Translated by John Petrie. New York: Praeger, 1970.

Kaegi, Walter E. *Byzantium and the Early Islamic Conquests*. Cambridge: Cambridge University Press, 1992.

———. *Heraclius: Emperor of Byzantium*. New York: Cambridge University Press, 2004.

Kazhdan, Alexander, ed. *Oxford Dictionary of Byzantium*. Oxford: Oxford University Press, 1991.

Keay, John. *India: A History*. New York: Grove Press, 2000.

Kennedy, Hugh. *The Armies of the Caliphs*. London: Routledge, 2001.

———. *The Prophet and the Age of the Caliphates*. Edinburgh: Pearson, 2004.

———. *When Baghdad Ruled the Muslim World*. Cambridge, MA: Da Capo, 2005.

Kennedy, Philip F. *Abu Nuwas: A Genius of Poetry*. Oxford: OneWorld Press, 2005.

Kirk, George E. *A Short History of the Middle East*. London: Methuen, 1959.

Lane, Edward William. *Arab Society in the Time of the Thousand and One Nights*. London: Chatto & Windus, 1883.

Lane-Poole, Stanley. *Medieval India Under Mohammedan Rule (A.D. 712–1764)*. Lahore: Sang-E-Meel, 1979.

———. *The Mohammedan Dynasties*. Westminster: Archibald Constable, 1894.

———. *The Story of the Moors in Spain*. New York: G. P. Putnam's Sons, 1898.

Lassner, Jacob. *The Shaping of 'Abbasid Rule*. Princeton, NJ: Princeton University Press, 1980.

Le Strange, Guy. *Baghdad During the Abbasid Caliphate*. Oxford: Clarendon Press, 1924.

———. *The Lands of the Eastern Caliphate*. Cambridge: Cambridge University Press, 1905.

Lewis, Bernard. *The Arabs in History*. New York: Oxford University Press, 1958.

———. *The Middle East: A Brief History of the Last 2,000 Years*. New York: Scribner, 1995.

———. *The Muslim Discovery of Europe*. New York: Norton, 1982.

Lopez, Robert S., and Irving W. Raymond. *Medieval Trade in the Mediterranean World*. New York: Norton, 2001.

Maalouf, Amin. *The Crusades Through Arab Eyes*. New York: Schocken, 1984.

MacMunn, Sir George. *Afghanistan from Darius to Amanullah*. London: G. Bell & Sons, 1929.

Mahajan, Vidya Dhar. *Muslim Rule in India*. New Delhi: Chand, 1965.

Majda, T. *Encyclopedia of Islam*. Vol. 5. New York: Brill, 1994.

Marcus, Louis Rautman. *Daily Life in the Byzantine Empire*. New York: Greenwood Press, 2006.

Masudi. *The Meadows of Gold*. Translated and edited by Paul Lunde and Caroline Stone. New York: Kegan Paul International, 1989.

Mawdudi, Abul Ala. *Towards Understanding Islam*. Lahore: Islamic Teaching Center, 1987.

Mayer, L. A. "Some Remarks on the Dress of the Abbasid Caliphs in Egypt." *Islamic Culture*, no. 17 (1943), pp. 36–38.

McBrien, Richard P. *Lives of the Popes*. New York: HarperCollins, 2000.

McEvedy, Colin. *The Penguin Atlas of Medieval History*. New York: Penguin Books, 1983.

Mehta, J. L. *Advanced Study in the History of Medieval India*. New Delhi: Sterling, 1979.

Metcalfe, Alex. *The Muslims of Medieval Italy*. Edinburgh: Edinburgh University Press, 2009.

———. "The Muslims of Sicily Under Christian Rule," www.medievalists.net/2010/02/16/the-muslims-of-sicily-under-Christian-rule/.

Morris, James. "The Silk Road." *Horizon* 9, no. 4 (Autumn 1967), pp. 4–22.

Muir, Sir William. *The Caliphate: Its Rise, Decline and Fall, from Original Sources*. London: Religious Tract Society, 1891.

Munier, Gilles. *Iraq: An Illustrated History and Guide*. Northampton, MA: Interlink, 2004.

Nadvi, Syed Sulaiman. "The Origin of the Barmakids." *Islamic Culture*, no. 6 (1932), pp. 19–28.

Nazim, Mohammad. *India: A History*. Lahore: Khalil, 1978.

———. *The Life and Times of Sultan Mahmud of Ghazna*. Lahore: Khalil, 1973.

Nöldeke, Theodor. *Sketches from Eastern History*. Translated by John Sutherland Black. Edinburgh: Adam and Charles Black, 1892.

O'Donnell, Terence. "Twenty-Five Centuries of Persia." *Horizon* 5, no. 3 (January 1963), pp. 40–72.

Ogg, Frederic Austin, ed. *A Source Book of Medieval History*. New York: Cooper Square, 1972.

Palmer, E. H. *The Caliph Haroun Alraschid and Saracen Civilization*. New York: G. P. Putnam's Sons, 1881.

Partington, James Riddick. *A History of Greek Fire and Gunpowder*. Baltimore: Johns Hopkins University Press, 1999.

Payaslian, Simon. *The History of Armenia*. New York: Palgrave Macmillan, 2007.

Perry, Charles. "Cooking with the Caliphs." *Saudi Aramco World* 57, no. 4 (July/ August 2006), pp. 14–23.

Philby, H. St. John. *Harun al-Rashid*. New York: Appleton-Century, 1934.

Powell, James M. "Frederick II and the Rebellion of the Muslims of Sicily, 1200– 1224." www.deremilitari.org/resources/pdfs/powell.pdf.

Prasad, Ishwari. *History of Medieval India*. Allahabad: Indian Press, 1966.

Price, B. B. *Medieval Thought*. Cambridge, MA: Blackwell, 1992.

Psellus, Michael. *Fourteen Byzantine Rulers*. New York: Penguin Classics, 1966.

Rautman, Marcus. *Daily Life in the Byzantine Empire*. Westport, CT: Greenwood Press, 2006.

Rawlinson, H. G. *India: A Short Cultural History*. New York: Praeger, 1954.

Read, J. *The Moors in Spain and Portugal*. London: Faber & Faber, 1974.

Rees, J. D. *The Muslim Epoch*. New Delhi: Asian Publication Services, 1978.

Riche, Pierre. *Daily Life in the World of Charlemagne*. Philadelphia: University of Pennsylvania Press, 1978.

Rogers, J. A. *World's Great Men of Color*. Vol. 1. New York: Macmillan, 1972.

Rogers, Michael. *The Spread of Islam*. Oxford: Elsevier-Phaidon, 1976.

Roland, Alex. "Secrecy, Technology, and War: Greek Fire and the Defense of Byzantium, Technology, and Culture." *Technology and Culture* 33, no. 4 (1992), pp. 655–79.

Runciman, Sir Steven. "The Empress Irene the Athenian." In Derek Baker, ed., *Medieval Women*, pp. 101–18.

Sachau, Edward C., trans. *Alberuni's India*. New Delhi: Rupa, 2002.

Scarfiotti, Gian Luigi, and Paul Lunde. "The Muslims in Italy." *Saudi Aramco World* 29, no. 6 (November–December 1978).

Scott, S. P. *History of the Moorish Empire*. 3 vols. Philadelphia: Lippincott, 1904.

Sedgwick, Henry Dwight. *Spain: A Short History of Its Politics, Literature, and Art from Earliest Times to the Present*. Boston: Little, Brown, 1925.

Shaw, M. R. B. *Joinville & Villehardouin: Chronicles of the Crusades*. New York: Penguin Classics, 1982.

Smith, Denis Mack. *A History of Sicily: Medieval Sicily, 800–1713*. New York: Viking Press, 1968.

Sourdel, Dominique. *Islam*. New York: Walker, 1949.

Stillman, Yedida Kalfon. *Arab Dress: A Short History: From the Dawn of Islam to Modern Times*. Edited by Norman A. Stillman. Boston: Brill, 2000.

Swisher, Clarice. *The Spread of Islam*. San Diego: Greenhaven Press, 1999.

Thorpe, Lewis, trans. *Two Lives of Charlemagne: Einhard and Notker the Stammerer*. New York: Penguin, 1984.

Turner, Howard R. *Science in Medieval Islam*. Austin: University of Texas Press, 1995.

Udovitch, A. L. "Islamic Sicily." In *Dictionary of the Middle Ages*, edited by J. R. Strayer. New York: Charles Scribner's Sons, 1980.

Vasiliev, A. A. *History of the Byzantine Empire*. 2 vols. Madison: University of Wisconsin Press, 1952.

Verhoeven, F. R. J. *Islam: Its Origin and Spread*. New York: St. Martin's Press, 1962.

Waines, David, ed. *Patterns of Everyday Life*. Burlington, VT: Ashgate, 2002.

Ward-Perkins, Bryan. *The Cambridge Ancient History: Empire and Successors, A.D.* Cambridge: Cambridge University Press, 2000.

Watson, Francis. *India: A Concise History*. New York: Thames & Hudson, 1979.

Welles, H. G. *The Outline of History*. 2 vols. Garden City, NY: Garden City Books, 1920.

Zaimeche, Salah. *Sicily*. November 2004. Foundation for Science, Technology, and Civilisation. http://www.fstc.co.uk.

Zipes, Jack. *Arabian Nights: The Marvels and Wonders of the Thousand and One Nights*. Adapted from Richard F. Burton's unexpurgated translation. 2 vols. New York: Signet Classics, 1991.

www.cyberbohemia.com/Pages/Islahammam.htm.

wonka.hampshire.edu/abbasidstudies/abbasids/cuisine.php.

www.saudiaramcoworld.com/issue/200604/cooking.with.the.caliphs.htm   (Charles Perry).

www.gay-art-history.org/abu-nuwas-gay-biography.html.

www.unhas.ac.id/~rhiza/saintis/biruni.html.

www.academia.emporia.edu/aberjame/histgeol/biruni/biruni.html.

www-groups.dcs.stand.ac.ukt~history/Mathematicians/Al-Biruni.html.

www.ucalgary.ca/applied_history/tutor/islam/learning/biruni.html.

www.members.tripod.com/~khorasan/TajikPersonalities/AlBiruni.html.

www.trincoll.edu/depts/phil/philo/phils/muslim/biruni.html.

www.voi.org/books/hhrmi/ch3.html.

www.workmall.com/wfb2001/pakistan/pakistal_history_islam_in_india.html.

www.chemheritage.org/explore/milestone_greek_fire.html.

custance.org/Library/Thesis/part_1/chapter4.html.

www.middleeastuk.com/culture/mosaic/arabian.html.

http://wonka.hampshire.edu/abbasidstudies/abbasids/barmakids.php.

http://wonka.hampshire.edu/abbasidstudies/Abbasids/fashion.php.

http://penelope.uchicago.edu/Thayer/E/Gazetteer/Places/Europe/Italy/_Texts/CRA
   ROS/home.html.

http://rupeenews.com/2008/02/12/islamic-sicily-muslims-ruled-sicily . . . renaissance
   -and-enlightenment-from-muslim-spain-to-christian-europe/.

http://thenational.ae/apps/pbcs.dll/article?AID=/20100911/TRAVEL/709109894/1196.

http://www.saudiaramcoworld.com/issue/197806/muslim.sicily.htm.

http://en.wikipedia.org/wiki/Sassanid_empire.

http://en.wikipedia.org/The_Book_of_One_Thousand_and_One_Nights.

http://en.wikipedia.org/wiki/Greek_fire.

http://en.wikipedia.org/wiki/Yahya_ibn_Khalid.

http://en.wikipedia.org/wiki/Jafar_bin_Yahya.

http://en.wikipedia.org/wiki/Irene_of_Athens.

http://en.wikipedia.org/wiki/Destrier.

http://en.wikipedia.org/wiki/Ali_ar-Ridha.

INDEX

Aachen, 134, 141–43
    Charlemagne's palace in, 127–28, 137, 141, 203–4
Abbasah, 50, 173–74
Abbasids, 11–12, 39–41, 73, 205, 212, 240
    alliances against, 145
    Barmaks and, 47–53, 82, 159–78
    diplomacy and, 139–43
Abd al-Aziz, 98
Abd al-Malik, 9
Abd al-Malik ibn Salih, 163–66, 175
Abd al-Rahman I, 12, 100–103, 209
Abd al-Rahman II, 211, 223
Abd al-Rahman III, 223–26
Abd al-Rahman (Hashemite), 164, 165
Abdullah, see Mamun, al-
abortion, 131
Abraham, cult of, 3
Abrash, Salam al-, 22–23, 172
Abu al-Abbas (caliph), 12, 14, 20, 41, 47, 48, 100
Abu al-Abbas (elephant), 141, 204
Abu al-Ahmad, 153
Abu al-Atahiyah, 87, 88, 89
Abu Ali al-Hasan, 87, 88, 89
Abu Bakr, 5, 10, 43, 76
Abu Hashim Masrur, 32, 61, 171–72, 175, 188
Abu Muslim, 12–13, 47, 183
Abu Nuwas, 87–90, 177–78
Abu Obeidah, 86–87
Abu Yusuf, 50, 56–58
Adelard of Bath, 240
Afghanistan, 6, 47, 76, 231–32
afreets, 72
Africa, 75, 129, 241
    see also North Africa; specific countries
Africans, black:
    in Baghdad, 21, 32, 92, 205
    in Sicily, 219, 221

as slaves, 21, 61, 75, 161, 212
    in Spain, 103
Aghlabids, 215–21
agriculture, 14, 49, 65, 76, 108, 217–18
Albania, 241
alchemy, 234–35
alcohol, 71–72, 88, 107, 130, 142, 218
Alcuin, 118, 128, 131, 135, 136
Aleppo, 233
Alexander the Great, 82, 232
Alexandria, 210, 219
    Battle of, 5, 7, 110
    learning in, 81, 82, 83, 207, 211, 238
Algeria, 214
Ali (Harun's son), 151
Ali (Prophet's son-in-law), 5, 10, 11, 23, 36, 71
Alids, 29, 41–42, 160–61, 162–63
    see also Shiites
Almagest (Ptolemy), 82, 207, 240
Almanzor, 226, 241
Amin, al-, 151–57, 193–202
    accession agreement of, 155–57, 185, 194–95
    Arab support for, 154, 163–64, 166, 188
    death of, 200–202
    as doubly descended from Prophet, 41, 53–54, 151, 189, 201
    education of, 152–54
    eunuchs loved by, 197, 198–99, 200
    Fadhl ibn Rabi and, 154, 168, 184, 194–95, 199
    Mamun's rivalry with, 151–57, 189, 193–202
    poetry and, 86, 89–90
    reign of, 193–98
amirs, 39, 43
Amman, 162
Anatolia, 43, 112, 122
Anbar, 169, 194